Pious Peripheries

Pious Peripheries

Runaway Women in Post-Taliban Afghanistan

Sonia Ahsan-Tirmizi

Stanford University Press
Stanford, California

STANFORD UNIVERSITY PRESS
Stanford, California

Printed in the United States of America on acid-free,
archival-quality paper

Library of Congress Cataloging-in-Publication Data

Names: Ahsan-Tirmizi, Sonia (Anthropologist), author.
Title: Pious peripheries : runaway women in post-Taliban Afghanistan /
Sonia Ahsan-Tirmizi.
Description: Stanford, California : Stanford University Press, 2021. |
Includes bibliographical references and index.
Identifiers: LCCN 2020037303 (print) | LCCN 2020037304 (ebook) |
ISBN 9781503614703 (cloth) | ISBN 9781503614710 (paperback) |
ISBN 9781503614727 (ebook)
Subjects: LCSH: Runaway women—Afghanistan—Social conditions. |
Women, Pushtun—Afghanistan—Social conditions. | Muslim
women—Afghanistan—Social conditions. | Women—Afghanistan—
Conduct of life. | Women—Religious aspects—Islam. | Promiscuity—
Afghanistan.
Classification: LCC HQ1735.6 .A65 2021 (print) | LCC HQ1735.6
(ebook) | DDC 305.4209581—dc23
LC record available at https://lccn.loc.gov/2020037303
LC ebook record available at https://lccn.loc.gov/2020037304

Cover art: Hangama Amiri, *Women Gathering*, 2017. Acrylic and oil on
wood panel (8" x 10").
Cover design: Rob Ehle

To Lila Abu-Lughod, the scholar par excellence

Contents

Note on Transliteration

Transliteration for Pashto, Dari, and Persian has followed the rules in Library of Congress romanization tables, with changes. Most diacritical marks have been omitted for clarity of reading except for the letter ‘ain. Diacritics in names of books, persons, and quotations have been retained. Names of famous poets are spelled in accordance with their common English usage—for example, Saadi and Khushal Khan Khattak. Non-English words in frequent English use are in their common spelling, such as *jirga*, *Quran*, *sharia*, *Shia*, or *Taliban*. For endings, *a* not *ah* or *eh* is used (e.g., *fahsha* not *fahshah*; *Hazara* not *Hazarah*), and for izafa, *e* not *i* (e.g., *namaz-e zuhr* not *namaz-i zuhr*). If words overlap between Pashto, Dari, and Persian, the Persian transliteration is used; for example, for the shared letter *waw*, the transliteration used is *v* not *w* (*vatan, vuzu, vali*).

Acknowledgments

The research for this book began in my youth during the years I lived in Peshawar. I owe tremendous gratitude to my father, who raised five opinionated daughters and encouraged us to ask questions and persist despite challenges. He was a strong, honorable man who was not afraid of raising strong women. I wish he were alive to read this book, and the hope that I will meet him again allows me to make this world mine in the moment. My mother taught me reading and loved me through the many struggles of life. The questions I ask in this book arise from the contested but loving relations I have shared with my family, especially my four sisters, Anita, Shazia, Bushra, and Lyla.

In Afghanistan, I am thankful to all the women, most of whom must remain anonymous, who allowed me to become a part of their lives at the khana-yi aman. I thank Omar Sharifi for his friendship and support in all stages of the project in Afghanistan and New York. I thank the many friends, relatives, and colleagues who helped me along the way: Aisha Saeed, Alberto Tiburcio, Anand Taneja, Andreas Chiovenda, Brooke Greene, Bushra Hamid, Erin Yerby, Eszter Daly, Faria Khalid, Farbod Honarpisheh, Gökçe Günel, Guangtian Ha, Homa Sorouri, Haroon Moghul, Hossei Wardak, Juana Cabrera, Jan Allen, Jyoti Ranadive, Mahbouba Seraj, Mariam Banahi, Marilyn Astwood, Mary Akrami, Melissa Chiovenda, Munira Khayyat, Nadia Kiyani, Nargis Nehan, Narges Erami, Natalia Mendoza Rockwell, Nauman P, Nauman Naqvi, Naysan Adlparvar, Neguin Yavari, Omar Sarwar, Özge Serin, Pasha Khan, Prashant Keshavmurthy, Sandra Peters, Sahar Sadjadi, Sarah Eltantawi, Seema Goestaneh, Sophia Stamatopoulou-Robbins, Saira Hassan, Shaharzad Akbar, Sonia James, Veli Yasin, Xenia Cherkaev, and Zainab Saleh. I thank Ashraf Ghani for his support in the research process. I thank the professors and colleagues who became a part of my life when I first immigrated to United States, especially Gary McGill, Jesse Boyles, and Charles Cromer.

At Columbia University, I am deeply grateful to Brinkley Messick, Elizabeth Povinelli, Valentine Daniel, Partha Chatterjee, and Manan Ahmed. Brinkley Messick introduced me to the wonders of anthropology, taught me that good anthropological writing is always historical, and has been a pivotal support through all phases of my intellectual development. Elizabeth Povinelli pushes her students beyond the limits of knowing, and has taught me the difficult art of critique. I am also grateful to Audra Simpson, Claudio Lomnitz, David Scott, Mahmood Mamdani, Neni Panourgia, Shah Mahmoud Hanifi, Sheldon Pollock, Stathis Gourgouris, Nicholas Dirks, Richard Bulliet, and Rosalind Morris for many spontaneous thoughtful conversations. I thank Saeed Honarmand and Roya for their support in Persian, and Professor Anwar for his support in Pashto. I am especially grateful to Partha Chatterjee for his kind and generous support through the years. I thank Jay Bernstein for welcoming me in his Torture and Dignity seminar and lectures on Hegel, and Simon Critchley for allowing me to attend his lectures on Heidegger. I also benefited from attending Richard Bernstein's lectures on Hannah Arendt. I thank Petra Shenk and Edith Klein for their careful reading of the entire book. I thank Michael Herzfeld for his engagement and guidance with my project, and for his intellectual generosity and kindness. Summer teaching at Columbia has been a joy for which I thank Ellen Marakowitz. The wonderful librarians of Columbia University, Peter Magierski and Sarah White, helped with primary sources.

I am grateful to Thomas Barfield for reading my book, giving feedback, and for believing in this project. I thank Nile Green for encouraging me at the beginning of my work and for publishing my writing, which gave me essential confidence to move forward with the book. Nazif Shahrani gave essential guidance for theoretical framing and ethnographic fieldwork, and invited me to participate in a wonderful conference in Indiana. Amin Saikal asked thoughtful questions at the beginning of this project. I am grateful to Alessandro Monsutti for reading chapters and giving guidance. David Edwards and Noah Coburn read this book with a careful and critical eye, and asked many important questions. Robert McChesney read some chapters and gave thoughtful feedback. I am deeply grateful to Dipali Mukhopadhyay, who believed in this project from its inception and organized a wonderful workshop for this book. My research was made possible with funding from Wenner Gren and the American Institute of Afghan Studies. I thank Hollings Center for International Dialogue, especially Michael Carroll, for its support. This book benefited from the comments of the anonymous reviewers, and at Stanford University Press I thank Caroline McKusick, Tim Roberts, Stephanie Adams, Michelle Lipinski, and especially Kate Wahl. I thank Hangama Amiri for the beautiful cover art. I thank Michele Jones for her careful copyediting.

My children, Ahad and Ibrahim, are the sunshine that guides my life. I hope they live to see a better world. I thank their father, Faisal, for giving me the space to write.

Lila Abu-Lughod, to whom this book is dedicated, has deeply influenced my writing. Her brilliance, thoughtfulness, and intellectual generosity open a space for new scholarship to emerge.

This book is a contribution to the growing scholarship on women who resist and subvert despite the tremendous risks attached to living and thinking differently.

Pious Peripheries

Introduction

Samia Sarwar was my neighbor, my older sister's classmate, and a close family friend. We grew up together, and I attended her wedding to her first cousin (her mother's sister's son) in Peshawar. In 1999, Samia acquired a lover and ran away from a miserable marriage to a women's shelter. Her own mother followed, found, and killed her at the shelter. Samia's family and friends, which included my family, did not give a single interview to the media. A shroud of secrecy fell on those nearest Samia, and no one close to her has spoken publicly since the day she was killed. Yet accounts of this killing saturate the public via television shows, articles, and books. For example, the BBC made a documentary about Samia called *License to Kill* without a single interview from a family member or friend. Princeton University professor Anthony Appiah wrote an impressive theoretical book called *Honor Code*, which includes Samia's killing as a case study, without ever visiting Peshawar or conducting a single interview with the affected families. Oxford University Press published a book called *Honor Killing* based on Samia's death, with no ethnographic insight. Even without any knowledge of Samia's life or how she was raised, everyone still had an opinion. Feminists and activists presented ideas about alleviating the conditions of downtrodden Muslim Pashtun women through education. Some academics spoke about poverty and destitution, others about Islam, the Taliban, honor, and pashtunwali.[1] But Samia and her family were educated, secular, and affluent. Her mother, who killed her, is a gynecologist, and her father is the president of the Sarhad Chamber of Commerce and Industry in Khyber Pukhtunkhwa. She was raised in a magnificent mansion in an affluent neighborhood of Peshawar, overlooking a golf course. Although her family practiced pashtunwali and Islam, they were not conservative. Like my five sisters and me, Samia and her younger sister, a medical doctor, were raised in an affluent, educated, modern, secular part of Peshawar city, where families also took pride in their Pashtun and Muslim roots. We studied at Peshawar Convent, a progressive school for Muslim Pashtun girls. How could her mother, a woman we cherished and loved, kill Samia? For the last twenty years, I have tried to solve this puzzle.

Samia's father and her *vali* (male patron) forgave her mother, and thus no legal action could be taken against her based on Qisas and Dayat laws, which allow the male patron to forgive a family member's murder. Samia was killed at a shelter run by a powerful women's rights activist, Asma Jehangir, which made her story famous. As a result of the international outrage, a bill was presented in parliament that would curtail such killings of women. However, the chairman of the Senate, an Oxford-educated lawyer, a Rhodes scholar and friend of Samia's father, vetoed it. No one has been punished. Samia's death has slowly receded into the past, but I have not forgotten. A few years later, my young cousin died under suspicious circumstances, leaving behind two toddler daughters, after she left her husband, also a cousin. Asna and I were very close.[2] There was no investigation into her death. Again, the family drama continued, with the specter of violence ever present but never spoken about.

After these deaths, I conducted private research and found similar deaths. My mother's sister Sophia was found dead one morning in her bed with her two young sons, ages seven and nine. When Sophia is remembered at family gatherings, her defiance, rebellion, and unruliness are at the center of our recollections. In some cases, the deaths garner international attention with endless news cycles of misleading information. Other deaths are relegated to obscurity. What do these deaths have in common other than that a woman is killed? In almost all cases, the woman is killed by a family member and then her in-laws and her birth family reach a tacit agreement to remain silent. In all cases, the dead women are labeled unruly, mad, disobedient, and promiscuous as a means of making her responsible for her own death.

Sheltering Runaway Women

This book is a reflection on the courage and bravery of ordinary women who persist and subvert despite the real threat of death. For example, I met Nurzia Athmar at the shelter—she had left her husband because he was abusive. She was a parliamentarian from Nangarhar province, and as an MP, was well known to the women of the shelter. There was also Gulalei, who had run away with her young son from her husband when he joined the Taliban. She was a long-term resident of the shelter who had been given the task of supervising the daily activities. One day when I was taking a break from the shelter, Gulalei called me. "Come immediately," she said on the telephone. When I arrived at the shelter, I saw Nurzia perched on a bed. Women sat around her on the floor. Her husband had arrived at the shelter to find her, so in order to protect the other women there, she could no longer stay. Thus, in 2014, she fled Afghanistan and still remains in hiding. Her position in parliament had given her no protection. Nurzia is a tall, stately, impressive Pashtun woman who is confident and well spoken. She articulated the reason for her running away in these words: "My family did not side with me after I told them about my husband's abuse. It was as if marriage made me another person, not their daughter."

Women's shelters across the globe are places of refuge against threats of violence. In Afghanistan, shelters are called *khana-yi aman* (home of safety) and house women who have been classified as "runaways" by the state and who are in the midst of legal and social sanctions. Women become runaways for a variety of reasons, including to get married or divorced, and/or to flee sexual and physical abuse. Many women at the shelter were the wives and daughters of the Taliban. Once women are ensconced in the shelter, the state can step into family arbitrations. What would have once and otherwise been resolved informally through *jirgas* (tribal councils) and family meetings can now be adjudicated by the state. This provides some protection to the women, but as the ethnography presented in this book demonstrates, it also subjects them to grotesque forms of violence, including mandatory virginity tests, indefinite imprisonment, forced abortions, and separation from infant children.

Women in the khana-yi aman are now at the mercy of the state without family safeguards and, in some cases, suffer gang rapes and other violence at the behest of the officials in charge of protecting them. Paradoxically, when such stories of rape and violence circulate outside the shelter in the public arena, they reinforce a stereotype of the runaway women as sexually licentious. A raped or sexually abused woman becomes part of the repertoire of promiscuity surrounding the shelter. Women in Afghanistan have few resources once they are marked as promiscuous (*fahhash*), licentious or prostitute (*randi*), or shameless (*bi-sharm*), which can happen for reasons that have little to do with actual sex or sexuality.[3] Yet the women persist and form a supportive community inside the shelters.

A lot of ink has been spilled about the oppression of Afghan women. This book is not interested in how those outside Afghanistan see Afghan women but is instead preoccupied with how ordinary Afghan women understand and inhabit their own worlds. The uniqueness of the khana-yi aman women is that their actions are in harmony with their principles. They are not simply taking a rhetorical position; they are enacting a socially risky, promiscuous position and endangering themselves in the process. In doing so, they are demanding equality and redefining what it means to be equal and pious. While deeply implicated within Western liberation discourses of modernity, the women at the khana-yi aman are unconcerned with debates in the West on Muslim women's emancipation. They do not run away to escape Islam, piety, and pashtunwali or to embrace freedom in its Western incarnation; rather, they run to own their Muslim piety and "Pashtun-ness" in ways unconstrained by Western or local patriarchal discourses. While their running away implies autonomous individual will, their fasting and praying demonstrate pious embodiment and religious self-discipline. By running, they lay claim to new possibilities of being Muslim women. These new feminine possibilities of being Muslim neither reject Islam nor entail obedience and submission to its nonegalitarian gender precepts. In inhabiting the contradictory positions between individual will and collective obligation, they transform the discourses that seek to subjugate them and demonstrate alternative ways of being pious Afghans.

Women run away for remarkably different reasons. Many run away after their husbands or fathers join the Taliban, others run to get divorced or to escape sexual and physical abuse, and others run away from conservative Muslim Pashtun families so that they can marry for romantic love rather than out of familial obligation. Ironically, still others run from secular-minded families who disapprove of their decision to become second or third wives. Each case has a complex history. The actions of the women at the khana-yi aman cannot be detached from the historical contexts embedded within the rich canonical sources through which piety is established. The women were proficient in Quranic and hadith sources and often recited them verbatim in Arabic and translated them spontaneously into Pashto or Dari. Women rendered intelligible their subject positions vis-à-vis pashtunwali and Islam through reflection on an Islamic past, and understanding the past was constitutive of how the women understood themselves in the present. Running away should not be read as a wholesale rejection of their Muslim identity, nor can becoming a willing second wife be read as a complete consolidation of their Muslim identity. The ethnographic work at the shelter dismantles the binary of tradition (pious) and modern (promiscuous) and demonstrates the historical complexity of each decision to run away at the risk of "becoming promiscuous."

Do public expressions of promiscuity render Muslim women modern in the way that public visibility of piety renders them traditional? What does it mean to be modern or traditional in the context of Islamic feminism? In Afghanistan, notions of modernity and tradition as they relate to female piety and promiscuity are entwined in complicated ways. The conditions of gender inequality affect almost all Afghan women. Despite its marginalization, the khana-yi aman was not completely outside the patriarchal discourse, and the women lived in accordance with most Islamic and pashtunwali precepts. They clearly saw themselves as Muslim. In many of our conversations, they described themselves as adherents of Islam, which they did not view as incompatible with being Afghan or with their decision to run away. Yet the women were ostracized from their communities, which constrained them through Islamic notions of pious womanhood. Running away was not always an abandonment of tradition but rather an embrace of tradition but toward a different end. For instance, some wanted to lay claim to a world in which their rightful inheritance was given to them, a world possible in a nostalgic Islamic past, but not necessarily in a secular future. In all these cases, binaries of tradition–modernity and Islam–secularism fall apart as women inhabit multiple subject positions, sometimes contradictory and sometimes complementary. This nomadic way of being, in which women rebel against some norms while inhabiting others, opens the possibility for alternative ways of being modern.[4] I call this notion *promiscuous modern*. Women rebel from a position of rootedness, not simply against tradition or Islam, but toward a future in which tradition and modernity cease to exist as simplistic binaries.

Islam and Feminism

The relationship between Islam and feminism has been well studied in recent scholarship on Muslim societies in the Middle East and Europe.[5] In this scholarship, the ritualistic inhabiting of normative structures is conceptualized as an alternative form of modernity that does not follow the telos of Western freedom. Within this framework, scholarship on Afghan women often situates them as pious moral actors seeking to consolidate their moral formations of pashtunwali and Islam.[6] This conceptual architecture relies on the Foucauldian understanding of subjecthood, morality, and ethics.[7] My book is situated within this scholarship of Islam and feminism, but asks a different question: What happens when pious Muslim women, who enact their piety through embodied gestures of veiling, praying, and fasting, also transgress the moral codes? What happens when a woman who wears a burqa sings a sexually explicit song or runs away from home to commit adultery? Do her actions consolidate or destabilize the power apparatuses that seek to subjugate her into conformity? For example, some women at the shelter chose their role of loyal mother while rejecting their role of loyal wife, thus fragmenting the traditional notion of pious womanhood that consolidates these roles.

Power apparatuses are inextricably tied to sexual relations; and in Afghanistan, sexual relations hinge on the notion of pious womanhood.[8] The willingness of some women to run away from home despite the risk of accusations of sexual promiscuity disrupts the relationality through which Afghan power hierarchies operate. The runaway women thus enable us to write an alternative history of Afghanistan by creating a space for rupture and irregularity in the form of ostensibly deviant or promiscuous sexuality.[9] They force us to question traditional representations of sexually rebellious actions as ventriloquizing a certain permutation of Western freedom. For example, local and international actors see an Afghan woman who claims to have an adulterous lover as Westernized. Her actions are seen as sexually rebellious, morally corrupt, and outside the purview of local frameworks of piety. However, running away has a local history not completely explained via Western frameworks of autonomy and freedom. Running away creates a new local space for difference. Communal connections may still be based on piety and chastity that accentuate familial lineage and maternal procreation. Nevertheless, running away allows for negotiation, challenge, and reproduction. What counts as pious can be reoriented toward unknown horizons (Weston 1991, 35). On the one hand, running away to the shelter creates a radical rupture within the frameworks of familial piety by directly inserting the authority of the Afghan state.[10] On the other hand, the gesture of refusal to obey and enact communal scripts of piety entails vigorous social dramas that reposition runaway women as active agents involved in a process of self-determination.[11] I argue that the shelter's residents actively inhabit the cultural repertoire of rejection of pious goodness and refusal of compliant obedience, and because they are not afraid to be called promiscuous, they demonstrate that all Afghan women are not voiceless, passive victims deprived of agency but rather are actively influencing the social hierarchies that implicate them.

What does it mean to be a Muslim feminist in Afghanistan? The life stories of women who live at the khana-yi aman illuminate the anxieties and ambivalences that undergird conversations about Islam, feminism, sexuality, gender, and sexual transgression. The narrative motifs of the khana-yi aman women demonstrate that the production of gendered knowledge regarding a proper Islamic moral ethos has more to do with modern systems of power and their enactment in everyday life than it does with specific interpretations of Islamic texts. Hegemonic discourses undoubtedly shape cultural stances, but cannot completely explain the attitudes and relations manifest in everyday life. The possibility of transformation emerges when norms are inhabited toward a different end than they are intended. And there are schisms between the societal ideals of Islam that the community has historically imagined for itself and how these customs are enacted in everyday practices. The khana-yi aman women create religious subtexts attached to dominant Islamic discourses that nonetheless potentiate space for different forms of communal relations (Das 2007, 63). For instance, as the ethnographic data reveal, alongside enacting their promiscuous selves by publicly admitting to sexual infractions deemed un-Islamic, the women also pray five times a day and fast during Ramazan. By inhabiting these fundamental and conventional Islamic practices of fasting and praying at the margins of Afghan society at the shelter, the women create spaces in the Islamic honor system within which they can fashion their own worlds.

Narratives of accusation and rejection surround the women who have been labeled sexually promiscuous, and in turn these narratives inform how the women construct, inhabit, and navigate their marginalized worlds. For Foucault, ethics is one aspect of morality, and morality comprises the prescriptive moral code, ethics, and concrete actions of social actors. In Afghanistan, the subject is historically and discursively produced within the regulative and disciplinary apparatuses of honor and Islam, which may be read as the prescriptive moral codes that form part of an ethical formation. These moral codes are definitional and prescriptive, but not definitive.[12] In not being definitive, they allow for the ability to maneuver. Within this historical and discursive framework, I read promiscuity as a "capacity for action," which Foucault, based on the Aristotelian tradition, has called askesis.[13] Foucault's conception of a moral subject is particularly pertinent to this book because he is influenced by the Aristotelian tradition that shaped Islamic pedagogical scripts on sexual ethics. Ethical work, self-discipline, and risk are at the core of acquiring freedom.

Honor versus Piety

There is precedence for the women's shelters in the form of shelter provided by friendly *khans* (leaders) under the Pashtun concepts of *panah* (sanctuary) or *nanawatai* (refuge). It is important to note, however, that safety provided by friendly khans for runaway couples or women, while providing some historical precedent, is far from the refuge provided by the shelter and the autonomy it provides the women. The khana-yi aman is a women-run organization, and the supportive community is almost entirely made of women, such as female politicians and judges newly appointed within the Afghan government. The reliance on an exclusively female network is without historical precedent and perhaps explains why the khana-yi aman in particular is viewed with suspicion and wariness by the public. This is an entirely different endeavor than one that relies on a patriarchal system within which a friendly male leader advocates on behalf of a runaway woman. As the many examples will demonstrate, women advocate their own cases in front of judges and at court, which is entirely dissimilar from a jirga, an exclusively masculine domain where women are spoken of in third person by supportive men.

The newness of the khana-yi aman necessitates a rethinking of analytical frameworks used to study Afghan women. Young Afghan women are creating new solidarities not completely bound by ethnicity, religion, or even gender. Some have suggested that honor is a more useful category of analysis than piety to understand the runaway women. In my analysis, I have deliberately included honor under a broader conception of piety. Although some women at the shelter had grown up with the honor principles of pashtunwali, this is not the case for all women. For young Afghan women practicing Islam, piety, in contrast to honor, is a more robust and expansive way of understanding their social position. This is well supported in current historical and anthropological works for Muslims outside Afghanistan, including works by Leila Ahmed, Lila Abu-Lughod, and Saba Mahmood.[14] In her recent book *Do Muslim Women Need Saving?* Abu-Lughod (2013) dismantles honor as a useful analytic frame to interpret the lives of Muslim women. Dicle Kogacioglu (2004) has done the same for honor as an analytical framework in Turkey. It is noteworthy that recent scholarship on Afghanistan (Coburn 2011) has also not applied honor as an all-encompassing framework of analysis, even in Pashtun-dominated areas such as Shinwar (Chiovenda 2019). Although many women are Pashtun, the khana-yi aman itself is not located in a Pashtun province. Family members are negotiating within modern state institutions such as family courts. This does not mean that honor is irrelevant, but that honor must be studied in conjunction with other mechanisms influencing the lives of Afghan women.

Piety and honor work in tandem to condition conventional Afghan womanhood. Piety, as an analytical framework for Afghan women, has explanatory potential and relevance beyond honor. Throughout Afghanistan's history, monarchs have used a combination of pashtunwali honor and Islamic piety to consolidate their rule. The two significant eras in which pashtunwali was evoked as a discourse of honor by the state to consolidate gender laws are the reigns of Amanullah (r. 1919–29) and the Taliban (1996–2001). In the early part of the twentieth century, an influential public intellectual, Qiamuddin Khadim (1901–79), began compiling and writing the book *Pashtunwali*, which he dedicated to Nadir Shah, whose reign followed that of Amanullah. Pashtunwali is perhaps the only code of honor to be written down by an emissary of the state. Today, pashtunwali precepts are embedded in permanent modes of governance. For instance, the *loya jirga*, a process through which the head of the Afghan state is chosen, originates as a precept of pashtunwali. While pashtunwali may not provide the conclusive structuring principles underlying honor and piety, it undeniably informs everyday lives and material practices. It describes the prescriptive and descriptive rules and laws said to govern Pashtun societies. It circulates both as an unwritten code of tribal law and as a written set of rules taken into account when writing the constitutions of Afghanistan and Northern Pakistan.

David Edwards (2017) describes pashtunwali as a set of practices rather than as a moral code or rulebook. He writes that pashtunwali should be understood in terms of "doing Pakhtu" (*pakhtu kawal*), which is a "cultural conceptual space in which identity is negotiated" (28). In this sense, pashtunwali not only enacts the honorable subject but also undergirds the discursive formations that condition the metaphysical assemblage of honor. Pashtunwali and Islam may be seen both as moral codes and as sets of practices, both prescriptive and descriptive.

Here it is useful to think of pashtunwali and Islam as discursive formations. Talal Asad (2009), in understanding Islam as a discursive tradition, notes that the theoretical underpinning for the anthropologist of Islam must be an analysis of "an instituted practice (set in a particular context and having a particular history) into which Muslims are inducted *as* Muslims."[15] He defines discursive tradition as a set of historical discourses that inform and condition practices, and tend toward achieving coherence (2009, 23). Thus, he writes, "Islamic discursive tradition is simply a tradition of Muslim discourse that addresses itself to conceptions of the *Islamic* past and future, with reference to a particular Islamic practice in the present" (20; emphasis in the original). This reading of discursive tradition is indebted to Foucault, who notes that discursive formations are regularized by rules that result in consequences that are not necessarily similar but are identifiable.[16] Whereas honor can be distilled into concrete rules and precepts, the way moral actions can be explained is in the ethical relations that moral actors form between moral actions and moral codes. These ethical relations originate in moral codes, but are not entirely encompassed by them. Nonetheless, the moral codes are key to understanding moral actors and their actions. Asad understands Islamic tradition as "deeply imbricated in the material lives of those inhabiting it" but not entirely encompassing those material lives. In this sense, pashtunwali, like Islam, is a discursive formation because it is not a unified narrative yet can be identified by rules or principles. For example, honor killings may be traced to Islamic or Pashtun notions of honor, but are not necessarily caused by those notions. After the killing, honor may manifest as an effect.[17] In many other instances, pashtunwali congeals into identifiable rules and principles that can be only vaguely articulated, such as love, friendship, camaraderie, and even nation (*qaum* and *millat*) and homeland (*vatan*). The theme of honor informs all these rules and principles. Qaum is often invoked by Pashtuns to mean family or tribe or those to whom one belongs or is close to. In a broader sense, this term may also be used as "nation."[18]

In Afghanistan, notions of state have been linked to an urban center, Kabul, while rural areas have come to signify nonstate. Khadim and his contemporaries designated pashtunwali as a state discourse even though it was seen by some as a tribal, rural, and even antistate ideology. But honor cannot be read through the binary logic of state (urban) and nonstate (rural), for honor permeates urban and rural, tribal and state functions.

Anthony Appiah (2010) reads honor codes across various geographical spaces as ethical motivators of moral revolutions and engines of history. Honor makes itself manifest at various points of intersection between the ethical and moral realms.[19] The principles of honor separate the laws of men from the laws of nature. In this sense, honorable behavior makes us human and has a civilizing effect. The honorable man is a good man, an ethical man, one who follows the righteous paths mandated by the Quran and sunnah (direct path of the Prophet).[20] Although the exegetical scripts have marked themselves as separate from honor systems, religion becomes, as Abu-Lughod (1986) has stated, conflated with honor in issues of morality. The precondition for this good and honorable life is the establishment and maintenance of an honorable state based on the mythical subject of honor.

The establishment of such an honorable state and maintenance of its corresponding power constellations have long been the subject of juridical knowledge and administrative discussion. Although honorable life was a preoccupation before the 1990s, the Taliban brought something new with them: the materialization of the honorable subject as the object of political occupation. The object of administrative concentration for the Taliban was not the rights of individual people or the limits of the state but the nature of the honorable subject whose attitudes were to be shaped by the laws of honor, which gained their credence through divine justice. In other words, the Taliban successfully consolidated Islam with pashtunwali in service of women's subjugation and did so more effectively than other rulers. In this sense, the Taliban demonstrate an epistemic shift, a historical rupture, in Afghan history.[21] While women had been subjugated before, Taliban oppression of women made a clear break from the past. Given the epistemic shift in governance the Taliban rendered through unprecedented draconian rule, promiscuous subjectivities, which are equally unprecedented, willfully emerged at the khana-yi aman. The stronger the oppression, the greater the possibility of resistance. An unintended consequence of Taliban rule was public recognition of shelters and the previously unnamable runaway or promiscuous women they house.

Book Outline

Pious Peripheries is a textual and social ethnography of the category of sexual promiscuity, variously defined and determined, in Afghanistan.[22] My work is deeply ethnographic in thought and content, which focuses on how Afghan women understand, inhabit, and interpret a world profoundly interested in saving them but that, in doing so, further oppresses them.[23] The conceptual and theoretical questions emerge from the speech, perceptions, and gestures of my interlocutors. I closely documented the words and concepts used by women to describe sexual violence and related concepts of chastity and promiscuity. Their words and gestures are not captured by the human rights categories recently developed by modern apparatuses of women's rights activism. To understand the recurring ideas evoked in narrative motifs of sexual violence, I conduct an intellectual history through oral and written poetry, theoretical canon, women's memoirs, fiction writing, and an extensive archive in Persian and Pashto that has seldom been used to contextualize how the categories of promiscuity and chastity (classified as piety for women) in relation to gender and violence have emerged in Afghanistan. The historical, religious, and literary sources I use are referred to in everyday conversations regarding sexual violence and gender inside Afghanistan. This book brings into conversation the historical, the archival, the literary, and the ethnographic.

The book consists of six chapters. The first three are concerned with resistance, and present the ethnography conducted at the Kabul shelter. The second three chapters are concerned with the formation of the power apparatuses of the Taliban, pashtunwali, and Islam. These later chapters perform an intellectual history of the concepts of chastity, piety, virtue, and promiscuity through a reading of Taliban publications, books, and articles written by literati and feminist newspapers.

Chapter One introduces the idea of the khana-yi aman within its Afghan context. Women who reach the shelter have uprooted themselves from their traditional communities bound by kinship ties of ethnicity, language, and religion to form a new community not bound by such ties. Here Pashtun women became friends with Dari-speaking women, Shia women with Sunni women. The loyalty among women, rather than to men, is central. This chapter provides a glimpse into the everyday struggles of ordinary Afghan women as they inhabit and resist patriarchal discourses and innovate social maneuvers and new vocabularies to challenge sexual (and other) injustices. In doing so, they redefine the meaning of kinship.

Chapter Two presents ethnography of multiple court cases of women at the khana-yi aman. I traveled with the runaway women and their families, friends, and lawyers through Kabul to resolve family disputes. The chapter shows how a wide range of runaway cases pertaining to forced marriage, sexual abuse, divorce, and adultery become subsumed under the ambiguous notion of promiscuity, as the khana-yi aman circulates in the Kabul imagination as a brothel. This chapter interrogates the linguistic permutations of rape used by women to narrate experiences of sexual violence. This vocabulary is not captured through the legal discourse on sexual violence and is deeply embedded within historical texts that shape the notion of pious womanhood in Afghanistan. Through long ethnographic vignettes that give voice to how women narrate their sexual subjugation, this chapter shows the madness and unintelligibility inherent in the division between piety and promiscuity.

Chapter Three discusses sexually explicit poetry in Pashto and Dari narrated spontaneously by women at the khana-yi aman to voice their protests and express their discontent. Poetry permeates the everyday lives of Afghans. Pashto poetry sung by women in short snippets called *landay* provide a vocabulary in Pashto for female sexual promiscuity. At the khana-yi aman, Dari-speaking women interweave Pashto landay with Persian verses. In all these poems, the lyrics depict motifs of love, abandonment, suffering, and violence. Some women used bold, sexually explicit poetry at the family courts to publicly register their protests. Landay allow women to take a risk and openly declare a sexually promiscuous self. At the core of landay is the risk of being different, mad, and promiscuous, but not vulnerable. Yet this poetry does make the women vulnerable to violence. Landay spoken by women in public give us insight into how honor is performed in public rather than enshrined in moral codes. What is significant here is not how closely the women adhere to pashtunwali or Islamic precepts but the strategic relationships they establish between themselves and these moral codes. The potential risk lies within the ethical relations that moral actors form with moral codes, and herein resides the possibility of difference. Landay allow women to "misinhabit" honor in subtle and defiant ways and invest their words with risk. This risk forms the basis of an emancipatory politics or a politics of difference.

Chapter Four considers ethnography in the form of conversations, interviews, and negotiations between the Taliban and their runaway wives at family court. This is supplemented with a reading of Taliban publications such as the *Shariat* newspaper and Taliban *fatawa* available in the form of gazettes. In focusing on the microhistories of the runaway wives and daughters of the Taliban, this chapter is motivated by the ethnographic question, What has changed in the everyday lives of ordinary Afghan women since the fall of the Taliban? The narrative motifs show that the Taliban exist as a powerful shadow state in today's Afghanistan. Therefore, as far as moral policing and disciplining of female bodies is concerned, not much has changed in the lives of women. By defining women's public comportment through a narrow interpretation of Islam, the Taliban rob women of their complex histories and plural subjectivities. Ironically, it is within this authoritarianism of the Taliban that the new radical subjectivities of women are rendered possible. The runaway wives and daughters of the Taliban at the khana-yi aman live their protest and resistance through subtle and surprising social maneuvers not entirely controlled by the Taliban.

Chapter Five provides an intellectual history of Afghan womanhood, which is grounded in notions of chastity and piety. It depicts an analysis of pedagogical Islamic texts, transnational pan-Islamism, and literacy and secularism campaigns that influenced the emergence of the modern Afghan woman vis-à-vis the modern notions of nation and homeland (millat and vatan). A reading of these texts is supplemented by extensive ethnographic vignettes that demonstrate how runaway women understand their own positionality in relation to classical texts that situate them as pious or promiscuous.

Chapter Six explores texts written by influential literati of the twentieth century to the present day that underwrite notions of honor and how women inhabit vocabularies of honor and piety in their everyday lives. Pashtunwali has an impressive repertoire of bodily conduct and comportment narrated through practices of sanctuary (*panah*), guest hosting (*hujra*), receiving guests (*mahman nawazi*), refuge (*nanawatai*), hospitality (*melmastia*), and love (*mina*) that socially define men and women as Pashtun and pious. The women at the khana-i aman access historically male-dominated practices to form communal bonds among themselves and, in doing so, simultaneously resist and consolidate the discourse of pashtunwali.

CHAPTER ONE

The Shelter

On a warm summer afternoon, I was accompanied by one of the khana-yi aman (home of safety, or safe house) workers, Haleema, to a hidden building behind a large garbage dump in Kabul.[1] As we walked quickly through the back alleys and narrow pathways to the khana-yi aman, Haleema vigorously went over all the instructions I had already received from the main office.

> You must approach these women with caution. You are responsible for your own safety once inside. You cannot leave the building, as it will be locked from the outside immediately after you enter. You cannot disclose the location of the khana-yi aman to anyone, not even your mother. You cannot bring a car or visitor here. Your phone and personal items will be taken from you. Do not try to hide anything. All will be revealed. All will be revealed. You have to stay continuously for lengthy durations. Temporary visitors draw unwanted attention from the neighbors. Oh yes, none of the neighbors know what we do.[2]

A woman in her early thirties, Mariam, ran a nongovernmental organization (NGO) that supervised the khana-yi aman. The khana-yi aman is a place where Afghan women who have run away from home live as they await court decisions about their cases. It houses women categorized generally as "adulterous" or "promiscuous" and who have been shunned by their communities. Women who run away from home to escape rape and sexual abuse or who have initiated divorces or marriages without family consent may also be sent to the shelter by the relevant ministries.[3] It also acts as a halfway house between prison and community reintegration.

Some women come to the shelter as they battle their families for their share of an inheritance. The shelter serves many purposes, yet this wide variety of purposes is subsumed under the vague label of *brothel*. It is as a brothel that encourages sexually licentious actions that the shelter was imagined and circulated in the Kabul imagination. As this ethnographic study will reveal, the shelters are a far cry from brothels. They house women from various walks of life who share a commitment to practicing Islam by fasting and praying, while also exercising their individual will by running away. In this way, the shelters both consolidate and destabilize the normative structures that situate them as subjects.

The main office of the khana-yi aman is located in a nondescript neighborhood of Kabul and poses as a skills-development facility for women. The two buildings that make up the khana-yi aman are concealed behind the large garbage dump that covers the rear portion of the main office. The operations of the khana-yi aman fall under the jurisdiction of the Vizarat-e-Umur-e-Zanan, the Ministry of Women's Affairs (MOWA), established in 2001 to handle women's rights issues. While MOWA's primary goal is ostensibly to protect women's rights, the relationship between the khana-yi aman activists and the politicians is a contested one. For example, a high official at MOWA has distanced herself from the khana-yi aman in public statements. One such official, whom I interviewed to gain permission to access the shelter to conduct fieldwork, said:

> I cannot encourage women to leave their homes and run away with strange men. This is not good for the women, nor for Afghanistan. I am an educated woman. I do not see the Taliban ideology as a threat to women's rights. We must move forward with the Taliban.

The MOWA administrator's stance was no different from that of other women in prominent positions. Even women who worked for women's rights activist organizations were quick to mark themselves as different from the women at the shelter. Because the shelter housed runaway women, it was an object of derision.

Running away from home is deemed immoral in Afghanistan. Although the women ended up at the khana-yi aman for a wide variety of reasons, many of which involved sexual transgression, they had in common their banishment from their communities. After the fall of the Taliban, the government had tried to protect women by allowing NGOs and women's rights activists to open shelters. Yet the shelters posed a threat to the legitimacy of women's rights organizations because they were viewed as protecting and encouraging noncompliant sexual attitudes. Running away, even to escape sexual abuse, is unprecedented and a cause for concern. Shelters are central to the perception that any form of women's rights activism is linked to sexual licentiousness, which is why the khana-yi aman was the first institution to come under attack in negotiations with fundamentalist religious groups, such as the Taliban, who wanted the government to shut down such places. While the Taliban posed a threat to the shelters, the perceived sexual licentiousness of shelter inhabitants also posed a threat to their own well-being. Most people I met had strong negative opinions about the shelter. This included both men and women from a wide range of classes, races, professions, and religious and ethnic affiliations. Even foreign workers in international organizations from ostensibly "progressive" countries shared this public perception of the shelter. It was for this reason that the khana-yi aman was hidden in plain sight in Kabul.

A few weeks earlier, I had attended a rooftop party with an American friend at another friend's residence in Kabul. The crowd was mostly expatriate Afghans and international workers. During a conversation with a white man in his fifties, he asked me my topic of research. When I replied that it was the khana-yi aman, he immediately said, "Oh, you are working with those prostitutes." This typifies the prevalent perception among the public that conflates the khana-yi aman with a brothel and the women inside with prostitutes. This perception was not peculiar to conservative Afghans. The other popular perception was that the women who came to the shelter were from lower-class families and were uneducated, rural, or tribal. None of these was an accurate description of the reality inside the shelter.

After getting special permission to conduct ethnographic fieldwork at the khana-yi aman, I spent some time in its main office. This particular day, I was to continue my fieldwork in the actual building that housed the runaway women, a building shrouded in secrecy, given the threats to the women. Haleema, a worker in the main office, volunteered to walk me to the undisclosed location away from the main office. After walking through multiple small, curving, and twisting alleys, jumping over several puddles, and avoiding trash heaps, we stopped at the gate of a small, unmarked building. I looked around. The neighborhood was quiet and unremarkable, the streets lined unevenly with differently colored houses. Haleema gave four sharp knocks and stepped back three feet, looked at me, made a gesture with her hands to signify madness, and said, "Good luck. These women are crazy and dirty. Crazy. Don't eat from their bowls." Then, with a quick good-bye, she walked hurriedly back to the main office as I stood alone and waited. A guard appeared out of nowhere and opened the large black lock on the gate. As soon as I stepped in, the door was closed with a loud thud and immediately locked. A small, dark corridor led to another locked door, which was opened from the inside, and a woman stepped out, followed by twelve others.

The thirteen women walked up to me with curiosity and suspicion. One of them, Gulalei, clearly the leader, spoke: "What brought you here? Whom did you sleep with? Did you just come from prison?" The candor of the questions was startling. "I am Sonia," was all I could say. She introduced everyone and mumbled, "We will figure you out and what you've been up to soon enough." It would eventually become clear to me what Haleema had meant when she told me that all would be revealed in here. Given the barred premises, the women lived close and intimate lives inside the shelter, where little could be hidden.

The shelter was housed in two residential buildings across from each other. This one was for transitory cases, those expected to last a few weeks. If the case became more permanent, lasting for more than three years, the woman was transferred across the street to the "permanent side." Although the building was referred to as permanent, the women could not stay there forever.

Another woman, Huma, one of the managers, gave me a tour of the building. I learned that Huma was a medical doctor by training and had received her degree from Quetta University in Baluchistan. Her family believed that she worked at a women's clinic. She showed me the other building of the khana-yi aman from the window upstairs. Although Huma said tightly, "We are not in prison," the thought of living in a locked building for more than three years seemed very much like being imprisoned. Gulalei shook her head, saying, "It is a prison. It is."

After the tour, it was time to pray. A *janamaz* (prayer rug) was ceremoniously brought out and laid for me in the center of the living area. I had no intention of praying, so I said, "I already prayed." Gulalei said, "I am sure you prayed namaz-e zuhr [noon prayer]. It is time for namaz-e 'asr [afternoon prayer]. The azan [call to prayer] happened a few minutes ago. Certainly, you heard! You better do the vuzu [prayer ablutions]. Sohaila will take you." Sohaila was an inhabitant of the shelter, whose story I would learn later. After I finished the vuzu under Sohaila's watchful eyes, the women formed a semicircle around the janamaz and watched me expectantly. This was the first time since I was nine years old that I had been observed so carefully while praying. My fieldwork was already beginning to invert my world as I became the one observed rather than the observer.

As the days passed, I became accustomed to the routine of the khana-yi aman. The women sat on carpeted floors and thin floor blankets that covered the corners of the living area. A large TV with bad reception stood on one side. Quarrels over the remote control could be heard intermittently. Because the khana-yi aman was under constant threat from the Taliban and the families of the runway women, the inhabitants were not allowed cell phones, in order to minimize contact with the outside world. Every material possession, including the clothes on their backs, was taken from them at the entrance and locked in one of the cupboards in a small room in the entrance corridor. Women shared clothes and other items collected in shared closets inside the shelter. Groceries were brought in daily by the guard, affectionately called *kaka* (uncle), who would knock at the door, open the outside lock, deposit the groceries, then leave for a few moments. The food was brought in by Gulalei and cooked in the kitchen on the ground floor. Cleaning, cooking, and washing obligations rotated weekly.

Some inhabitants were rebellious teenagers, others claimed to be wives of the Taliban, but most had come either to get married or get a divorce. Most women were between the ages of fifteen and thirty, but there were inhabitants as young as two and as old as eighty. Some women were highly educated and prosperous; in fact, one was an acting member of parliament. The khana-yi aman had a makeshift parlor where women put on makeup, did their hair, and dressed each other. The attic had been converted into a sewing room where women formed circles and chatted daily. Most women wore the clothes tailored in this room, although there was a community tailor who came for special occasions, such as Eid. There was a marked feeling of friendliness and hospitality that united the women here, and, since no one could leave the building, strong bonds formed among the inhabitants. Unlike the nondescript façade of the main office, the inner space of the khana-yi aman, as the ethnography will show, was defined by chaos, madness, hospitality, and unpredictability, and also friendship and love.

This ethnography reveals a wide range of social and political beliefs among the women of the khana-yi aman, who represented an array of political ideologies and modes of social belonging. Despite such variation, all had been rejected and shunned by their local communities. What they had in common was their stories of abandonment. They shared their respective failures of communal integration regardless of the community to which they belonged. Naila, a shelter inhabitant, narrated the necessity of the khana-yi aman in terms of protecting all forms of love and belonging. According to Haleema, the need for shelters materialized as a response to the widespread notion that a particular form of Islam was the only way of organizing their social worlds; any other way of thinking had been increasingly ostracized under modern configurations of Islamic governance. As a result, women ran away from home. Feminist activists who operated the shelter voiced concerns about the increasing Islamization of Afghanistan, a historical consequence of imperialism and modernization, which had increasingly restricted the possibilities of communal belonging. Despite the managers' fears of Islamization, the inhabitants fully practiced the rituals of Islam through prayer, fasting, reciting the Quran, and veiling. Adding to this paradox was the bias against the actions of the inhabitants by secular-minded activists who rallied against Islamization while simultaneously practicing it.

Fiscal Apparatus of the Shelters

The shelter where I conducted fieldwork functioned within the NGO apparatus, particularly the Afghan Women Network and the Afghan Women's Skills Development Center, founded in 1999 in Pakistan and moved to Kabul in 2001. At the time when I was conducting fieldwork, attempts to nationalize the shelters were thwarted by women's rights activists.[4] During my stay at the shelter, a Sri Lankan nonprofit organization interested in providing funding was invited for a brief observation. During this time, we were told not to speak about the court cases but to act as a "skills development" center where women were trained in sewing and knitting. This example shows how difficult it is to obtain funding for places like the khana-yi aman. The shelters do not want to openly claim they are helping women escape their families, even though their role is known and has been debated in parliament. As one manager told me, "Shelters must operate behind veil of discretion." These are unspoken and unwritten rules that are difficult to quantify and put on paper.

The shelters are funded by a variety of sources and have a difficult time staying afloat. Funding for the shelter is filtered through various women's rights organizations.[5] During my time working in the main office of this particular shelter, lack of funding was often brought forward as a concern. Precariousness of funding, along with political insecurity, undergirded the feeling of uncertainty. Mariam, who ran the shelter, along with Waniza, a women's rights activist, would often advocate for ad hoc funding. I saw them travel to various embassies, United Nations events, and influential international women's rights organizations to ask for support. Mariam was not fluent in English, so Waniza was the main person giving presentations in front of international donors. The language on the website uses the familiar phrases of human rights, development, and peace building. As is evident from a comparison of websites, the shelter is not well funded and is more fiscally precarious than others.

Waniza and Mariam also participated in monthly or bimonthly trainings for shelter employees in which staff gathered at the main office for various educational and awareness-building programs. There were periodic workshops, literacy groups, and skills training to expose the residents to various forms of knowledge and activities. The trainings guided women in general ways to attain self-confidence and advocate for their rights. However, the shelter administrators were not trained lawyers. The four shelter lawyers, two male and two female, were responsible for all legal argumentation in the courts. They were assigned to women based on linguistic or geographic affinity, and they often developed a rapport with the women and became their link to the outside world. I saw the lawyers use all possible means, including their legal knowledge, personal contacts, skills, and legal maneuvers, to achieve favorable outcomes for the women.

Topography of the Shelters: What Is a Khana-yi Aman?

Shelters are not peculiar to Afghanistan, and the idea of shelters is not specific to gender. Shelters across the globe are places of refuge from economic disenfranchisement and social marginalization. Shelters in Afghanistan almost exclusively house women who have been classified as runaways. As noted earlier, runaway cases arise for a variety of reasons, including marriage or divorce. Women subjected to sexual and physical violence will also be sent by administrative officials to a shelter while their cases are processed. Shelters allow the state to step into family arbitrations. What would otherwise be resolved informally through jirgas (tribal councils) and family meetings is now adjudicated by the state. This can provide protection to the women, but as the ethnography demonstrates, it also subjects them to grotesque violence. Once in the shelter, women are at the mercy of the state without family safeguards and, in some cases, suffer rape and other violence at the hands of the officials in charge of protecting them.

The cases are not only about sexual infractions; they range from disputes over inheritance to sexual abuse. Despite the wide range of cases, the khana-yi aman circulates in the public imagination as a place of moral corruption. How do simple disobedience, claims to inheritance, escape from an abusive family, and even rape all become viewed as sexual immorality on the part of the woman? That puzzle is at the heart of this study. These various claims from variously marginalized people become connected to and subsumed under the generalized notion of promiscuity. As I will show throughout this book, promiscuity is not a character trait but a social label placed on women who strive to be different.

Ethnographic fieldwork over a prolonged period demonstrates the futility of using statistical metrics to classify and explain such cases, because each is complex and cannot be reduced to a data point. Ghazi Hashmi (2017), a professor at Kabul University, explains why running away may be conflated with prostitution or sexual crimes: "While Islam may not expressly prohibit running away from home, it is considered to run counter to Islamic principles"[6] (214). Running away is often conflated with sexual and moral crimes such as prostitution, fornication, and adultery, even though it is not explicitly a crime under the Afghan constitution. Nevertheless, "law enforcement authorities often arrest, jail, and even prosecute girls for running away, usually qualifying the charge as 'intention' to commit adultery [*zina*] which is a crime" (214).[7] It is for these reasons that women are subjected to virginity tests to ascertain whether they have committed a sexual crime.

Runaways or Escapees?

The Supreme Court of Afghanistan made a distinction in 2012 between running away because of domestic violence and running away with the intention of committing a moral crime (Hashmi 2017, 216). The decree states that "running away" should be used for cases in which women have run away to escape abuse and, therefore, should not be prosecuted. In practice, however, this decree has not stopped the prosecution of runaway cases based on abuse. It also does not stipulate that a mandatory waiting period be observed before divorcing missing husbands, but does leave open the possibility of charging women for moral crimes if an intent to commit zina (adultery) is established.

Many women claim that their husbands joined the Taliban and have gone missing (*ghaib*). '*Iddat* (*Edat*) is defined as "separation due to absence" and is part of the Islamic divorce process (Afghanistan Legal Education Project 1977).[8] In these cases, women must complete the mandatory waiting period ('iddat) enshrined in the Afghan constitution, which varies according to case, but can be up to three years. The concept of a mandatory waiting period is rooted in Hanafi jurisprudence (one of the four schools of Islamic thought), upon which the Afghan constitution is based.[9] The law mandates that the husband be notified by the court if a woman files for divorce in his absence. Moreover, divorce due to absence is reversible if the husband returns to the wife before the mandatory waiting period is over. When runaway cases are presented in front of judges, they are decided on a case-by-case basis, and judges have complete discretion. When cases are unclear, judges will revert to their understanding of Hanafi laws. Evidence gathered through testimonies of family members is used to establish the moral character of the woman, and if doubts are raised about her chastity, her credibility in front of the judge is in jeopardy. Because many women cannot stay at the shelter indefinitely, they are aware that charges of licentiousness would have a negative impact on their lives after returning home. It takes tremendous courage to run away and fight court battles in these circumstances.

Even women who are educated are often unable to understand the complexity of the documents they are signing. This is especially the case when women are made to sign away their property rights or confess to adultery. In my interviews with police and lawyers, I often heard adultery and rape being used interchangeably, especially for women whose morality was put into question because of prior sexual encounters. As a Human Rights Watch report states:

> [P]olice often treat a report of rape as an admission of *zina* [adultery], arresting the victim along with the perpetrator. Many police officers, prosecutors, and judges accept a mere counter-allegation of consensual sex to trump a complaint of rape and transform it into a complaint of *zina*, instead of treating consent as a defence that can be pleaded by a person accused of rape during a criminal investigation or trial. In this way many complaints of rape are never even investigated. The result is the double victimization of a complainant. And this makes the process so traumatic that it is even more unlikely that women and girls who have been raped will seek justice by informing the authorities. (Human Rights Watch 2012, 37)

This was corroborated during my fieldwork. Runaway women faced tremendous obstacles as they circulated through the Kabul courts to prove sexual abuse. Women who left their husbands were often accused of adultery. For example, Sarah, a twenty-five-year-old woman who ran away from her husband to file for divorce, was accused of loose moral character by her family, along with her in-laws, who were distant relatives. She had accused her husband of repeatedly raping her during her five-year marriage. She was eventually sent back to her husband with the proclamation that rape did not exist in a marital union. With no place to go, Sarah contemplated killing herself, but decided to postpone her suicide so that she could raise her daughters. When I met her at the shelter, she said the following:

> Why am I waiting to kill myself, tomorrow and not today? I have to raise my daughters. That is the only reason to live in the present. My husband beats me repeatedly during sexual intercourse even though he is neither drunk nor on drugs. He is a respectable civil servant. If you meet him, you would sing his praises. And yet he rapes me every day.

Before I could formulate a coherent question, she continued.

> My daughters will face the same fate [*kismet*]. It is in our destiny. Should I wring their necks to save them from this agony? But I have faith that their fate is different than mine. Do you know how it feels to have your hands tied behind your back while a man penetrates you? Do you know how it feels to be raped until you are unconscious, only to be woken up by your toddler daughters?

I stammered to tell Sarah that marital rape became a criminal act recently in the United States, but only in some states. However, this information seemed irrelevant, almost discourteous to her narration. How would it make her life better if I shared with her that husbands rape their wives in the United States as well? She had no ambition to emigrate, nor was she sharing her story to draw a comparison. I asked whether she had a support system should she succeed in leaving her husband, Karim.

> I have no one. My in-laws and my own family have told me that I should be grateful that my husband wants me, desires me. They say a Muslim wife should be pleasing to her husband. They tell me that he has to rape me because I say no to him. Why are you saying no, they

ask me? Do you want someone else? My mother said, "Poor Karim has to bring a rope and tie your hands, you stupid woman. Why are you resisting your husband? He is young, and he is attractive. Even if he were old and ugly, he would still be your husband, and have rights for sexual intercourse. You should be willing to please him. What are you teaching your daughters, you mad woman?"

When I met Karim at one of the family negotiations at the family court, he was polite and courteous. He spoke softly without raising his voice for emphasis. The shelter lawyer representing Sarah made a passing comment in front of Sarah: "Unlike Sarah, her husband seems composed and not driven by emotion." As we waited for the judge, I asked Karim, "Why are you here?" He replied, "I want my wife back. She is dear to me. She is the mother of my daughters. I have deep affection for her." I made a vague reference to the violence by asking, "Why do you treat her this way then?" He understood, because he answered, "I have not touched her while fasting or when she was on her break." The reference to "break" is to menstruation, which releases a wife from her sexual obligations to her husband. The reference to fasting relates to the month of Ramazan, in which sexual relations between husband and wife are forbidden except between the nonfasting hours, which are from dusk to dawn. Karim did not think forcing his wife for sexual relations was immoral because it was neither against his religious tenets nor against the law. He claimed, "Being intimate with your wife is neither illegal nor un-Islamic."

Karim's interpretation was shared by many. The concept of forcing a wife to have sexual relations was difficult to argue in front of a judge. Sarah's appointed shelter lawyer told me that judges would laugh when they brought up issues of marital rape. By contrast, if a woman complained about lack of intimacy or impotence, it would be a serious issue and grounds for wife-initiated divorce. Because the marital unit pivoted on sexual relations between husband and wife, the idea of marital rape was almost impossible to argue. In these cases, the lawyers reverted to the precedent set in the sunnah, or how the Prophet behaved with his wives. They spoke about affection and tenderness, which would be incompatible with coerced sexual relations. Sarah's lawyer told me that her case was almost certain to fail in front of any judge, male or female. In the coming days, Sarah was told to go back with her husband. Gulalei gave her and the other women a talk before Sarah was to leave with Karim. She used her interpretation of Quranic and hadith references to guide Sarah's behavior toward her husband. She was advised to show a positive attitude when he wanted to have sexual relations with her and to be grateful that he was physically attracted to her.

Historicizing the Shelters: Governing Women's Rights Apparatuses

MOWA, which oversees the shelters, is an ostensibly new organization developed through Western influence in post-Taliban Afghanistan. Yet MOWA's institutional framework has a long history in the form of precursor organizations. Progress in Afghanistan has long been measured by how various governments enact gender rights reform in their agendas. Almost all governments have implemented measures to transform women's rights along either conservative or progressive trajectories. The Taliban are viewed as the game changers on women's rights issues in Afghanistan, and their influence on sexual morality has indeed been deeply influential. This book devotes a chapter to the Taliban's Islam, as it is my contention that they continue to be the most influential drivers of sexual morality in contemporary Afghanistan. To this day, the Taliban are in negotiations with the Afghan government and the Americans, and sexual propriety and women's issues are at the heart of these negotiations.[10] However, gender reform has a longer and more complex history.

A number of significant gender reforms pertinent to the establishment of MOWA, and by extension the shelters, have taken place in prior decades. In the twentieth century, the first significant gender reforms on record took place under Amir 'Abdur Rahman (r. 1880–1901), who prohibited cousin marriages, even though there is clear precedence in Islamic history for these. The Prophet's daughter Fatima married the Prophet's first cousin, 'Ali, and the many Afghans I know suggested that the Prophet favored 'Ali for his daughter over other suitors because of 'Ali's family connection to the Prophet. Likewise, Zaynab bint Jahsh was a first cousin and wife of the Prophet. Thus 'Abdur Rahman's ban on cousin marriages was not without controversy. He also instituted a mandatory limit on bride price, which nevertheless did not constrain the practice (Dupree 1984). Paradoxically, he instituted other measures that can be interpreted as against women's rights—for example, stoning for adultery, which is also grounded in Islamic law. He would later come to be known as the Iron Amir. Why would 'Abdur Rahman ban a seemingly innocuous Islamic practice of cousin marriages while also implementing stoning for adultery? I argue that the legitimacy of Afghan leaders is anchored in legislating women's sexual virtue in the public sphere. The intensity with which Afghan rulers have attempted to establish, perpetuate, and redefine moral codes of sexual conduct has created the space for tragic errors. The issues I saw during my fieldwork as narrated in the subsequent chapters are more complicated than forced cousin marriages. Many women loved and wanted to be married to their cousins. Thus it is not surprising that a blanket ban on these would not have alleviated women's condition.

The next major campaigners for gender rights were Amir Amanullah and his wife, Queen Soraya (1899–1968). They are the most memorable reformers of gender rights in Afghanistan to this day and are spoken about with nostalgic fondness. Amanullah and Soraya lived a fashionable and Westernized life. Soraya, the daughter of the influential intellectual Mahmud Tarzi, wore skirts and dresses. Tarzi (1865–1933) was a prolific intellectual and wrote about important women in Islamic history, such as the wives of the Prophet. During Amanullah's reign, schools for girls were opened, and women were encouraged to reinterpret veiling as a modern garment evincing modesty rather than an old style of covering (burqa). Conservatives of all strains who contended that national honor was linked to protecting the honor of women resisted Amanullah's reforms (Dupree 1984, 307). Modernity was often juxtaposed with tribal customs emanating from outside Kabul. Throughout the gender reforms of the twentieth century, a notion of Pashtun tribalism emerged in opposition to gender progress. After a revolt against Amanullah and a yearlong war, Nadir Shah (r. 1929–33) became the king, followed by his son Mohammed Zahir Shah (r. 1933–73), during which time women's reforms progressed slowly. The 1964 constitution gave women the right to work, vote, and pursue education.

During these and subsequent eras, women's progress and gender reforms were grounded in appeals to Islamic precedents. The Saur Revolution of 1978 abrogated the constitutions of 1964 and 1977 and established the rule of the People's Democratic Party of Afghanistan (PDPA). As during Amanullah's rule, here, too, heroic images of women from the past were used to inspire change. During the reign of the PDPA, public narrations about the maternal heroines of the past—such as Zargunah, mother of the famous king Ahmad Shah Durrani (r. 1747–72); the tenth-century tragic heroine Rabia Balkhi; and Malalai of Maiwand, who inspired rebellion against British soldiers in 1880—were evoked to encourage women to defy custom and seek change. Also during this time, the Ministry of Social Affairs, headed by Dr. Anahita Ratebzad, a relative of Mahmud Tarzi, was instituted. As minister, Ratebzad (d. 2014) worked relentlessly for women's rights, but she was dismissed after a few months when women's affairs became the domain of the Ministry of Education. Despite its short stint, the Ministry of Social Affairs can be considered a predecessor to MOWA.

In 1965, the Democratic Organization of Afghan Women (DOAW) was instituted to promote change for ordinary women, with the claim that women's rights had become a business of the aristocracy. DOAW later became the Khalq Organization of Afghan Women (KOAW), which focused on increasing the presence of women in the public sphere. The communist era was inundated with a concern to make women's rights accessible to ordinary women. Images from this era often circulate in public media to depict a secular and modern past for Afghan women by showing women in Western-style skirts and dresses walking on streets and speaking with men. Even though the rhetoric at this time was toward mainstreaming gender reforms, the nostalgic images emanating from this era are far from mainstream. Only elite women from upper-class Kabul society experienced such liberties.

While these heroine images certainly depict courage and inspire change, the grounding principles undergirding this imagery were maternity, chastity, and piety. After the fall of the Taliban in 2001, Hamid Karzai became the president of Afghanistan, serving until 2014. Karzai's government placed a particular emphasis on women's rights, more especially because of international interest in Afghanistan. Karzai signed the Elimination of Violence Against Women (EVAW) instrument into law through a decree in 2009. Many cases at the shelters made appeals to this decree, but the judges had discretion to adjudicate on cases based on their own interpretation of Islamic law.

Running Away as Agentive Action: Becoming a "Fahsha"

Is running away from home a form of agency? What does it mean to run away from home, and how should we understand women who make this decision? Women who run away are not always running away from sexual abuse or to save their lives from an existential threat of death. An example would be Nirmeen, a sixteen-year-old Pashtun from Paktia province whose parents had arranged a marriage for her with her first cousin. Nirmeen did not have a lover, nor was she opposed to the marriage. However, she wanted to finish her schooling before she married. In my conversation with her, I asked how her life would change if she finished school, since she was committed to marrying her cousin soon after. I asked her, "Why did you run? Does this make your life easy or difficult?" Nirmeen, a bright and opinionated young Pashtun woman, chose to speak eloquently in Persian about her decision to run.

> It is not about making life easy or difficult. This is about respect [*'iz-zat*] for my decisions. I know that my in-laws will not let me work after I get married. They think a working woman is a prostitute [*fah-sha*]. I know I am taking a risk. I know I am endangering myself [*man dar khatar hastam*]. My end goal [*maqsad*] is not to work but to gain respect for my decisions.

This was one of the first deeply startling ethnographic conversations I had. As a woman who grew up in Peshawar, I am well versed in Pashtun norms. While the idea of a "working woman" as linked to being a prostitute was familiar, redefining *'izzat* was not. The notion of respect or *'izzat* is linked to proper comportment and adherence to social values. This is true for both men and women, and endangering one's life in the service of higher ideals does accord respect. If it compromises one's sexual reputation, however, respect is not a common outcome.

I was baffled. How could Nirmeen link respect with running away, which was necessarily tied to the notion of promiscuity? I asked her, "How can you gain respect by running away? As you said yourself, not adhering to societal norms [*rasm v ravaj*], such as becoming a working woman, will render a loss of reputation. How will you become respectable by running away, which some would see as far worse than becoming a working woman?" Nirmeen smiled and said, "I am putting myself at risk. I am taking a risk [*man dar khatar hastam*]." Nirmeen was linking the risk to her personhood with the acquisition of respect, even though it compromised her reputation. In subsequent ethnographic conversations with runaway women, the notion of risk (*khatar*, which variously translates as "endangerment," "danger," or "risk-taking") was frequently mentioned. Such a risk of promiscuity was at the core of finding an alternative trajectory to a respectable personhood, which was largely unintelligible within common perceptions of piety and promiscuity. Singing landay, sexually explicit Pashtun poetry, best exemplifies this kind of promiscuous risk.

Nirmeen was not a promiscuous woman within a Western framework. She had not engaged in promiscuous relations even within a local framework of sexual desire. Yet her reputation was compromised by her decision to run away. Instead of justifying her decision by speaking about her oppression, she asserted her independence by redefining the normative structure that situated her as marginal. Nirmeen redefined the link between promiscuity and sexuality and, by extension, promiscuity and morality. By purging the act of running away of its sexual connotations while embracing the risk of promiscuity, she made the risking of promiscuity a moral decision. The nuance and complexity of Nirmeen's position were often lost in conversations with her family. Even in negotiations with the state by feminist organizations, which purported to be experts on runaway women, the complexity of everyday micropractices was not captured. The failure to understand the perspective of runaway women resides in a broader failure to parse the particular notion of promiscuity willingly inhabited by these women.

In the weeks that followed, I met with Nirmeen's parents and her fiancé's family. Her affianced man, named Raza, explained the situation in a different way: "Nirmeen's decision to run away is deeply confusing.

Why would she do this? She is not under immediate threat of death. No one is threatening her life. Her family loves her. I want to marry her. Why is she doing this? The purpose seems only to hurt us. What can she gain from this?" Nirmeen's father attributed her running from home to immaturity, and expanded on the perceived childishness of running away. The distress of the families was obvious in all our conversations, and, a few weeks later, Raza broke off the engagement.

The only telephone in the shelter's administrative room rang loudly with the news. Raza had notified the lawyers in the main office building, who had called the shelter to notify Gulalei. Gulalei called me to witness her breaking the news to Nirmeen. I waited for Nirmeen's reaction, but she was uncharacteristically stone-faced, and remarked, "Raza's true character has been revealed." Gulalei raised her eyebrows and said, "You mad woman. You put yourself in this situation. Raza broke the engagement because you ran away. How can you be so dense?" But Nirmeen replied again, "Raza's true character has been revealed." I waited a few days before asking Nirmeen about her cryptic remark. She gave a detailed reply:

> Raza is my first cousin. I have known him since I was born. He is deeply selfish and narcissistic. The truth is, I do want to work. I was just testing Raza to see what he would do. It is obvious that he would not have let me work. I will finish my education and find a job.

"What about marriage?" I asked slowly. Nirmeen seemed so much stronger than I, despite her situation in life. Nirmeen replied, "I am not thinking that far. I have achieved what I wanted." Nirmeen left a few days later with her family. A year later, she had finished school. She eventually got married to a different cousin, and the memory of this incident receded. While Nirmeen's decision to run away did not end in death or violence, other women were not as fortunate. Some, as mentioned earlier, like Samia Sarwar, suffered death, and Nurzia Athmar endures a life in permanent hiding.

Nirmeen was an avid reader of Persian poetry, particularly feminist poets such as Forough Farrokhzad. In some ways, Farrokhzad's life was worlds apart from the khana-yi aman women, the latter sharing nothing with the former's privilege, fame, and affluence. Yet the trajectory of their lives is remarkably similar. Farrokhzad's life, like her poetry, was tumultuous. She married a relative against her family's wishes and endured public vilification after her affair with Nasser Khodayar, a writer for whom she had written the poem "Gonah" (Sin), which expresses carnal feminine desires outrageous for some. Khodayar betrayed Farrokhzad by publishing a serial story containing great sexual detail about a promiscuous protagonist heroine who uncannily resembled Farrokhzad. Perhaps as a result of this, Farrokhzad had a nervous breakdown and was admitted to a psychiatric hospital, where she was given electroshock therapy after she attempted suicide. Her marriage ended in divorce, and she lost custody of her son. Farrokhzad died in a car crash in 1967 at thirty-two years of age. Her writing was banned after the 1979 Islamic Revolution in Iran, but this only increased her fame. Her poetry was later co-opted by the Islamic state.

Samia Sarwar, Nurzia Athmar, and Forough Farrokhzad exemplify how economic privilege does not prevent a woman from being labeled as marginal, licentious, and senseless. Ironically, Farrokhzad has been called the Sylvia Plath of Iran. Plath's suicide at age thirty demonstrates that women's struggles are not unique to Afghanistan and that economic privilege and intellectual talent have hardly ever protected women against labels of promiscuity and madness.[11] But, what is more important, these life stories express how women have always endangered themselves and put themselves at risk of being called mad and promiscuous in order to forge alternative life trajectories. They demonstrate how many women have embraced this risk of promiscuity. Farrokhzad was aware of her controversial position in Iran when she noted, "Perhaps because no woman before me took steps toward breaking the shackles binding women's hands and feet, and because I am the first to do so, they have made such a controversy out of me" (Radjy 2019). The following is from Farrokhzad's 1955 poem "Captive":

I think about it and yet I know
I'll never be able to leave this cage
Even if the warden should let me go
I've lost the strength to fly away. (Radjy 2019)

The women at the khana-yi aman, not unlike their favorite poetess, were not free. But they also did not consider themselves un-free. While they seemed caged inside the shelter, many considered reaching the shelter an achievement. Those who arrived willingly at the shelter took great pride in their accomplishment.

To understand these women and why they run, we must move beyond the binary category of freedom and oppression. Saba Mahmood's work on a particular women's piety movement in Egypt has been pivotal to scholarship on Islamic feminism. Mahmood's approach is that we must move away from deterministic theories of agency toward "a grammar of concepts within which [agency] resides" (2005, 34).[12] Her work asks us to consider the modes of sociability that women enact in everyday practices of piety to foment a political movement. Western frameworks of resistance and oppression do not capture these modes of sociability. Neither do these modes engage directly with institutional arrangements usually connected to the political domain (2005, 34–35). Mahmood's work is a major breakthrough in the move away from Western explanations of non-Western feminist movements. Although the main thrust of her influential book is to reject secular-liberal trajectories of progressive feminism, her work posits Egypt as a secular-liberal state against which the piety movement is positioning itself. In this way, her theoretical framing never really breaks away from the hegemony of a Western understanding of resistance and oppression. Nevertheless, despite these limitations, her analytical intervention to expand the notion of critique to include various modes of resistance and sociability underpins my work.

Mahmood (2005) describes her repugnance and discomfort studying the seemingly patriarchal and oppressive modes of belonging in the piety movement. She notes how she often felt this repugnance "against the practices of the mosque movement, especially those that circumscribe women's subordinate status within Egyptian society" (37). In dealing with this repugnance, she seeks to move beyond a foreclosed notion of feminism that requires equality between genders to be realized. The women who run away face a different form of repugnance as they are viewed as promiscuous, loose, mad, and licentious. It is a repugnance that is shared across various social and moral systems. In running away and then offering alternative interpretations of their actions, the women rewrite what it means to be moral and ethical and, by extension, desirable or repugnant. Mahmood claims that because the Egyptian piety movement is not interested in taking over the state—an interpretation that has been contested by other scholars of Egypt—we must read it differently than other illiberal movements that do aim to take over the state, such as al-Qaeda (37). Whereas the women who manage the Kabul shelter are deeply embedded within an institutional framework of state politics, most women who run away, like the piety movement women of Egypt, had no direct engagement with state structures. Despite the lack of a political public platform, the runaway women at the Kabul shelter demonstrate that alliances can be formed across all kinds of social marginality.

The khana-yi aman allows for transitory bonds to form between marginalized runaway women. Most residents of the permanent side eventually leave within several months or a few years. Although the shelter is not the first nonfamilial institution to allow women to access the public, it is unlike other spaces of female communal bonding, such as dormitories, hospitals, and schools. Historically these spaces have prohibited actions that rebel against or challenge codes of proper comportment, especially behaviors such as adultery or fornication, which are viewed as directly disobeying Islamic precepts of sexual conduct. Because the shelter houses runaway women, an official status that already marks them as marginal, it is by definition a peripheral organization. However, the issue of sexual morality makes the shelter central to the Afghan state (Ahsan 2017). The khana-yi aman itself has some emancipatory potential, but it is deeply implicated within the disciplinary mechanisms that necessitate its existence in the first place. It is not the existence of the khana-yi aman then that potentiates the possibility of political difference but the actions, practices, and interpretations of everyday women who either run away and live to tell their stories or, like Samia, run away and die.

The khana-yi aman faces criticism from many sides. Some consider it ventriloquizing a specific Western notion of agency. This Western permutation of freedom necessitates a subversion of the normative structures of oppression. This means that without subversion there can be no agency. Running away by definition is subversion and rebellion, a failure to integrate. While this may be a correct reading of the runaway women's actions, it is an incomplete story. Demonstrating subversion by running away does not preclude the possibility of inhabiting other aspects of a patriarchal discourse. Thus the women veil in complete burqas while out-side, pray and fast during Ramazan, and many even choose to be second or third wives. These actions cannot be subsumed under the singular cat-egory of consolidation or resistance to the normative structure. Rather, women inhabit a multiplicity of nonteleological subject positions toward various modes of ontological becoming.[13] The subjects of piety in this sense are always already in unfinished processes of becoming.

CHAPTER TWO

Portraits of Pain

The Mobile Phone

Mobile phones were coveted inside the khana-yi aman. When I entered the shelter, Sadaf, a Pashtun from Jalalabad, tried to convince me to get her a mobile phone from outside. Her soon-to-be husband, Habib, had a first wife named Suha. Suha and Sadaf were friends, and Sadaf missed their daily telephone chats. "I thought you wanted the mobile phone to talk to Habib," I said to her one day. "No," she said, "Habib is boring on the telephone. We have nothing to talk about. I miss Suha."

Inside the shelter, Sadaf was friends with Hangama, a tall, stately Pashtun from Helmand. Hangama was at the shelter to complete her *'iddat*, or mandatory waiting period, for a divorce, which can be up to three years, and three months for cases in which husbands are missing. Hangama had filed for divorce because she said her husband had joined the Taliban and disappeared (become *gum* or *ghaib*). *Ghaib* and *gum* both literally mean "lost," "not there," or "invisible." A divorce initiated by a wife (called *khula* or *khol*) must follow different rules from one initiated by a husband (*talaq*).[1] A man can effect immediate divorce by orally announcing to his wife, "I divorce you" three times. As described elsewhere in detail, for khula cases based on missing husbands, the judge has discretion in deciding the length of 'iddat for women. A judge can lessen the waiting period by months. However, the law favors the husband if he appears before 'iddat is over and wants a reunion. During the 'iddat, there can be no visits (any private visit is interpreted as conjugal by the court) between the husband and wife. Hangama had a great Pashto wit that would send us into peals of laughter. She would say, "lar sho, rok sho, Talib sho," which translates from Pashto as "He went, he got lost, he became a Talib."[2] Hangama and Sadaf, who had both arrived at the shelter six months before, were inseparable.

Hangama insisted I join her for her court dates in front of the judge. On one such court date, we waited outside until we were called into the judge's chambers.

Judge *(speaking Dari)*: Are you married?

Hangama *(speaking Pashto)*: Yes.

Judge: Are you a Pashtun?

Hangama: Yes. I am from Helmand.

Judge: Why did you leave your husband? Is this what good Pashtun women do?

Hangama: I did not leave him. He left me. He disappeared. He had been talking about joining the Taliban.

Judge: How convenient for you that he *suddenly* [*yakdam*] wanted to join the Taliban when you decided to leave him.

Farooqa *(the lawyer)*: Judge, actually—

Judge: I am speaking with Hangama.

Hangama: It is not convenient. He did not suddenly join. He was talking about it for years.

Judge: I see you did a marvelous job of stopping him from becoming a Talib.

Hangama and Farooqa: *(Nervous laughter)*

Judge: I cannot decide anything today. Speak to my assistant and schedule another date.

We made the next appointment with the court secretary and left for the day. On the next court date, the judge discussed Hangama's case in more detail. She asked when Hangama had last seen her husband, which was a rhetorical question because it was assumed that her 'iddat began when she arrived at the shelter six months ago. Surely there was no way she could have met her husband, given the security mechanisms at the shelter. However, perhaps Hangama had lost count or deliberately wanted to confuse the judge, because she told her that she had seen him three weeks before, in effect restarting the clock on her 'iddat. The judge became visibly angry and made a gesture of a large zero (*sefr*) and said, "Zero. This is your 'iddat." She had written "zero" on a piece of paper, throwing it at us, "Go back to the khana-yi aman. Get out." Hangama seemed unaffected. On our way home, she gave me a sideways glance and smiled, "I guess I forgot the last time I saw that Talib donkey [*khar*]." The lawyer, Farooqa, was not amused and told Hangama that she was not taking her for another court date soon given her antics. "Te kho akhpal tol kar auran ko." (You messed up your whole case yourself.) Hangama only shrugged.

The subtext in Hangama's gesture to destabilize her case may not be evident to a Western audience, but it is easily understandable to locals. Viewed from the outside, Hangama's actions may seem like a result of hapless and perhaps illiterate confusion over her circumstances. But read by a fellow Pashtun woman, Hangama's actions demonstrate an extraordinary understanding of the mechanisms of her subjugation, and a courageous and strategic ability to calculate risk. Her gestures are intelligible within the power apparatuses that implicated and limited her decision-making. Hangama explained her actions that evening by saying, "I do not want to go back to him. And I do not want to leave the khana-yi aman. I am waiting for Sadaf to get married. I want to be here to support her." By reducing her 'iddat to zero days, Hangama had ensured her stay at the shelter for the foreseeable future. Here, social challenge was possible through actions that did not overtly challenge the patriarchal discourses. In misinhabiting patriarchy through subtle forms of sabotage, Hangama demonstrated surprising maneuverability. This was a recurrent theme at the shelter, where women created friendships and a supportive community around which to navigate their lives with clever maneuvers not perceptible to outsiders. Hangama had found a new family at the shelter that she did not want to leave. Her friendship with Sadaf, a strong homosocial and cohesive bond, had given her comfort and confidence. She did not know what her future entailed, but she wanted to spend her present with Sadaf and the other women at the shelter, whom she considered kin.

Sadaf, with Hangama's help, was relentless in trying to find a mobile phone. She would constantly talk about it, much to Gulalei's chagrin. Then one day, out of nowhere, a mobile phone was found stuck in the crevice between a large closet and the wall. One of the women discovered it while cleaning. Where had it come from? When the phone was opened, it did not have its memory card identifier. Where was the SIM card? This was a major breach of security. An extensive search was launched, in which no one was above suspicion. The managers questioned Sadaf and Hangama as obvious suspects, given their vocal desire for a mobile phone. They accused one of the lawyers, and when that did not work, they accused one of the managers, but this was also refuted. By the end of the day, Hangama had become agitated by the accusations, and a loud fight broke out between her and one of the managers. Hangama yelled, "Am I marrying your father that I would need a mobile phone to speak to him?" She then ceremoniously brought out a Quran and said, "I can place my hand on the Quran to declare my innocence" As the drama of the mobile phone unfolded, Hangama advanced multiple subject positions.[3] She inhabited a promiscuous self who had need for a cell phone to connect to the outside world, a clearly unlawful action at the shelter. Paradoxically, she relied on the Quran to perform a pious self who was bound by the laws of Islam. She reinforced her Muslim identity by establishing her trustworthiness through her conformity to Quranic principles. By inhabiting multiple, often contradictory, subject positions, Hangama destabilized her identification with the power networks of Islam and pashtunwali.

In these clever social maneuvers lies the cunning of the khana-yi aman, which frees women to disconnect from patriarchal discourses and ethically fashion themselves toward new social positions not bound by traditional notions of Islam, Pashtun kinship, or gender. At the khana-yi aman, every identity becomes negotiable and flexible, unpinned from hegemonic ideals of piety and honor. For instance, in her keenness to find a cell phone, ostensibly to talk with a lover, Hangama refused to perform the role of pious wife who waited patiently for her husband's return during 'iddat. Through subtle maneuvers of sabotage at court, she deliberately confused the system that sought to subjugate her. Hangama's friend Sadaf ostensibly inhabited the position of a pious second wife to a traditional Pashtun man. Yet, through Sadaf's loyalty to her girlfriends—Hangama and her husband's first wife, Suha—the homosocial bonds of friendship were as strong as her devotion to her husband. With all the women I met, I observed schisms in the trajectories laid out for them by society, which they utilized to fashion their own worlds.

Trials of Motherhood

Loud screaming woke me up one morning. I ran downstairs to see all the women lined up in a row, with a visibly angry Gulalei walking up and down the line. The women looked terrified. Some had turned red, and others were protesting in loud voices. An unwrapped bloody menstrual pad had been found in the bathroom, and no one was claiming responsibility. Suddenly Rahmin, who had the most serene demeanor, lifted her clothes to reveal that she was not on her period. Gulalei looked at everyone else and made a gesture threatening to "use her hands." Some women showed reluctance, but everyone lifted her clothes. No one was on her period. Where had the pad come from? As we looked at each other, Tania strolled into the room. Quietly, we all walked back to bed. Gulalei disposed of the bloody item by wrapping it in plastic and putting it in the garbage. The pad was not mentioned again.

"Tania is mad," I had been warned. "Do not get bitten by Tania," Haleema had advised as we had walked up to the shelter. "At the very least, you will get your hair pulled." In the past few weeks, I had seen Tania slap and punch inhabitants during sporadic outbursts. But no one complained or resisted. When I was eventually bitten on my leg by Tania, I cried out in pain. Gulalei rolled her eyes at the lameness of my crying at an inevitable event. "Everyone told you. You knew this would happen." She used her scarf to cover the wound. These bite marks eventually fade, she reassured me. Reluctantly, Wahida recounted to me how she had picked Tania up from the street: "When I tried to bring her to the shelter, she bit my hands and punched me. Should I have left her on the streets to continue being raped?" She described how this was a pivotal moment in her activism. "Something changed for me that day. I was exhausted from trying to rescue women from themselves. I used to live at the shelter. Then I moved out. I was able to bring Tania here, but now I do not have the same enthusiasm about picking women up from the streets. If they want to come, they will walk here themselves. They will find us."

Tania personified the paradox of the shelter. The purported madness of Tania reveals the madness of a system that posits women as pious or promiscuous, sane or insane, dirty or clean. It was difficult to talk to Tania. Even though she had suffered one of the worst forms of violence, she had not come to the shelter voluntarily. Her gestures revealed and concealed clues to her suffering. Ostensibly, she was "mad," but her insanity revealed more about the systems of injustice that brought her to the shelter than it did about her. Her madness revealed the madness of a system that categorizes women as either pious or promiscuous, while allowing men to rape them with impunity. Sometimes Tania would not speak for days, and if addressed, she would growl or grunt. She had a separate room, given her eruptions in temper or because she had special funding because of the risk she posed. Ironically, she was the designated babysitter when the women with children had to run errands. Tania was very protective of children and would indiscriminately punch anyone who approached a child placed in her care. She would sit like a bear guarding the children. Her own five-year-old daughter, Karishma, whose name means "miracle," was the result of a gang rape. Her daughter would brush her hair and help her bathe. She would advocate on her mother's behalf for food and other items, especially on the number of naans (bread) she received each evening. Tania would describe Karishma proudly as "more than a hundred sons."

On occasion, I would see Tania circle the house. The building was surrounded by large gardens, and the women washed clothes outside on the ground. A long pipe attached to the faucet brought the water around to the front, where a clothesline had been hung. Tania would sit by the clothesline, holding her body, rocking back and forth, crying and moaning. Karishma would sit next to her. The women washed the clothes and put them on the clothesline, without disturbing Tania. I had seen Tania take small toys and bury them outside by the water pipe. Each day, she followed the same ritual of placing a toy gently on the ground, digging a small hole, putting the toy inside, and covering it with soil. Then she would water it. Her astute and talkative daughter explained her mother's actions: "She is burying all my brothers and sisters she has lost." I could not utter a question. Karishma continued, "My mother lived on the street. She brought me with her here in her stomach. Men did bad things to her. She says I had many brothers and sisters who were lost." Over time, I understood that Tania had experienced multiple miscarriages because of multiple rapes by different men, none of whom she knew. Tania was giving her lost children a proper burial. Karishma commented, "I do not have a father. My mother is all I have."

In some ways, Tania was unique, but in many other ways she shared similarities with other women. For example, Rukhsana left home to get a divorce. She told her husband, Naeem, during a legal arbitration that I witnessed at the court that she did not want to cook every day for the whole family. Naeem insisted that it was her moral obligation to take care of his entire family. He looked at me and commented, "A man brings a bride to take care of his family. Otherwise, I can have children with prostitutes." He implied that not fulfilling her marital obligations, which he construed as cooking and cleaning for the whole family, was a form of wanton promiscuity and madness. Rukhsana put up an admirable counterargument. She argued that the Prophet washed his own clothes and cooked his own food and did not expect his wives to do household chores. It was because of the freedom of his wife 'Aisha that she was able to document hadith (sayings and doings of the Prophet) and become one of the first female scholars of Islam. Rukhsana also gave the example of Khadija, the Prophet's first wife, a successful businesswoman and the Prophet's employer. Her argument was intelligible and grounded in Islamic history. Umm al-Muminin (Mothers of Believers) are the wives and daughters of the Prophet and are deeply respected in Islamic history.

But Naeem answered by accusing her of madness and adultery with a male relative, and questioned the daughter's paternity. During this interaction, Naeem's male cousin Nasirullah persistently interrupted and insisted that Naeem be stronger in his stipulations. Naeem did not ask after his daughter, a beautiful child who played outside by herself, occupied with the pebbles and stones on the pavement. The negotiations ended with the husband commenting, "What kind of mad woman [*lewani khaza*] brings her sexual matters into public? We have been publicly disgraced, and *your* daughter tainted by *your* immoral actions. What kind of madness is this? [*Da singa pagal pan de?*]" As Naeem walked out with his cousin, he made a show of ignoring his daughter. Rukhsana was reassured by the lawyer, Farooqa, that, if she persisted, eventually the judge would concede and give her a divorce. But it could take months or years. Her future was uncertain. Eventually, Rukhsana returned to her husband because of her fears for her daughter's future: "Who would marry my daughter; how would she face the world?" she said as she returned to her husband. Mothers dreaded the consequences, such as physical beatings and loss of extended family support from their husbands, of their failure to properly parent a daughter. Given the powerfully negative effects associated with the perception of sexual permissiveness, most women, even after reaching the shelter, endeavored to temper their rebellion with conventional standards of female piety. Most women, like Rukhsana, did not want to be called promiscuous. Even a baseless accusation of promiscuity and its link to madness was enough for her to return to her husband. In these conversations, madness and promiscuity are linked and then mapped onto a disobedient female body, and the threat extended to her daughter.

Rukhsana feared the label of madness and promiscuity for herself and her daughter. Other women, such as Zara, had lived as prostitutes in their past and were not afraid to be called mad or promiscuous. But they also feared for their daughters. Zara had worked as a prostitute; in one of her sexual encounters, the man noted that she was eight months pregnant and gave her extra money. She used it to travel to the shelter. Her daughter, Naba, was born before her arrival and turned two years old during my stay at the shelter. When groceries arrived, they were counted meticulously; every item had to be accounted for. Naba would sit on the staircase waiting patiently for the counting to end, when she would be handed an apple. There was always an extra apple for Naba. With great ceremony, she would bring both hands together, and the apple would be placed in them. She would turn around and take the apple upstairs, climbing one stair at a time. Zara did not have any court dates and so helped with the sewing. From curtains to clothes, she sewed everything. Zara and Tania had an especially contested relationship, and their relationships with their daughters were markedly different. For example, Zara would sometimes pull up Naba's shirt and beat her with a stick as a punishment for small mishaps, at which point Tania would run upstairs when she heard Naba's cries. Zara often lamented what was to become of her child when there was no future for the girl as the child of a prostitute.

Tania's care and concern for Zara's daughter, despite their contested relationship, was characteristic of the bonds women formed inside the shelter. In the community of the shelter, everyone had a role, and women supported one another and their children. The way the women formed bonds of love, care, and concern for one another was not visible to outsiders. In all my conversations about the shelter, people imagined it as a place of licentiousness and wanton debauchery, an image that circulated among locals and foreigners. Although some women at the shelter did not shy away from being labeled as promiscuous or adulterous, their lives were nevertheless rooted in care and concern, and their daily practices of friendship and hospitality complicated the cultural category of promiscuity. We observe, emergent from daily shelter life and a cultural context labeled as immoral, an alternative form of promiscuous being that is neither immoral, bad, wanton, nor mad. Here, I argue that (the risk of) being called promiscuous potentiated the women's lives with possibility and allowed them to redefine morality.

Promiscuity cannot exist without its other, piety, just as madness cannot exist without some notion of reason. What conditions the possibility of promiscuity is pious womanhood. Zara inhabited the notion of promiscuity in her work as a prostitute and for years sold sexual intercourse for money. Yet she is also a caring and loving mother, which is a central attribute of pious womanhood. Taliban newspapers and other publications are replete with references to mothers and their central role in bringing up children (*tarbiat* and *parvarish*).[4] Both tarbiat (upbringing) and parvarish (rearing) are fundamental concepts in Islamic literature, and imply an educational element. The role of mothers is central to an Islamic and Pashtun community. For all three women, Rukhsana, Zara, and Tania, motherhood was central to their lives, even though other parts of their lives were not traditional, Islamic, or Pashtun. The women had found an alternative family, and although their lives at the shelter forecast uncertain futures, in the present they formed a supportive community based on the shared precepts of love, care, friendship, and motherhood, moral codes central to community formation in pashtunwali and Islam. Zara and Tania fragmented the notion of pious womanhood and, despite their differences, created distance between the moral code and its intended moral iteration. The moral codes of pashtunwali and Islam that hinge on pious womanhood are not intended for promiscuous women.

Yet Zara and Tania owned and lived these moral formations in their own ways. In the iterations of moral codes by ostensibly immoral women, the possibility of difference manifests. Rukhsana, by contrast, consolidated the notion of pious womanhood by seeking to close the gaps between the moral codes and her moral actions. The lives of these women show that moral actors and their actions cannot be predetermined or fully explained by strict moral codes, even as those codes condition the women's actions. In the Foucauldian sense, pious and promiscuous women exist within the matrixes of pashtunwali and Islam, which condition but do not limit their existence.[5]

Women arrived at the shelter for remarkably different reasons. No two cases were exactly alike. The way women spoke about their past and the gestures they used rendered visible the violence they had endured. Every woman I met was acutely aware of the difficult path ahead. Some would talk casually about death as an option to escape the trouble of this world. Yet none saw herself as a hapless victim of her circumstances. Their families either supported or rejected their choices, familial decisions that were never reached easily or taken lightly by those involved. The ambivalence and anxiety associated with decisions to either accept or reject female family members illustrate the far-reaching consequences pertaining to the actions of women.

Nazira had fallen in love with her mother's sister's husband, Aasif. In this case, the mother and her sister Safia had brought charges of sexual immorality against Nazira. At court, I saw Nazira's mother and Safia plead with her. They begged and cajoled, but Nazira said she was in love. "This is not love. This is selfishness," her mother said, but Nazira was undeterred. The judge ruled in Nazira's favor. She had packed all her belongings in a small cloth bag and was bathed and dressed by the women at the shelter. Nurzia, the female parliamentarian, applied her makeup, and Gulalei let her put on henna. The night before the court marriage, the women sang wedding songs and brushed Nazira's long hair. They teased her about what was to come. Her new husband said he had nothing to give her, and the *mahr* was set at 100 Afghan rupees.[6]

The next day, the lawyer and I accompanied Nazira to the family court where she and Aasif were officially married. Aasif had used a friend's connection to allow their case to be heard by a judge who, under direct pressure from women's rights activists, had ruled in the couple's favor. I met with Aasif at the court where he shared his worry that he did not have money to bring a car. "What about your first wife, Safia?" I had asked. He shrugged. As they were leaving, Safia, who had come to make one last plea to her niece, could be heard crying behind us. Aasif had chosen not to divorce Safia. He wanted to keep both wives, which is not against the law. The judge had encouraged Nazira and Safia to resolve their differences for the unity of the family. The lawyer and I watched as Nazira and Aasif jumped on a crowded bus that had slowed down in front of us outside the courthouse. They waved to us as the bus faded into the distance. After returning from court, I recounted the story to Waghmina, a friend of Mariam's and a powerful women's rights activist who worked relentlessly to support the shelter. She said, "We have worked very hard on this judge for a long time to get her on our side." Ironically, in this particular case, Safia and Nazira's mother told me that they had both been disadvantaged.

If one knew nothing more about Nazira than that she was a willing second wife to Aasif, one might construe her as a passive victim of her circumstances. Nazira's actions did consolidate the moral codes of Islam and pashtunwali, which intended men to have more than one wife. But her actions of defiance against her mother and aunt differentiated her from the same moral codes. Thus there is no predetermined trajectory from which their actions can be predicted. Each woman made her decisions from within her historical circumstances of subjectivation. For Foucault (1978), subjectivation consists of ethical work based in an ethical substance toward a telos. Reading each woman's actions from within her own imbrication of her power mechanisms provides a deeper understanding of her subjectivity. Rather than arguing for a binary of resistance and subjugation, in which women either consolidate or destabilize normative structures, a careful historical ethnography reveals the complexity of the women's social positioning. It also reveals more about how mechanisms of power subjugate and create their subjects not uniformly toward a singular telos but in complex and unpredictable ways.

Negotiating the Law: The Lawyers

The four lawyers appointed by the shelter to argue the cases of the runaway women had an astute understanding of how honor functioned in
Afghanistan and how to navigate and fight for women's cases. They used
knowledge of written and unwritten rules on how Kabul courts moved and
how cases about runaway women were normally decided.[7] For difficult
cases, the shelter managers used personal connections with female politicians to effect legal outcomes. For example, I witnessed a case in which
a man accused of killing his wife was about to be released from jail, ow-
ing to his friendship with the governor of that province. In this instance,
Mariam quickly mobilized her female friends in government to stop the
release. Friendships with politicians were integral to winning cases.

Farooqa, one of the female lawyers, spoke Pashto and Dari and was
assigned to Pashtun women. Walwala spoke Dari and understood Pashto.
The men, Nadir and Ahmed, spoke Dari and understood Pashto. The lawyers used a combination of legal knowledge and social skills to navigate
the courts. When the two female lawyers, Walwala and Farooqa, would
enter the khana-yi aman, women would crowd around them pleading to
be taken to court. Even as the lawyers worked diligently on their legal
cases, they could not hide their disdain for the actions of the runaway
women. The lawyers did not eat or socialize with the shelter inhabitants
and spent most of their time in the main office. When they entered the
building, they would stand near the door and answer questions collec-
tively from the crowd of women.

I traveled with the lawyers around Kabul as I followed the legal cases. On one of my excursions with the lawyers for Aafia, who wanted to
marry a second time but had not been divorced yet, a legal drama erupted
in the judge's office. Farooqa noted that it was important to underscore
for the judge that Aafia did not know where her husband was. The judge
was clearly annoyed with this and said, "Even if your husband is buried
a hundred feet deep in the earth, I will find his bones and bring them to
court to stand in front of you. You will sit at the khana-yi aman for a
hundred years. I will make sure you do. You cannot get married again
until your first husband divorces you." In the courtyard, Aafia's family

waited to convince her to return to her current in-laws. It was usual to find, in the courtroom gardens, families confronting and entering into lengthy arguments with the runaway women. The fact that the women had found an alternative family at the khana-yi aman allowed them to be direct about their sexual attitudes and future plans. They also found encouragement from the lawyers, especially the female lawyers, with whom they identified. Farooqa stayed calm in front of the judge and reassured Aafia that she would keep coming back to court until the judge relented. Aafia would address Farooqa as *khor* (sister), and, despite her disdain for running away, Farooqa was clearly fond of Aafia and the women whose cases she was arguing. As the women risked their lives to fight their cases, deep bonds, even if sometimes antagonistic, formed among them. In all cases, the women rallied and supported each other to forcefully demand their rights from their families, in-laws, and the justice system. Aafia told me that without the supportive community of the shelter, she would have continued living with her in-laws and quietly waited for her husband to reappear. Eventually, and as Farooqa predicted, the judge relented, and Aafia obtained a divorce and married her lover.

The lawyers employed a combination of persistence and shrewd navigation of the judicial and political systems to help the women. The laws are unclear and applied arbitrarily. I saw many cases being decided through intervention by politicians or highly placed officials in the Ministry of Justice whom the lawyers knew and who were amenable to helping the women, but who did not want to be named for fear of political retaliation. Very few cases were decided in the courtroom. Deals were made clandestinely in politicians' and judges' offices rather than in court, as I saw with the case of Arshia and Parwaneh. During Ramazan, the lawyer Nadir promised fourteen-year-old Parwaneh that he would bring her mother, Arshia, from jail before Eid. Arshia's sons and brothers had bribed the police to put her in jail after she had asked for her Islamic share of inheritance. Nadir told Parwaneh, "You will spend Eid with your mother, I promise." Parwaneh and I had visited her mother in Pul-e-Charkhi prison with Nadir. (The female lawyers avoided the prison if possible.) Parwaneh had packed a small bag with soap, knitting needles, wool, and oranges. She was crying the entire time, but upon seeing her mother, Parwaneh put on a smile and gave her the bag. They hugged tightly and cried as the guards watched. After our visit to the prison, Nadir dropped Parwaneh at the shelter and then visited an official in the Ministry of Justice with a handwritten plea for Arshia's release. Nadir let me accompany him. As we entered the very large office of this official, we saw people lined up with similar pleas. Nadir and I sat on one side of the office waiting to be noticed. After three hours of waiting, during which time we saw him pray and attend to his employees, he finally acknowledged us. As Nadir pleaded with him to release Arshia, given that it was the holy month of Ramazan, which called for mercy, the official waved his hand to quiet him. Then he signed the document without reading it. We left, with Nadir visibly excited at having fulfilled his promise to Parwaneh.

Two days later, Arshia was released from prison. She came to the shelter days before Eid, with the gift bag unopened. She had not opened it for fear of the items being stolen in jail, and had given it to the warden for safekeeping. The day Arshia was to arrive, Parwaneh and I cooked *bolani* (a special bread) for her. The lost girl who would sit in a corner in silence for days had magically come to life. Arshia and Parwaneh giggled and opened the bag, feigning surprise as if neither knew what it contained. On Eid, several dishes were cooked in addition to dessert, unlike the usual single dish that was cooked on all other days. Traditional sweets had been sent from outside. Parwaneh and Arshia had no idea how Nadir had managed to get her out of jail, nor did they know what the future held or whether Arshia would have to go back to prison. The official had signed Arshia's release without reading the document. Her release had been entirely dependent on the moment that Nadir presented the document to the official. Nadir later told me that he chose a time when he knew the official would be busy, and a day when he knew the possibility of showing mercy was higher because of Ramazan. The rhythm of the shelter was underpinned by such shrewd calculations and estimated risk.

Masked Virgins

In 2011, a new television series called *Niqab*, translated by the producers as *The Mask*, began to be telecast on a local channel. The show depicted women concealed behind blue-and-white masks (Damon 2011).

Although it challenged some social taboos about publicly speaking out about violence, it entrenched others. Some thought the show obscured the vitality of the women by hiding them behind masks, the blueness of which symbolized the blue burqa for which Afghan women have come to be known. The show's creator, Sami Mahdi, a fashionable young Afghan man, described the show as enabling women to speak about experiences of sexual violence they would otherwise not be willing to share. About the women who had endured sexual or physical assault, Mahdi said in an interview, "They don't have a tongue. They don't have a voice to talk about what they are suffering" (Sundby 2011). For their part, the women were unsure whether the series was helping alleviate their concerns about sexual violence or causing to further alienate the victims of said violence.

The shelter inhabitants complained that the show's producers would "lift women" from shelters and place them in front of the television camera. When I discussed this show with Wahida, she disagreed with Mahdi's assessment: "We do have a tongue. We do have a voice. We need people to listen." Huma chimed in, "And why are they calling it a mask? Niqab is not a mask." The translation of *niqab* as "mask," rather than as its proximate translation of "veil," was ostensibly a gesture toward uncovering or unmasking the unseen gender violence. Paradoxically, the women were told to wear a mask, instead of a face-covering veil, in front of a camera, and their voices were distorted for protection. Many women at the shelter thought the combination of mask and distorted voice gave the women an eerie quality and otherized them. Several women told me that the masked women evoked fear in them rather than empathy. It is ironic that while this program gave a platform to women who have been marginalized, it simultaneously created an enigmatic impression of otherness that, in turn, caused the women viewing the show to feel fear. "The mask is scary," I heard frequently. Women who had also suffered abuse could not get past the mask to identify with the woman behind it.

Wahida told me, "Afghan women are either shown in the blue burqa or with cut off and distorted limbs, and now through this terrible mask." Wahida's mention of distorted limbs was a reference to a *Time* magazine depiction of Bibi 'Aisha, whose nose and ears had been cut off by her husband's family, and whose photograph had been put on the cover of *Time*'s

2010 summer issue (Stengel 2010). With the global circulation of print media, these images reached Afghanistan and instilled horror, especially among women. Wahida said that while such grotesque images increased their donor funding, the women felt that their dignity had been taken away nonetheless. "Would you pose for a photo with your nose cut off? Would you look at the camera like that?"

While such horrifying depictions illuminate the violence perpetrated on Afghan women by the Taliban, they also render invisible all other forms of quotidian violence. Some women referred to a preexisting grid within which they had to fit their stories of violence in order to be intelligible to international actors. Even Bibi 'Aisha's story was narrated in *Time* magazine in snippets. Bibi had been promised to a Talib fighter by her father, and when she tried to escape, she was captured, mutilated, and left to die on a deserted mountain. But she did not die. Bibi 'Aisha received free reconstructive surgery and immigration to the United States. She found many supporters because she made the cover of *Time* magazine; however, it is extremely rare for Afghan women to migrate to America as a result of domestic abuse cases. Bibi 'Aisha's story is simultaneously extraordinary and commonplace. Extraordinary because of the international outcome; commonplace because Bibi 'Aisha is one of many who suffer gendered violence.

At the shelter, I met many women whose husbands had joined the Taliban and whose life histories were always far more complex than any depicted in the media. Gulalei's husband was a powerful member of the Taliban who would often appear on television. She was in hiding because he wanted their seven-year-old son and had tried to kidnap Gulalei and their son several times. Given his influence, she was one of the few who could never leave the shelter, even to go to court. The lawyers were not willing to argue her case for divorce for fear of reprisal by her powerful Talib husband. The shelter managers let her stay indefinitely. Gulalei was well educated and given the responsibility of day-to-day management of the shelter. Sakina's husband had also joined the Taliban, but in a lower-ranking position. When it was discovered that she was pregnant, she was arrested for adultery, because her husband had been away and could not have impregnated her. She told the police that in her husband's absence, his younger brother had raped her. On one occasion I saw her brother-in-law's name written in henna on her hand. When I asked her about it, she said that her friends in jail had put it on her arm. Then she said that she loved her brother-in-law. This was the main cause of dispute between the brothers, who were her first cousins; she had wanted to marry the younger brother instead. Sakina's story kept changing depending on who was asking the questions. In their conversations with her, judges and lawyers attempted to produce the "truth" about the illicit nature of her relations. As it turns out, these kinds of conversations between the accused and their lawyers often became a path to self-discovery, as many women would have to think through their decisions during intense interrogations. For example, Rukhsana displayed knowledge of Islamic history and grounded her protest in a notion of Umm al-Muminin (Mothers of Believers), wives and daughters of the Prophet. Hangama demonstrated a variety of subject positions that sometimes contradicted and sometimes complemented each other. Even though their stories saturated the news, it struck me how little was known beyond a few paragraphs about the women and how difficult it was for women like Gulalei and Sakina to explain their life histories in snippets. An ethnographic perspective reveals these narratives as a diagnostic of power mechanisms (Abu-Lughod 1990).

Many runaway women at the shelter were resentful and felt surrounded by people who exploited their misfortune yet still held them in contempt. For example, they saw shelter administrators ridicule them through spoken and unspoken gestures. It was commonplace for the administrators to place bets on how long their marriages would last. Nasreen, for example, was often ridiculed by shelter administrators because she had left the khana-yi aman several times only to come back again. Her husband was a drug addict who would beat her up, and, although he made promises to change, he always reverted to his old behavior. Nasreen told me that everyone was benefiting from their suffering. The shelter managers had a job, and the NGO running the shelter obtained funding to engage with women's issues. The entire women's rights apparatus was built on the suffering of ordinary women like Nasreen. But was anyone listening to them? Were the women more dehumanized in the process of being "saved"?[8] While stories like those of Gulnaz and Bibi 'Aisha made headlines and drew international attention to their plight, were the women reduced to caricatures? In order to become visible, women had to acquire a specific public persona; but this acquired persona erased their particular trauma, self, and memory.

Although shelter inhabitants and some outside observers accused them of benefiting from the trauma of ordinary women, the Afghan women who ran the NGOs lived complex lives themselves. For example, while Mariam was running the shelter, her own life was falling apart. Her husband had left her, and her family had abandoned her. On most mornings, Mariam was distressed about her failing marriage. While I was at the shelter, the father of Walwala, one of the female lawyers, was brutally murdered. The shelter managers went to her house for *namaz-e janaza* (funeral prayer); Walwala returned a few days later with red eyes, and continued her job fighting cases undeterred. Nameen, a close friend of mine and a successful businesswoman and supporter of women's rights, had chosen not to get married. Her friends and family told her that she would regret it, but she only laughed. Eventually President Ashraf Ghani handpicked her for a cabinet role as minister. Her position was not ratified by parliament, however, given her strong reformist opinions. Another Afghan friend, Mehreen, in an official placement on the UN Gender team, told me that she wanted to move out to a mainstream post. By "mainstream," she meant anything not related to gender. She said, "Whenever we start talking about gender in a room full of men, they become bored. They stretch and yawn. They already know what we have to say. No one takes us seriously. Why not join economics, infrastructure, mining, positions where men do not expect to see us?" Another friend who ran a gender-related NGO believed that men had to be forced to change their perceptions about gender. I saw her enacting this stance in real life many times. She frequently hired men to speak about gender equality. The male employees would often complain, and she would reply to them, "This is called breaking a stereotype. I want to break one stereotype a day. You are a stereotype." While running an NGO for gender equality, Nahida, another friend, was strict about women's comportment in her firm. During one of our trips to Mazar-e-Sharif to open a new local office, the male employees complained about the behavior of the young woman, Akeela, who had been hired as manager. Akeela was seen flirting and laughing loudly with the landlord of the new office building. Various employees said that Akeela's behavior reflected lewdness or promiscuity (*fahhashat*) and bad character (*bad-akhlaq*).[9] Nahida terminated the young woman's position the same day. A young man was hired to fill her role. The same men who had complained about Akeela recommended the new employee. In this case, it was difficult not to make a connection between the self-interest of the men in bringing a friend aboard and a baseless accusation of Akeela. When I brought up this connection with Nahida, she laughed it off.

The issue of moral and immoral sexual intent is central to the shelter and to women's rights. It is what necessitates policy controls such as virginity testing. Most women, especially those in prominent positions, did not want to be connected with what might be construed as sexually lascivious actions, a general category of actions with which almost anyone could be easily associated. The shelter managers had to uphold their image as pious Muslims and could not openly advise the shelter inhabitants and employees in ways that might contradict Islamic principles. Indeed, many of the shelter managers told me that they lied to their families about their occupation. The shelters had reluctantly instituted mandatory virginity testing upon the government's insistence. A virginity test is a medical examination in which the hymen is inspected to determine whether sexual intercourse has taken place. I had seen Huma, the manager who was also a medical doctor, conduct the test, which most women did not object to. They understood that it was mandatory to gain access to the shelter. Others did object, but their objections were ignored. Alia described Huma putting two fingers inside her vagina to determine the status of the hymen, which in her case was intact. Alia noted how the police, prosecutors, and shelter managers had become sympathetic to her after this examination, which she deemed necessary to separate herself from the nonchaste (or promiscuous) women without hymens in the shelter. In Fawzia's examination, the hymen was not intact. She had run away from an abusive father and had been stopped by police and brought to a police station. She described how the medical personnel inserted two fingers inside her vagina and rotated them clockwise and counterclockwise to find the hymen. Fawzia's memory was fragmented. She was not sure why her hymen was not intact given that she had no memory of having sexual intercourse. She recalled being raped but was not certain if that had broken her hymen. The purpose of this test, as Wahida explained, was to separate the chaste women from the promiscuous women. The logic behind it was that if a woman ran away claiming she did so to escape abuse and her hymen was intact, it followed that she did not run away to commit sexual intercourse. However, the absence of a hymen signified immoral intentions. But such logic falls apart quickly. What if the woman was escaping sexual abuse, in which case she would not have a hymen but also would not have immoral intent? And what about married women running away to get a divorce? No hymen would be found in these cases, and such questions did not have clear answers.

Fawzia had been raped all night by a series of men after her hymen was discovered not to be intact. She had been taken to a police official's house after her virginity test had concluded that she was not a virgin. In the morning, she was brought back to the police station. The shelter managers were called to pick her up in the morning and found her unconscious at the police station. I learned of the grotesque violence she had been subjected to by overhearing a conversation between Huma and Amara, who described in graphic detail how much semen her body had been covered with. It was clear to me that they were recounting the story so that I would write about it. Fawzia said to me months later, "The first police officer called me a whore. He said that the medical doctor had determined that I was not a virgin. He said I had already been opened. Then he used *zabardasti* [force]. He called all his friends. I passed out after the fourth and woke up the next morning." Her story shows that a woman who is not a virgin is deemed promiscuous and thus deserving of rape. Paradoxically, when such stories circulate outside the shelter in public, they act as evidence in support of the belief that runaway women are licentious. A raped woman becomes part of the repertoire of promiscuity surrounding the shelter, which then feeds into a circular logic that categorizes women as either virgins or whores. A whore, who is defined as sexually licentious, deserves to be raped. Raped women are called promiscuous whores. This is the vicious cycle of the madness of promiscuity.

Practices like virginity tests operate on the binary logic of female chastity and nonchastity (what I have been calling promiscuity). Women like Fawzia who run away from home to escape abuse were often rejected by their families and then left to the mercy of state officials who, tragically, subjected them to more abuse. According to a decree by the Supreme Court of Afghanistan that placed protections on women running away from abuse, Fawzia should not have been subjected to the virginity test.[10] In Fawzia's case, however, the police officer decided that a medical examination was necessary, based on "how she looked," Fawzia told me. When I asked her what "how she looks" meant, she did not give an answer but looked away. It is important to note that most law officials, including lawyers, prosecutors, and even judges, do not implement the law as it was intended, so that even though virginity tests are not intended for women running away from abuse, Fawzia and many others are nonetheless subjected to them. The status of gender laws was uncertain, and no clear instructions on how to apply the laws existed. Police officers had tremendous discretion in how cases were processed and classified. The women's rights activists would pressure the judges and prosecutors to apply laws in a way that favored women, but it did not always work.

When I began fieldwork, I was encouraged to review the files on the women entering and exiting the shelters, kept by the main office, which is how most researchers accessed information about the women and their cases. Few spoke to the women or their families. Even when journalists or researchers interviewed the women, they did so in less than an hour at most. On one occasion, I saw a Western journalist get special permission from shelter managers to speak with one of the shelter inhabitants, Gulnaz, who had been pardoned by Karzai and had made international news. Note that in these cases, the women themselves are not asked for permission, but rather the shelter managers give permission. The journalist came to the main office at 10:00 a.m. with a translator who spoke only Dari. Gulnaz, who is a Pashtun, had been transported briefly to the main office, where she sat uncomfortably in a chair waiting for the journalist to arrive. The journalist went through a pamphlet of standard questions in about fifteen minutes. Gulnaz answered in Pashto, which was then translated to English by the Dari-speaking translator. After the journalist left, we never saw her again. In these interviews, women would repeat their file information in short snippets. It is impossible to obtain an accurate historical picture of the complexity of each woman's life in fifteen minutes, which is why more sustained ethnographic fieldwork is necessary to study systems of injustice and how women are positioned within them.

Having grown up in Peshawar, one of five sisters, and having completed most of my schooling and early university there, I am intimately aware of the difficulty that women face narrating abuse and violence to administrative officials. After immigrating to the United States at the age of nineteen, I saw women facing similar struggles in the West bringing cases of abuse against close family members to the authorities. After I began living at the shelter, I realized further how little was captured in the narratives documented in the women's files, which reduced the complexity of the cases to a few prescribed data points. Moreover, some women would deliberately lie during these pro forma interviews, in which case the accounts brought to the public are not just inadequate but inaccurate.

Linguistic Permutations of Rape

Amara, a khana-yi aman worker, and I became close friends. She was from a Dari-speaking family and had married a Pashtun. Amara walked to the khana-yi aman every day for work and had often been threatened. She had endured physical violence in the courtroom at the hands of angry family members who blamed her for misleading their daughters and wives. Once, as we walked together from the main office, a young boy said to us, "Your father must be turning in his grave. Look how you are walking, you shameless whores." Amara replied, "How do you know our fathers are dead?" To which he had responded, "If he is not dead, he must be a *bi-ghayrat* [one without honor], which is worse than dead." Amara told me that men would often call her names like *randi*,[11] which in Pashto means prostitute, whore, widow, and divorced woman.[12] How one lexical item, randi, can mean both prostitute and widow is a puzzle I have tried to solve most of my life. Most people answer this question by stating that any woman without a male patron becomes, by definition, sexually promiscuous. Hangama, who was not averse to creating trouble, asked a prosecutor in one of her court hearings why she was being referred to as a randi. He answered that because her husband was missing, her sexual propriety was questionable. Out of embarrassment, most would stop here; however, Hangama continued: "So if a woman runs away, her husband is a randi?" I admit I almost jumped out of my seat at her boldness. The prosecutor raised his hand as if to slap her, but was restrained by his colleague. Hangama's question is important for understanding how the categories of promiscuity attach solely to female social actors. For example, the category of nonvirgin makes a woman a whore, which, in turn, deems her "already opened" and promiscuous and thus subject to rape. This category does not attach to men in the same way.

Rape was added as a legal category separate from adultery through the Elimination of Violence Against Women (EVAW) instrument signed as a presidential decree in 2009.[13] The legal vocabulary to describe rape, *tajavoz-e-jinsi*, which literally translates as "sexual coercion," is rarely used by survivors of rape. In my years of fieldwork, I have rarely heard raped women describe assault using these legal terms. Lawyers sometimes use the legal vocabulary in front of a judge or among themselves; however, outside the Kabul courts, in the lives of the women and their families, this language is nearly meaningless. In Pashto, rape is spoken about by the women using general references to coercion, as in "He used force upon me." For some women, there are literally no words to describe rape beyond *zabardasti* (force). Many women used the word *force* in a passive-voice construction that does not indicate an agent of the force—for example, "Force was wrought upon me." Women who spoke Dari also did not use the official sexual vocabulary to describe rape, instead using gestures rather than words. Some would say, "Bi-namus shud" (I was rendered without honor.) *Bi-namus* was used by both Dari- and Pashto-speaking women to describe sexual assault. Families often used *zina* (adultery) to describe sexual assault, even though in Islamic usage, zina implies consent. Sometimes they would say "zabardasti zina," or "zina bil-jabr," which means forced adultery.[14] Adultery, by law, means illicit relations outside marriage, yet adultery was used in the context of unmarried women. During fights, men sometimes make references to raping the other's mother or sister. In Pashto they use the word *umandum*, which literally means "will run over" her. "Sta mor be umandum" literally means "I will run over your mother." Women I met did not use this word to describe voluntary or involuntary sexual encounters. Men rarely use these words in the presence of women unless intentionally disrespecting or intimidating them. Such complications that arise from the insufficiency of language urge us to think more deeply about the complexity with which women's lives are organized. This is not a mere call to conduct deeper or more reflexive ethnographic fieldwork but a call to rethink the need to make general (and eventually futile) arguments about feminism and women's rights that can be applied universally. And here I submit a plea to allow Afghan and Muslim women to write their own histories of oppression and narratives of violence.

Wahida noted that the difficulty was with the laws regarding sexual relations including zina (adultery) and rape. She explained that despite attempts to establish one, there remains no robust legal framework to distinguish between rape and adultery. Therefore, most cases of rape come to be defined as adultery, which in Islamic belief is a sin, and in Afghanistan a punishable offense. The most difficult work for women's rights activists is to bring cases of rape to the forefront and create a local mechanism to distinguish forced from voluntary sexual encounters. Wahida said, "This work is extremely sensitive [*nazuk*]. Most women would rather say that they have been raped than to admit to adultery, which is punishable by death. However, doing so ends in unintended consequences." For instance, many women end up in jail for illicit sexual encounters even when they claim to have been raped. Moreover, it is difficult for women to narrate events, given the vocabulary of rape available to them. As Dina Siddiqui (2015) has shown in Bangladesh, the category of rape is used by women when a man fails to fulfill his promise of marriage (sexual intercourse by fraud).[15] This amounts to any sexual encounter outside a marital union conceived as coerced retrospectively by the woman if the man fails to marry her. These complications, in addition to the legal confusion inside Afghanistan on the distinction between rape and adultery, and what gets construed as lawful versus forbidden, places raped women in a double bind.

Localizing Assault and Divorce

Cultural influences have always marked the Islamic permutation of marriage, which is locally customized in many forms. As scholars such as

Vikor (2006) and Messick (1993) have shown, Islam has a proper place for local mores and makes accommodations for customs (*'urf*). Some oppressive practices were clearly un-Islamic and easy to challenge through appeals to Islam (even though they had been practiced as Islamic until now). I attended several theatrical shows funded by international organizations that challenged the practice of *baad* in pashtunwali, for which a woman is given as compensation to settle a debt. Baad can be isolated as a practice not grounded in Islam, but anchoring women's rights within an Islamic framework is not without risk. The Taliban and conservative elements frequently advocate their positions through Islamic frameworks. Julie Billaud (2015) writes,

> For Afghan women's rights activists who have a historically informed understanding of justice as a social field tightly connected to existing norms, social structures, ideologies, and power hierarchies, one way to reconcile the antagonism between the competing normative orders that composed the legal landscape (human rights, customary law, and sharia) was to root women's rights within an Islamic framework and to distinguish between customs that enjoyed Islamic support and customs that were not Islamically grounded. (102)

But this strategy does not always work in practice. For example, Islamic law does not require parental consent for marriage, and women's rights activists have advocated that couples be allowed to marry independently of their families. The couple needs two male witnesses and a *qazi* (officiator or Islamic cleric) to officiate the marital union. However, the qazi will not conduct marriage ceremonies for runaway couples. If he suspects that the couple is a runaway, the police are notified and have the discretion to decide what to do—ostensibly to protect the girl from forced and fraudulent marriage or abduction. Although parental consent is not necessary in Islam, Afghan courts have made parental involvement integral to marital unions. Because the participants in the marriage may be children, the state emphasizes the importance of parental guidance. The focus here is on making marriage a communal responsibility rather than increasing the age of consent. A prosecutor told me that men often swayed young girls to marry them without their parents' knowledge, only to divorce them shortly after sexual intercourse. With no family to return to, these girls either kill themselves or become prostitutes.

Female consent for marriage has been a problematic issue in Afghanistan, as women are assigned a *vali* (male patron), who acts as a representative for the bride and has authority to speak on her behalf. In fact, for my own marriage, my paternal uncle was assigned as my vali. In cousin marriages, a vali is a mutual relative and typically not partial to the bride's interests. The role of the vali is to advocate on behalf of the bride for alimony (mahr) and other rights. *Mahr* is translated into English as "alimony," although the rules of mahr are significantly different. In Islamic law, the bride is entitled to mahr on her wedding day. Even though mahr is supposed to be paid at the time of the wedding, the groom and his family often fail to do so, and when a woman demands divorce, it becomes incumbent on the husband to pay the mahr at this time if the divorce is being officiated formally and the question about the payment of mahr is asked by a judge or qazi. If a woman initiates a divorce, she is pressured to forgo her mahr in order to speed up the process. To avoid giving mahr, the husband may prolong an already lengthy process. Divorces initiated by men, by contrast, are very speedy and often only require the man to say the words "I divorce you" three times. If a man gives his wife a divorce of his own volition, it is almost impossible for the wife to ask for her mahr. Moreover, men can lie and claim that they paid the mahr on the wedding day, and women cannot disprove it. In informal negotiations, men will often cite expenses their wives incurred while living in their house, treating the unpaid mahr as a form of compensation, thus further distorting the concept of mahr. In some cases, I saw mahr exchanged between male members of the families, a modern form of bride price in which the bride gets nothing for herself. In all these cases, accusations of promiscuity serve the interest of avoiding paying her mahr. Slandering a woman's character discredits her in front of the law and her family, and makes it easier to forgo paying her due financial compensation. She is pressured to consent to giving up her share, and the male patron assigned to protect her interests will not act on her behalf if she has been established as promiscuous.

Most women at the shelter shared the frustration of not being able to advocate for their Islamic rights at the time of signing the *nikah* (marriage contract). I often heard it said, "You never know what the vali will do on that day." On the day of the nikah, the vali accompanies the qazi to meet with the bride. Given that wedding ceremonies are segregated by gender, the bride's close female family members and friends surround her, at which point the qazi asks the bride whether she agrees to the nikah, and recounts the mahr and other stipulations of the marital contract. The question is asked and answered three times. Silence is construed as acceptance. Wahida told me about her own wedding, in which she expected the vali, also her close uncle, to enter into lengthy negotiations on her behalf. A proficient vali can negotiate to have property transferred to the bride. I saw property transfers at the time of a wedding for a few affluent families; I was told that this was not common, however. This might happen if the bride's family is influential and had appointed a powerful vali willing to advocate for her. However, for Wahida, as for many other women, the vali ended up siding with the bridegroom's family and negotiated a paltry sum of mahr.

If getting married is tough, getting divorced is even tougher. The male lawyer Nadir had attempted to plea for a khula divorce for one of the shelter inhabitants, Nosheen, on the basis of her giving up her mahr. In this divorce process, based on Article 156 of the Afghan Constitution, a wife can obtain a divorce in exchange for giving property to her husband. This stipulation was rarely used by the lawyers, even though, if successful, it can hasten a divorce. Nosheen's family attempted to use mahr, which had not been paid, as a substitute for khol. Although Nosheen had been entitled to mahr on her wedding day, she, like many brides, did not receive it. In khol divorces, women can sometimes write off the mahr and obtain a speedy divorce. This practice, though popular, is entirely against Islamic law. As noted, Nosheen tried to substitute the khol payment with her mahr, but the judge rejected that plea. In order to get a speedy divorce through khol, Nosheen had to pay either cash or property to her husband. Like Arshia, she had rights to her father's property, but her brothers were not willing to give over her share. The male members from both sides reached an agreement in which mahr would not be claimed, and ten thousand rupees of khol would be given to the husband for the divorce. But how would Nosheen earn that money? The judge suggested getting a job, but Nosheen was not literate and could not work in an office. And because she did not have a car, transport was an issue, not to mention that she had an infant son who was breastfeeding. A guard at the court offered to pay the khol if Nosheen agreed to marry him. After a short marriage, during which he frequently raped Nosheen, the guard divorced her by saying "Talaq" three times. It was accepted by the judge, and Nosheen came back to the shelter a few weeks later.

Most of these cases are considered routine, and do not make headline news. One that did garner international media attention was the case of Lal Bibi, who was raped by four police officials. It was said that her rape was an act of revenge because a close relative of hers had offended a highly positioned police officer. The defense argued for one police officer that it could not be rape because a local mullah had performed a religious marriage ceremony before sexual intercourse took place (Rubin 2012). During the court proceedings, a distinction was made between forced marriage, here subsumed under the category of baad, and rape. As mentioned earlier, in baad marriages a girl may be given as compensation to settle a debt between families. This practice is increasingly rare in Kabul, although practiced in some provinces. The police stipulated that Lal Bibi had been given in exchange for the offense, which thus constituted a baad marriage. But Lal Bibi's parents claimed that it was rape, not baad (construed as forced marriage). According to Lal Bibi's family, she was abducted, forced into marriage, and then raped. By arguing that the violent sexual act occurred within the context of baad, the police attempted to render legitimate the violence of a forced marriage. In this case, the argument did not succeed. The four police officers were each sentenced to sixteen years in prison (BBC 2012).

In Afghanistan, the conception of marriage in Islamic history shifts between the domains of economic transaction and reciprocal personal/ sexual companionship (Ali 2010, 96). Both economic transaction and sexual companionship orient marital trajectories. Marriage evolves from financial logic to compensate social debts (baad and *badal*[16]) to the logic of love and companionship, which still remains embedded within a transactional economy.[17] While the official form of marital union has remained

Islamic, it is now conditioned with modern notions of love, sexual attraction, and friendship. At the shelter, the managers often scoffed at the notion of love that brought many women there, calling it modern and shallow, incompatible with traditional conceptions of marriage. For them, marriage is meant to protect families and secure a place for women in society. Love must conform to Islamic ecologies of belonging and occur only within the transactional economy of marriage. The runaway women, however, redefined love and marriage in unexpected ways through subtle and open manipulations of the system.

Promiscuity is intrinsically linked to piety, as reason is linked to madness. They exist in differential opposition to each other.[18] In Afghanistan, the historical conditions that propelled the need for the shelter were embedded within notions of piety and promiscuity, categories that have existed and circulated for centuries. Sexual promiscuity was never legally permissible in Afghanistan, but the Taliban created conditions that expanded the category of promiscuity to encompass a vast swath of behaviors that included washing clothes, laughing, flying a kite, and going to school. As the governance of female bodies became more draconian during Taliban rule, I argue, so did the will for difference. By "will for difference," I mean the struggle to become different, subvert, or resist what is deemed normal. Many women at the shelter are wives of the Taliban; they risked being labeled promiscuous or even killed for running away. While Afghan women have always resisted power mechanisms that situate them as second class, after the Taliban the will to resist created a vociferous possibility of difference. Shelters arose to contain the problem of "runaway women," a problem that proliferated after the fall of the Taliban.

The existence of shelters reinforces the categories of *runaway* and *promiscuous* and maps them onto female bodies. For example, practices that regulate the shelters, such as virginity tests, are intended to distinguish chaste bodies from promiscuous ones. Virginity testing, discussed earlier, is a vaginal examination that has only two possible results: virgin (pious) or nonvirgin (promiscuous). Even though loss of virginity can occur as a result of marriage and rape, the reason a woman is no longer a virgin is not considered relevant as she is subsumed under the category of promiscuous. Such a vast category manifests as an effect of patriarchal power after a woman has been raped or abused, or has conducted voluntary sexual relations within or outside marriage. What is more, virgins who run away are considered promiscuous, as are women who have mental health challenges or are impoverished. In this sense, the virginity tests are more a mechanism of punishment for running away, which renders leaving home the original sin that calls for retribution by the state.

One difference between the containment centers described by Foucault in *Madness and Civilization* (1965) and the shelter I examine here is that shelters also house affluent women who have taken a position of difference. Thus a woman like Nurzia, an affluent parliamentarian, becomes linked to Gulnaz, who comes from an impoverished world. What links them is their running away and ensuing banishment, which both create and reinforce the notion of promiscuity. Female piety and promiscuity exist only as an effect of institutional power networks that organize women according to such categories. The organizing practices of the shelter that mark women as either pious (virgin) or promiscuous (nonvirgin or nonchaste) manifest these categories. Ostensibly, shelters provide protection for runaway women. At the same time, however, shelters also create and congeal the category of promiscuity, link it to female runaway bodies, and criminalize them. The mechanisms instituted by the shelters and the concomitant vocabulary that describes them reveal an imperative more complex than protection. In all the institutional measures that undergird the administrative processes of the shelter, promiscuity as a category manifests and differentiates itself against piety. As madness is grounded in a history of reason, promiscuity is grounded in a history of piety. Promiscuity, like the modern forms of madness described by Foucault, is contained in custodial centers and banished from the pious sphere of visibility. Promiscuity cannot exist without its other, piety.

The draconian measures meted out to female bodies do not preclude the possibility of forming a community inside the shelter. At the Kabul shelter where I lived, women inverted conventional male practices of guest hosting (*hujra*), hospitality (*melmastia*), and refuge (*nanawatai*). The women prayed and fasted together in a community that was not bound by familial or patrilineal bonds. In doing so, they found an alternative means of forming a family. Women rooted themselves in these conventional practices and feminized them, creating homosocial female bonds among themselves and fragmenting the notion of womanhood mapped onto motherhood and piety, by choosing motherhood but rejecting piety. The promiscuous self of the shelter is always in a process of becoming and consolidates some but not all norms of the normative structures of Islam or pashtunwali. This unfinished process of becoming founds the basis of what I call the promiscuous modern (discussed further in Chapter Three).

The Promiscuity Effect

This chapter provides a glimpse into the everyday struggles of ordinary Afghan women as they inhabit and resist patriarchal discourses and innovate social maneuvers and new vocabularies to challenge sexual injustices. In doing so, they redefine the meaning of kinship. Women who reached the shelter had uprooted themselves from traditional communities bound by ties of ethnicity, honor, language, and religion and formed a new community not bound by these conventional ties of kinship. Here Pashtun women became friends with Dari-speaking women, Shia women with Sunni women. The loyalty among women, rather than to men, became central. In this sense, the women in the shelter redefined familial relations and formed a supportive community, which, though meaningful within conventional notions of kinship, was not bound by them. For example, when women invoked the Umm al-Muminin (Mothers of Believers), they used a model grounded in Islamic belief, but uprooted it from its history. By doing so, they engendered Islamic history by creating and claiming a space for themselves. When Mullah Omar, the leader of the Taliban, took over Kabul, he famously wore the mantle of the Prophet and called himself Amir al-Muminin (Leader of Believers), a phrase associated with the male companions of the Prophet. When women call on the example of Umm al-Muminin while living a promiscuous life, they destabilize a system that seeks to position them as inferior. In doing so, they redefine what it means to be equal.

The women at the khana-yi aman were subsumed under the interlinked categories of madness and promiscuity, which situated them as deviant from traditional notions of piety and honor. Kogacioglu (2004) adapts the Foucauldian understanding of subject as an effect of institutional power networks to honor-related crimes in Turkey. She notes that honorable tradition congeals as a retroactive effect in issues related to Muslim women and becomes the primary analytical paradigm through which to understand violence upon the bodies of Muslim women. She writes:

> [To] tackle the tradition effect, feminists around the world do not need to agree on what "tradition" is or who is authorized to speak about it. All they need to do is to look closely at institutional policies, especially when those policies imagine that they themselves are contesting tradition. (Kogacioglu 2004, 143)

In Afghanistan, shelters ostensibly rescue women from a patriarchal grip, and in that sense contest traditional notions of honor. Yet, closer ethnographic fieldwork suggests that shelters play a role in congealing the categories of piety, madness, and promiscuity, and mapping them onto female bodies. Thus shelters can hardly be read as innocent or emancipatory. They are deeply embedded within the disciplinary mechanisms that condition the possibility of pious reasonable womanhood and differentiate promiscuity and madness from it. If a woman runs away and reaches the shelter, she becomes neither free nor emancipated. She becomes subject to grotesque forms of violence, including rape and virginity testing, and is labeled promiscuous and mad. Yet, in the act of running away, she sets herself apart and reveals the networks of power within which her subject position is located. Running away is meaningful and reveals something. Abu-Lughod (1990) asks us to "respect everyday resistance not just by arguing for the dignity or heroism of the resistors but by letting their practices teach us about the complex interworkings of historically changing structures of power" (53).[19] For Afghanistan, I argue that this is accomplished by sustained ethnographic fieldwork through which we can observe the historically contingent subjectivities of runaway women that situate them as mad and promiscuous, but which also shows their practice of everyday resistance.

CHAPTER THREE

Poetic Risk

Every day at the khana-yi aman, the Pashtun women sing landay, short verses of Pashto poetry. *Landay* translates as "short, poisonous snake," likely for its short form and biting themes. Almost everyone at the khana-yi aman was conversant in both Persian and Pashto, and the non-Pashtun women would also participate in these spontaneous poetic outbursts with their own verses of Persian poetry. The verses often referenced legendary Persian folklore classics, such as "Laila and Majnun" and "Shirin and Farhad," as well as pashtunwali and Islamic precepts.[1] At times, women would take opposing sides, man and woman, God and human, but many poems also reflected the love and friendship between women. Although there is no consensus about the origin of the genre, Eliza Griswold writes, "Landays survive because they belong to no one" (2014, 6). Such anonymity (singing from under the burqa) and community ownership (many sing the same landay) ensure the survival of both the poems and the women who sing them. Landay are a form of oral literature, and writing does not play a role in their transmission. They are narrated spontaneously, and the same verses may change depending on who is voicing the content. Anonymity and orality, the two main features of landay, afford them tremendous fluidity and offer the women who use them a modicum of freedom. Landay enable women to orally inhabit an alternative voice that is anonymous, pithy, short, witty, and biting. For example:

> You sold me to an old man, father.
>
> May God destroy your home, I was your daughter. (Griswold 2014)

Having grown up in a Pashtun-dominated area for the first nineteen years of my life, I am very familiar with such poems; yet the boldness of the poetry at the khana-yi aman was inimitable. Many of the women's husbands were missing (ghaib), and many of the women did not know whether their husbands had been captured by the Americans or the Taliban or had willfully joined the Taliban. Still other women had chosen to run away themselves. Thus themes of abandonment were common. Although many women were married, the poetry of love was almost always addressed to lovers, men and women, and the critical mentions of their husbands would rarely be possible outside the poetic context without tremendous consequences. Women sang about their amorous love for other women and men, often not their spouses.

Landay have been described as poetic laments of wretchedness by Pashtun women unable to escape the patriarchal constraints of their subjugation. Sayd Bahauddin Majrouh (d. 1988), the revered Afghan poet who had an astute understanding of women's suffering, collected landay during his research with Pashtun women in refugee camps in Peshawar. Majrouh's book of Pashtun women's poetry was adapted and published posthumously by Andre Vélter, who notes that the lyrics rarely complain about the immediate physical aspect of the women's suffering: "[T]hese women never bemoan their slave labor. Rare are the *landays* in which they mention their 'velvet fingers' that gather the kernels of wheat or the all too heavy jars that make their backs ache." Vélter notes that the landay do not refer to men as beasts, nor do they question whether the perpetrators of their violence are human. Vélter writes that most women sing about their moral subordination through poetry of love, death, and honor (Majrouh 2003). He answers the question of how a Pashtun woman lives her moral degradation in the everyday:

> She performs her duties like clockwork. She accepts and suffers the value system that makes her just an object among so many others. And yet, if one takes a slightly closer look, it turns out that in her innermost self the Pashtun woman is indignant and skeptical, feeding her rebellion. From this deep-seated and hidden protest that grows more resistant with each passing day, she comes out with only two forms of evidence in the end—her suicide and her song. (Majrouh 2003, xv)[2]

Benedicte (1992; see also 2004) deploys a sorrow–joy or *gham–x̄adi* paradigm to narrate performance of emotion among Pashtun women. While Grima's work provides an interesting glimpse into the lives of Pashtun women, superimposing the gham–x̄adi framework does not allow for a range of emotions that are not easily encompassed within this binary structure. Grima posits suffering or gham as the primary interpretive framework to understand the lives of Pashtun women, and asks why Pashtun women do not "seek alternatives to the system, despite their awareness of its oppressive qualities" (1992, 163). Her answer to this question posits the honor system as all-encompassing, in which "challenge is not an option" for women (164).[3] In her well-known work on Maduzai Pashtun women, Nancy Tapper (1991) states that "few men or women are able to exercise much individual control over their lives" (238).

The women at the khana-yi aman defied such descriptions of suffering victims. They were vocal in their protests and courageous in their confrontations. They did not merely sing about resistance; they performed it by running away. They did not perform their duties like clockwork, and they did not quietly accept the value system of pashtunwali and Islam that made their suffering possible. Majrouh posits only two possibilities for a Pashtun woman's suffering: she either sings landay or commits suicide. The women at the khana-yi aman navigate their worlds in far more complex ways than singing their suffering or killing themselves.

Most Pashtun women speak and write Persian, the official language of the state and the education system. At the khana-yi aman, Pashto verses were heavily influenced by Persian literary ideas, such as divinity and homoerotic desire, which is also not uncommon for landay sung by educated women in rural Pashtun areas.[4] The intertwining of Pashto and Persian in poetic discourse sits well within the literary tradition of the great Pashtun poets such as Khushal Khan Khattak (1613–89), who wrote effortlessly in both languages. The themes of love and protest are shared across these poems.

It would be easy to assume that as subjects of global capitalism, the women protested their subjugation by inhabiting a secular or nonlocal position. However, most women who sang landay came from rural areas with no access to global media. Many had not watched television shows or movies, nor had they read international publications. The khana-yi aman had a television with minimal reception that aired only local news programming, and there was no radio or computer access. Where, then, were these ideas of freedom and emancipation originating? Landay exceed the binaries of tradition and modernity, Islam and secularism. As a form of protest against male domination, they can be viewed as modern, secular, and nontraditional. But the ideals of emancipation, autonomy, and egalitarianism are locally invoked, and, in this sense, the landay are traditional. When women sing landay, the emancipatory ideals are not embedded within or originating from the West. Both the Taliban and the runaway women invoke references to an exemplary Islamic past embedded in the precepts of the Quran, sunnah, and hadith. While the Taliban do so in the service of domination, the women do so in the service of emancipation.

The Taliban's Embodied Honor and Poetic Promiscuity

We can understand honor in Afghanistan as embodied practice in the way that veiling and modesty have been understood elsewhere.[5] In these embodied practices, the role of the body is central to pashtunwali. Taliban fatawa (religious edicts) make specific references to the noise a feminine body can make through striking feet while walking, wearing bangles, or laughing. The Taliban's disciplinary program targeted the female body and viewed female sexuality in public spaces as a threat to social sanctity. Juan Cole (2008) describes the conditions under which some women lived:

> Girls could not go to school—according to the Taliban, schools were a gateway to Hell, the first step on the road to prostitution. Women were not allowed to laugh or even speak loudly, because this risked sexually exciting males. High heels were banned because their sound was also declared provocative. Makeup and nail varnish were banned. Women who failed to respect such edicts would be beaten, whipped, or stoned to death.[6]

The *Taliban Official Gazette* explicitly bans women in public. Article 4 of this gazette, written by the Ministry of Promotion of Virtue and Prevention of Vice (Vizarat-e amr bil ma'ruf va nahi 'anil munkar), states:

A lady who launders by the side of a spring in a village or in a temporary dwelling place, shall be prohibited by any necessary measures, her residence shall be identified and landlord shall be punished as necessary. (16)[7]

Ladies shall be prevented from dancing and singing loudly in weddings and on other jovial occasions. If such an act is detected, the landlord involved will be punished severely. (16)

Such enforcements were a means of protecting a woman's chastity for her present or future husband. Loyalty to a husband, as demonstrated by sexual chastity, became the regulatory domain of the Taliban community. But the measures introduced by the Taliban were not entirely unfamiliar to Afghans, especially in Pashtun communities. Pashtun women are taught from a young age that the sexual satisfaction of men, specifically their husbands, is their primary obligation. The duty to one's husband takes precedence over duty to God. For example, shelter inhabitant Gulalei narrated a hadith familiar to most women at the khana-yi aman and with which I was also familiar: A woman asks the Prophet how she can fulfill her obligation to her husband. He answers that if her husband is taken ill such that his entire body has erupted in boils, and if she cleans the pus out of every boil with her tongue, she has still not fulfilled her entire obligation to her husband.[8]

Men are not obligated to their wives in the same manner. This hadith underscores the role of a woman's body in marriage and demonstrates how Islamic virtues vary when performed by male or female bodies. On the surface, this hadith represses and denies the feminine body in service of the male; yet the women read it differently. For them it centers the role of the female body in the sexual satisfaction of men. In this sense, it does not seem repressive to the women who narrated it. When I asked Gulalei how she interpreted this hadith, she replied that it shows men's dependency on women. Despite her contested relations with her husband, she demonstrated impartiality in reading this hadith. She said, in Pashto, "khawand shifa zama zaban sara ki gi," which translates as "My husband's wellness depends on my tongue." She implied that without her tongue he would remain sick, which she interpreted as investing her with influence.

As this chapter will show, women in Afghanistan read such hadith and other classical sources differently than do men. Gulalei's reading was understandable within a moral formation that prioritizes the duty to the husband as the pivot of her pious character.

Two decades after the fall of the Taliban, piety remains the primary social currency for women in Afghanistan. Men control social, economic, and political resources; pious behavior enables women to access resources and ascend social hierarchies without destabilizing normative formations undergirded by Islamic scripture and pashtunwali.[9] Women's chaste comportment is at the center of Afghan communities, and feminine piety is earned through proper sexual comportment, which foregrounds fidelity in the marital union. Socially sanctioned forms of sexual freedom accessible to men, such as polygamy or immediate divorce, are not available to women. Yet the same women who present themselves as chaste in social situations and who emphatically renounce sexual promiscuity depict themselves differently through the lyrics of landay. In these poems, women confess emotions of sexual desire that cast them not as passive and helpless victims but as active participants shaping their worlds.

Why women can express through poetry sexually explicit sentiments that violate honor codes and Islamic principles is aptly explained by Lila Abu-Lughod, who notes that threatening sexuality is controlled by embedding it within the code of morality (1986, 208). Abu-Lughod's work on *ghinnawas* (Bedouin poetry) in Egypt notes the incongruity between poetic and nonpoetic forms of expression.[10] Women express bold emotions through poetry that are not socially accepted outside poetic expression. She shows how, in a society bound by honor, matters of love, demonstrations of weakness, and expressions of deep attachment are possible only within poetic expression (208–9). Abu-Lughod depicts how the Arabic notion of *'agl* (reason) operates as social sense (165).[11] In this logic, piety makes social sense if one possesses 'agl, the opposite of which is *nafs* (passion), which is considered misguided by the individual self or ego.[12] Thus, in Afghanistan, displaying promiscuity demonstrates a lack of *'aql*, which amounts to madness, or unbridled passion misguided and governed by desires of the flesh. Abu-Lughod posits a dichotomy between the world of honor and the world of poetry, even though the latter is not clearly outside the former (209). The poetic world hinges on vulnerability, whereas the domain of honor pivots on strength. Although landay at the khana-yi aman function in a different and more urban context than ghinnawas, they nonetheless share important similarities.

Landay are a demonstration of courage that enables women to risk openly expressing a sexually promiscuous self. At the core of landay is the risk of being different, mad, promiscuous, but not vulnerable. Landay spoken by women in public give us insight into how honor is performed in public, not just how it is enshrined in moral codes. Following Foucault, what is significant here is not how closely the women adhere to pashtun-wali or Islamic precepts but rather the strategic relationships they establish between themselves and these moral codes. The risk of difference is within the ethical relations that moral actors form with moral codes. It is within these relations that the possibility of difference exists. Landay allow women to misinhabit honor in subtle and defiant ways and invest their words with risk. This risk forms the basis of an emancipatory politics or a politics of difference. For example, consider the following landay I heard often at the shelter:

> For nine months I hold my sons in my belly.
> In nine years, they pierce a dagger through my heart.

The following is another landay that exemplifies illicit same-sex relations:

> As I lay with her sharing a dream
> My husband calls her my sister, but we know she is not.

Saba Mahmood's work (2005) on devout women in Egypt shows that one is not born pious but becomes pious through deliberate effort. Thus shyness or modesty is learned through self-cultivation of bodily acts, such as veiling, praying, and fasting.[13] Through embodied practice, the architecture of the self is created in a way that aligns outward behavior with inward disposition (159). A woman who is not shy at first can become shy through the repetitive embodied practice of veiling. In this conception of piety, the interior of the woman is created through ritualistic embodied practice. In contrast to Judith Butler's (1990) example of drag queens whose reiteration of a norm puts the entire system of heteronormativity at risk, pious excellence does not endanger the Islamic referential system but rather consolidates it.[14] In Butler's conception, the excellence of the drag queen's performance reveals the weakness of the heteronormative referential system. For Mahmood, by contrast, pious performance labors to close the gap between the referential Islamic structure and its iteration. Thus each instance of veiling or praying as an iterative performance seeks to consolidate the Islamic referential system encapsulated in the Quran and sunnah. In other words, women veil to become better Muslims and to consolidate their subjectivity with the referential system of Islam. They veil and pray to become closer to Islam, which demonstrates the strength of the system.

In the same way, women at the khana-yi aman sought to consolidate their Muslim selves by fasting, praying, and veiling. But they add another dimension to this, which puts the system at risk at the same time. The performance of promiscuity by ostensibly pious women singing landay in public does not consolidate the referential system. But neither does it fully destabilize it. Landay create possibility beyond consolidation or destabilization of the normative structure and show that the subject's relationship to moral formations is variable and will rarely follow the trajectory determined by moral codes. The most cogent framework for this intertextuality and multiplicity is Bakhtin's idea of the dialogical self (1983), which allows for a multiplicity of subject positions that can be simultaneously contradictory and complementary. As I show in this chapter, the promiscuous self makes possible what I call the promiscuous modern. Promiscuous modern is neither consolidated nor seeking to become consolidated but is in a process of ontological becoming, and, as such, is always in flux (Bradiotti 2012). This nomadic way of being modern, in which women root themselves in some traditional norms but detach themselves from others, forms the basis of the promiscuous modern.

I Cut My Wrist, but the Knife Was Not Sharp

The promiscuous self, which is simultaneously rooted and nomadic, is seen at the khana-yi aman specifically in landay. Poetry permeates the everyday lives of Afghan women, who, even outside the khana-yi aman, often exchange poems with each other. At the khana-yi aman, lyrics sung by Afghan women may be understood as poetry of love and protest, which women recite to express sentiments about their world. Although many of the women's lyrics did not follow the exact grammatical rules of landay as described by Griswold, they nonetheless expressed the same sentiments.[15] Griswold (2014) divides landay thematically into major categories, including love and abandonment. The other three are mourning, homeland, and war (3–4). At the khana-yi aman, the poetry centered around the themes of love (mina), friendship and hospitality (melmastia), and separation (*juda shudagi*). Love poetry about the friendship shared between women had homoerotic elements, and the women often displayed physical gestures of intimacy such as kissing and embracing. Because the women shared a common experience of abandonment, the thread that united the lyrics was the suffering and wretchedness of their station in the world. Women repeatedly voiced protest against men, God, or a divine being. Given their confinement within the walls of the khana-yi aman and the uncertainty of their future, imprisonment of the soul and body was also commonly expressed.

Katiba and I spent several evenings preparing meals for *iftar*, the breaking of the fast. She told me that she had run away after discovering she was pregnant. She could not be certain about the paternity of the child, and I did not ask her more about the matter. She had prayed that the child would die in her womb, and before reaching the khana-yi aman she had a miscarriage. Some days she was inconsolable and spoke only in lyrics, and some days she spoke slowly enough that I could transcribe her words. On occasion, she would not speak for days. *Akhir ʿashara*, the last ten days of Ramazan, are marked by special prayer, especially on odd-numbered nights. Of these, the twenty-seventh day is *laylat al-Qadr*, the night of blessings in Islam.[16] As a practicing Muslim in childhood, I was well aware of its significance, and at the khana-yi aman we prepared special snacks because no one would sleep that night. On this night, Katiba put her prayer rug next to mine and, in between prayers, would whisper in my ear:

My son's blood soaks my shawl today
yesterday he lived inside me

Have you seen a dead child, my dear?
the horror will take your breath away, I promise

Why did God kill this innocent child?
I lament, I lament, I lament

Do you know how wretched my soul has become?
but how will you know since I have stopped speaking?

She told me her father-in-law had raped her frequently, and this caused uncertainty about the paternity of the child. She blamed herself for the rapes: "I used to wear red clothes around the house. I brought this upon myself," she whispered. I thought of contradicting her supposition, but instead asked whether her husband knew about the rapes. She said she had not told him, but it was possible that he had guessed. There were clues. In the beginning she had wanted the child to die, but its actual death caused grief that she had not expected. She described it as her flesh being cut from her body. The pain was unbearable. "I tried to cut my wrists, but the knives were not sharp enough." At this, she burst out laughing and resumed her prayer. The next day, I tried to speak to her, hoping to say something about the absurdity of her blaming herself for her predicament. She blinked and said that she did not recall the details of our conversation from the night before. That night we prayed next to each other again. After we finished, she said, "I killed my own child by wishing it dead. For three days, I walked dripping in his blood refusing to change my clothes. I wanted him to stay with me. Everyone called me mad. Is it madness to mourn a child's, your child's, death?" After her miscarriage, she had a procedure with an unofficial medical provider that left deep scars on her body. She lifted her shirt to show me. After placing my hand on her scars, she said, "If I had this child today, I would have had a token from God. I could forgive my violator. I could forgive my husband. Now what do I have? I have nothing but the scars on my body. I am like an empty vessel, a wrecked ship sailing in the night waiting to sink." She was able to articulate her grief to me outside poetry once I became aware of why she had not initially wanted the child. Yet she did not deliberately attempt to lose the child and carried it for many weeks after running away from her house, until it met its own death. For those around her at the shelter, Katiba's mourning for her dead child became her madness. When she ran away, she became labeled promiscuous in addition to mad. Katiba exemplifies how madness and promiscuity become linked through systematic marginalization undergirded by model notions of piety. Her landay narrated the impossibility of her situation and revealed the power mechanisms that conditioned the possibility of her madness and promiscuity.

Landay elucidate the formation of the subject in its contradictions and complications. Katiba's subject position in her family was fractured through experiencing multiple rapes. She was betrayed by her father-in-law and her husband, who became a silent witness to the brutality she endured. Katiba's poetry reveals a world that pivots on women's subjugation through sexual violence. Landay do not just depict violent events that happen to women but rather illustrate how suffering is enfolded into women's everyday relations. Katiba defined her relationships through the notions of love and care for her family, and the violence of rape by her father-in-law disrupted the ways in which she could perform care. The poetic recollections of her dead son were not simply a recounting of the past; they were a lament for the death of her motherhood. It was protest for carrying her rapist's child and the devastation of enduring the child's death. It was the helplessness of enduring rapes within her family and the sadness at the loss of her family, who had abandoned her. The complicated relationships that Afghan women must navigate require them to inhabit various modalities of subjecthood, all of which originate in violence.[17] The women were familiar with the widely shared stories of the brutalities done to women by the Taliban and the mujahideen. Their particular narratives of brutality were woven into the tapestry of violence without justice. Katiba's verses exceed the binaries of inner and outer, power and resistance, crime and punishment. They grant her the ability to speak and to make the violence in the interstices of her past life publicly known in the present. But to what end? There is no chance of jail for her rapist. There is no chance to bring her child back. There is no chance of reconciliation with her husband. There is no chance of support from her own family, who disowned her after she told them about the rapes. The concept of retribution ('azab) or justice ('adl) for the violence she has endured is outside the parameters of her social world.

How is death in connection to love and loss understood in a world without justice? Abu-Lughod (1986, 206) observes, "ideology of honor provides the guiding concepts behind responses to that most radical of loss situations—death," and through ethnography shows how women speak of the death of infants through lyrics of sorrow and resignation (121). In Sayd Majrouh's view, Pashtun women are dehumanized by experiencing the deaths of their children, and such dehumanization renders them incapable of maternal love.[18] This observation does not describe the women I met at the khana-yi aman, whose devastation from witnessing death did not decrease their love for their children. Death was at the core of their humanity. Most of the poems—at least the ones I heard at the khana-yi aman—underscore how love and death are entwined in the lives of ordinary Afghan women. Love, loss, and the danger of death are ever present within these poetic lyrics. This is what renders the women human. Theorists of subjectivity such as Achille Mbembe (2003) centralize the role of violence in the formation of the subject. Vocalizing the experiences of brutal pain reveals the power structure that makes the pain possible. Violence, in this conception, to use Elaine Scarry's (1985) words, "makes and unmakes" the world. The violence of rape and death was central to the making and unmaking of the women's worlds.

Given the risk of promiscuity as a child grows up, many girls are married at very young ages—twelve, thirteen, even nine and six. But how does a girl as young as six understand the marital union? What does it mean if she says she has taken on a lover? How does she explain it to others who have not shared this common experience? Many children have their hands tied behind their backs on the wedding night. The violence of the wedding night is deeply understood without question.

One evening, a poetry game erupted among the women. The following verses were recited sequentially without interruption, each woman inhabiting a different voice.

My father sold me no doubt
to quell the gossip, I did not pout.

Abandonment will not abandon me, my friend
it has swallowed all my lovers.

That night I was cast upon the sword
Hands tied behind my back, my mouth was still open.

After the first blow, I felt my face turn blue
not like the sky you fool, it froze like ice.

Throw the stones at me if you will.
Each stone is a letter from my lover.

My lover saw my wedding henna the other night.
I said it was my sister's wedding.

Hush, my lover, lest my husband wakes
blood will be splattered like pomegranate seeds.

My wretched hands rested by you and did nothing
Tonight I will knit my white coffin.

The shared experience of abandonment makes possible this poetry in which each verse is a rendition of their suffering. They speak about being sold at a young age by their fathers to their husbands. They speak about abandonment and the violence of marital rape, without using the vocabulary of marital rape. Yet the women give voice to the pain caused by forced sexual intercourse. The reference to throwing stones is to the Quranic punishment for adultery, which the Taliban officially instituted (although it existed in various forms before then) and has sporadically carried out after its fall. These verses take a position outside the discourses of pashtunwali, honor, and Islam, yet are rendered intelligible by these discourses. The women both inhabit and resist the power formations to which they are subjected. In their abandonment, they knowingly inhabit a promiscuous self, but this promiscuous self is undergirded by the moral formation of piety.

Subject Vulnerability and Poetic Risk

Improvisational prowess and ability to narrate poetry are highly valued in Afghanistan. A musical voice is considered a divine gift, and singing at auspicious occasions such as weddings or childbirth is encouraged.[19] When landay are sung, they are meant to demonstrate the quality of the deliverer's voice. Neelam had been told not to sing in the garden lest the neighbors heard her voice, which did not stop her from singing inside the house. I could often hear her sing in the kitchen and would join her in the cooking preparation. The khana-yi aman managers told me that Neelam had delusions of grandeur. She had been married to an older man: "Despite my beauty, I was a virgin. Do not think there was no temptation." Gulalei had remarked, "The fool thinks she could have had an affair and her beauty would have saved her. It is her beauty that brought her here." Her expectations were unreasonable, they whispered. Nevertheless, Neelam was popular because of her voice and her spontaneous wry and pithy wit. She would talk boldly about her sexual dissatisfaction in her marriage, which would cause great amusement. She repeated this verse so often that it became a mantra among us.

> I made love to him in many winters
> when his maleness would shrink in the bitter cold.

Men's virility is often compared to cornstalks. When a woman gets pregnant, if her next of kin, especially her mother-in-law, dreams of a cornstalk, it signifies that the baby is male. An apple or pomegranate signifies a girl. A famous Pashto landay often heard on the radio station is,

> Making love to an old man
> Is like having sex with a shriveled cornstalk blackened by mold.[20]

Women would talk explicitly and in poetic metaphors about the sexual inadequacies of their husbands. This was one of the most popular topics of discussion. Neelam was soon to be married to a public official who had taken a fancy to her; however, she first needed her current husband to divorce her. Neelam was not in love with this official. She had encountered him at the courts after she had already left her husband. I had accompanied her to the court visits where she would complain about her husband and his family in a loud voice. The lawyer commented that it was an astute strategy to provoke her husband's anger so that he would let her go willingly. It had not worked, however. When she called him ugly or old, he would smile and shrug off her insults. In one of the visits, she told him about a lover, which I knew she did not have. She recited a cryptic and bold poem whose meaning was not immediately revealed in its narration:

If you hear about my death from Khusru
Know that Shirin awaits Farhad by the river

My husband is like a joyous child with a toy
Playing with my body, does he know where my heart is?

I roam the streets as a mad woman
villagers talk about me, I laugh at them

When you see me naked you will know
why my husband will not let me go

Be quiet or I will kiss you in public
Your blood will be on my veil

Touch your face, my darling
I lie in between those beautiful hands
I pray you become a thread on my veil
I touch you to soothe my soul

I told the yellow spring flowers to get lost
they reminded me too much of you

My husband smells like a pig
I would rather make love to a dog

He was wearing your perfume last night
I made love to him thinking it was you

Here Neelam invokes the legend of Shirin and Farhad in the first verse. She inhabits the figure of Shirin by speaking of her death in this legendary

tale of rivalry between two men, Farhad and Khusru. The Persian classical poet Nizami Ganjavi (1141–1209) wrote this and the other famous
tragic romance epic popular among the khana-yi aman women, "Laila
and Majnun." In Nizami Ganjavi's version of this epic, Khusru falls in
love with Shirin without meeting her. He learns of her beauty from his
friend and embarks on a journey to find her. Many local versions of this
tale exist among the local women. The story is a long and convoluted
one in which Farhad appears as a commoner and rival to Khusru, who
is himself interested in Shirin. When Farhad learns of the false news of
Shirin's death, he jumps from a mountain to kill himself. Shirin kills herself eventually to avoid marrying another suitor, Khusru's son, who has
also fallen in love with her. Although Neelam did not know the entire
epic, she was familiar with parts about the rivalry between Khusru and
Farhad, and the death of Shirin and Farhad. Neelam used this popular
legend to signify that she had another admirer, and perhaps a new lover.

Neelam voiced the verses loudly, ensuring that everyone in the vi-
cinity heard them. She did not sing these but recited them in a slow me-
lodic voice. Despite my own discomfort, I managed to raise my eyes and
glance at her husband, who had been listening quietly with his father.
They turned pale, and after she finished, they left. The next week, we
heard that her husband had agreed to the divorce. I asked her to explain
the poem, but she said it had served its purpose. A few days later, she
brought it up on her own: "I have always showed respect to my husband.
I did not leave him because I fell in love with someone else. I left because
I did not love my husband. He does not understand it. He thinks I should
have stayed. How should I explain this to him? I had to make up a lover.
There is no other way." She said she was not interested in marrying the
official who had taken a liking to her. "What will you do?" I asked her.
She shrugged her shoulders and looked to the sky: "He will find a way
for me." Eventually she did marry the official. I saw her a year later, and
she said she was content with her decision. It may seem odd that she left
her husband because she did not love him only to immediately marry
another man whom she also did not love. Neelam explained it in these
words: "At least I tried to change my kismet."

It is not common for men to engage with women directly. When women talk with their fathers, brothers, or husbands, most do not look directly at them. It is not uncommon to have a conversation without making eye contact. Men do not mention their wives' names outside the home, and women are given names like Bibi Shireen (Sweet Madam) or Shireen Gul (Sweet Flower). In almost all circumstances, men will refuse to engage in direct confrontation with the women in the family. General references to mothers and wives among men often occur during fights and are almost always deprecatory. For instance, as mentioned before, "I will rape your mother" (*sta mor be umandum*) or "I will rape your sister" (*sta khor be umandum*) are commonly used in anger between men.[21] As Neelam's husband later told me, "It is a matter of great dishonor to even speak to my wife in public. We have already been dishonored." The emotion he felt was not anger but dishonor. The two were not to be conflated, he insisted. When I asked him what it meant to be dishonored, he replied, "It is helplessness and detachment. She has detached herself from my world."

Neelam used the lyrics to direct her world to a place she wanted to live. She demonstrated that poetry is not ineffectual in everyday life and, when used astutely, had tremendous sway. Could another woman utilize poetry in the same manner? Neelam's rendition conveyed her emotions to her husband, which led to a subjective transformation that altered both their worlds. Neelam's landay gave voice to her anguish and despair through a performance of sexual promiscuity. By acting sexually promiscuous through an imagined lover, she used honor discourse to a favorable end that depended on participation from her husband and his father. It is not unusual for such situations to erupt in violence. It took courage, skill, and an astute understanding of her subjectivity to peacefully achieve her objective. Neelam had taken a calculated risk. Her poem showed that attainment of nonconformity was not easy, and her husband's reaction showed that respect is accorded to those who are willing to endanger themselves to acquire freedom.

Landay entwine the experiences of women by referring to shared legends familiar to and loved by Afghans. The lyrics contain known images embedded within a historical and cultural literary corpus. Familiarity with cultural and historical metaphors, such as the stories of Laila and Majnun or Shirin and Farhad, enables us to understand the richness and intertextuality of the landay.[22] Although some landay may invoke love tales from a distant past, entrenching them within tradition and decreasing their social risk, most break with tradition to conjure a new world of possibility. The stories of the character pairs of Laila and Majnun and Shirin and Farhad are commonly invoked in everyday conversations. These are legendary folktales about the sorrow of love, separation, and abandonment. In the former epic, Laila marries someone else, and Majnun dies tragically while seeking her in the wilderness. In the latter story, Shirin kills herself to avoid marrying someone she does not love. These stories had profound resonance in the khana-yi aman. In Afghanistan, given the high incidence of nonliteracy in women, literary texts live through discursive practices not entirely controlled by educated Muslims or men. Landay impart new meanings and valences to male-dominated discourses. Despite Neelam's lack of formal education, her poetry often invoked literary images such as the legend of Shirin and Farhad and religious sources such as the Quran and hadith. Her awareness of these sources came from orally transmitted stories. She was especially familiar with the common hadith and Quranic verses related to women, and incorporated these effortlessly into her poetic narrations. Her understanding of literary and religious sources was markedly different from her husband's engagement with the same literary corpus. He later said, "Neelam is seeking Majnun. A madman who will die a wretched death. She is destined to doom." He emphasized the unrealistic madness of her verses. In the epic of Laila and Majnun, also written by Nizami Ganjavi, Majnun falls in love with Laila and sends her a proposal that is rejected by her father. Laila marries someone else, and Majnun wanders the wilderness heartbroken and mad, and dies a tragic death. In some versions, Laila, too, dies of heartbreak. Majnun's character is central to an understanding of love as madness (*junun*). When Neelam's husband invoked Majnun, he did so deliberately to underscore the madness of love outside the marital union, which is destined for death and destruction.

Abu-Lughod (1986) reads ghinnawas as culturally and socially embedded within conventional forms of constraint (238–39). Formulaic constructions render the poetry impersonal and nonindividual, and thus decrease the social risk associated with the transgression. Although they are markedly different forms of expression, ghinnawas and landay share important similarities. Both are anonymous and ambiguous, both narrate emotions not commonly expressed outside poetic form, and both are linked to honor as a moral code. But landay are not linked to honor in the same way that ghinnawas are linked to tradition (240). Landay are not completely bound by Pashtunwali or Islam, although they are differentiated against these systems. In this sense, in singing landay, women do not abandon the honor system but situate themselves differently within and against it. Neelam's husband said that she had detached herself from his world by performing a promiscuous self. For him, female promiscuity was a form of madness not possible within his world. But this form of madness was linked to traditional folklore, in the figure of Majnun. Thus the possibility of this promiscuous madness was well within his world. Neelam had shown an astute understanding of her world by taking a calculated risk and invoking shared ideals. This careful disruption did not completely destabilize their worlds, but it conjured the possibility of something different.

From the outside, it may seem that these poems would define the women as outcasts or as mad. The women at the khana-yi aman were certainly different if not exceptional. Most Afghan women do not run away from home. Most are not imprisoned. Most will not end up at the khana-yi aman. But the stories of the khana-yi aman women nonetheless give a glimpse into the everyday lives of ordinary Afghans. Griswold (2014) notes, "Landays are mostly sung, and singing is linked to licentiousness in the Afghan consciousness. . . . Much of an Afghan woman's life involves a cloak-and-dagger dance around honor—a gap between who she seems to be and who she is" (5).[23] The khana-yi aman closes that gap between perception and reality. Women inhabit their licentiousness and do not shy away from explicit sexual expressions and, in this way, demonstrate the Pashtun notion of courage.

In Pashtun legends, brave women are idolized. Scheherazade's story from the Arabian nights is a popular legend in Afghanistan. In its Pashtun narration, Scheherazade is married to a king who is enraged with his existing wife because of her adultery. Through exquisite poetry and erudite prose, Scheherazade wins the king's favor and saves the lives of potential future wives. Growing up, I would often hear stories about Malalai of Maiwand, after whom Malala Yousafzai is named. (Malala is a common name for Pashtun girls.) As a young child, I thought of Malalai as a distant aunt, because the story was shared in a familiar and socially intimate fashion. The legend says that Malalai of Maiwand called on crestfallen Afghan soldiers on the brink of failure to increase their efforts against the British. It is believed that Malalai raised her veil singing a landay, which uplifted the spirits of the Afghan soldiers, leading them to victory. The popularity of Malalai's legend in Afghanistan shows that women's bravery is lauded. Nevertheless, women carefully navigate social risk between piety and promiscuity, between conformity and rebellion. Even though the cultural milieu in which poetry narration occurs epitomizes shared ideals of bravery and courage, Afghan women daily walk a tightrope between pious obedience and promiscuous insubordination. Landay, like the khana-yi aman, thrusts this concealed everyday struggle into the public. In a Geertzian sense, one can say that the risk taken by the women is not completely irrational and may even have some rewards (Geertz 1973).[24] When a woman runs away from home, it seems irrational, risky, and dangerous. On closer view, women like Gulalei and Neelam take calculated risks that combine pious reason and promiscuous madness in the service of changing their worlds.

This high-risk social drama unfolds every day at the khana-yi aman. Because most poems contain explicit sexual images, they summon a world that is not entirely captured by honor or Islam and is rarely visible in public. Judith Butler (2009, i) argues that "reproduction of gender is . . . always a negotiation with power" and "there is no gender without . . . reproduction of norms that risks undoing or redoing the norm in unexpected ways, thus opening up the possibility of a remaking of gendered reality along new lines." In this sense, poetic expressions are not mere passive laments on the state of the existing world; they are calls to action and, in some cases, drivers of change. Afghans often say that poetry has the capacity to bring change. Landay's power resides in their calculation of risk. Unlike ghinnawas, which are associated with dependency and weakness (Abu-Lughod 1986, 243), landay are upheld as ideals of courage.

Malalai's legend shows that using symbolic femininity, epitomized by her use of voice and veil, can change unfavorable circumstances.

Linguistic Enactment of Poetic Promiscuity

If we turn from the reaction of her kinsmen to Neelam's conception of her own world, a set of questions presents itself. Most women would deny having a lover even if they had one. It is rare for a married woman to admit she has a lover, even under duress. Neelam claimed to have a lover, boldly and in public. And even though she did not actually have one, that fact was deliberately obscured in order for her to take a position of promiscuity. Her statement was not true, but it was also not false. Her utterances had a performative value that should not be measured by truth or falsity but by their ability to facilitate change in her life. To use the vocabulary of the linguistic philosopher John Searle, her poetic utterances had an illocutionary force that was meaningful to her father-in-law and husband. J. L. Austin (1975) describes performatives as sentences that perform an act through enunciation. In this sense, performative sentences do not merely report a situation but have the force of action. Performatives *do* something.

Landay entwine piety and promiscuity in ways that cannot easily be disentangled. A woman who wears the burqa, prays five times a day, and fasts during Ramazan will voice illicit sexual sentiments through these lyrics. In its Foucauldian incarnation, the subjectivity of the women may be located in the microcapillaries of power as power's effect, rather than in opposition to power. For Foucault, power creates subjects and informs its resistance. Women like Neelam consider themselves to be within the power networks of Islam and pashtunwali, but they use these mechanisms to form a resistance. Foucault's understanding of subjection does not leave space for resistance. Butler's reconceptualization of the Foucauldian subject expands the notion of subjectivity to consider language as a system of signification through which subject formation takes place. For Butler, each reiteration of the social norm opens a possibility for agentive action. An understanding of the performative constitution of pious subjectivity allows us to also see how promiscuity is performative.

Butler (1993) invests performativity with the possibility of difference. Given the historical and social relations that undergird the performative subject, enacting a promiscuous self through landay is not simply a performance of choice or freedom. Rather, it is a "forcible citation of a norm, one whose complex historicity is indissociable from relations of discipline, regulation, punishment" (232). Promiscuity is embedded within intertextual references to a shared past, such as invocations of Shirin and Farhad, Laila and Majnun. In other words, promiscuity is made meaningful by citations of Islamic, Pashtun, and Persian norms and ideals such as folklore, veiling, and praying. Landay are replete with references to veiling, but these traditional references are inverted. When landay invoke the veil, they associate it with lovers rather than husbands. Thus landay reveal the disciplinary and regulatory mechanisms that make veiling possible. But the citation of veiling in landay is toward subversion. This calculated risk furnishes the possibility of difference. Landay forcibly cite the norm of veiling, which is indissociable from the moral formation of piety in Islam and pashtunwali, but in doing so differently than intended, they open a possibility of changing that moral formation.

Speech is integral to feminist theories of subject formation, and for Butler social reality is enacted through performing the convention. Butler (1993, 13) states, "a performative is that discursive practice that enacts and produces that which it names." In this sense, Neelam's verses may be understood as performatives because they enact a promiscuous self.

Be quiet or I will kiss you in public
Your blood will be on my veil

I pray you become a thread on my veil
I touch you to soothe my soul

The veil invoked in Neelam's landay does not refer to a sense of modesty or to the familiar blue burqa through which Afghan, particularly Pashtun, women are known to the world. Many landay speak of the lover's proximity by turning him into a woman's veil. Veiling here is a metaphor for a woman's lover and not her entrapment in her system. Landay take on the visual image of sexual obedience and piety inscribed in public veiling and deliberately invert it. Neelam once remarked, "Afghan women have been devastated through decades of war and poverty, and yet it seems as if only their sexual chastity could provide an index of their suffering." In a remarkably astute statement, she captured the importance of piety: "Afghan women are known through the burqa." Landay abound with metaphors of veiling. A married woman veils to save her chastity for her husband to whom it rightfully belongs. Women also veil to strengthen their relationship with a divine being and to become better Muslims. Neelam, by contrast, associated her veil with her lover, which was unbearable for her husband, who had once said to me, "A wife's veil is her husband." This was an obvious reference to the popular Quranic verse that refers to marital spouses as each other's clothing, who must cover and protect each other.[25] Adultery, even if only ostensible, is the ultimate betrayal. Although the marital unit centers on fidelity, Neelam told me that men are rarely considered promiscuous. As a rule, men's piety centers on their relationship with God, while women's piety and their relationship with God is mediated through their husbands. Most women at the khana-yi aman were familiar with the hadith that situates the husband next to God.[26] A husband is a *majazi khuda*, or earthly incarnation of God. Obedience to the husband is a primary virtue.

Failure to become a proper sexually pious woman in Afghanistan leads to social sanctions such as imprisonment, ostracization, and even death. A woman becomes pious through repeated actions that enact her piety. To the extent that piety is performative, it exists as fiction (Butler 1988). The social fiction of piety hinges in binary opposition to its other, promiscuity. The words of Neelam's poem recited outside this context would not have challenged the representational framework of honor. However, narrated in this particular instance and in this particular manner, they conjectured an alternative interpretive logic of honor, which caused a disruption. Mahmood (2005) notes that pious and nonpious dispositions are learned and embodied through repetitive virtuous actions, which is why only a deep understanding of the historical system that underwrites piety could lead to a resignification of Islamic practices such as modesty (166). Neelam demonstrated profound engagement with the honor system that undergirded her subject positioning as a pious Pashtun woman, and successfully appropriated landay, an already noncompliant discourse, toward meaningful subversion. Through her speech acts, poetry became invested with possibilities not entirely predetermined. Even Neelam herself could not have predicted the outcome. Butler (1988, 521) notes, "one does one's body . . . different than one's embodied predecessors and successors." In this sense, Neelam had done landay differently from others who shared her predicament. Butler states that the "possibilities of gender transformation are to be found in the arbitrary relation between [repetitive] acts, in the possibility of a different sort of repeating, in the breaking or subversive repetition of that style" (520). Neelam's subversive repetition of well-known conventional norms rendered arbitrary the relation between moral action and moral code, between act and norm. It is within this gap between norm and action that the possibility of transformation exists.

While courage and rebellion are valorized as ideal traits in Afghanistan, so is submission to a notion of divine destiny, a common theme in Persian and Pashto poetry. A famous Pashto adage, *Kismet pe mando na, pa thando derzi*, means, "Destiny comes not by running after it, but by waiting for it in tranquility." This means that good fortune (here "destiny" means good fortune) will come to those who wait patiently. Men and women use the adage to encourage patience (*sabr*).

Not all women had Neelam's boldness or capacity for risk calculation. Arshia was an elderly woman. As described earlier, she and her teenage daughter, Parwaneh, ended up at the khana-yi aman after asking for their Islamic share of inheritance from their brothers and sons. Pashtunwali does not explicitly give women rights to property, but Islamic law clearly does. David Edwards (2017, 31) states, "Pakhtuns assume without question that belief in Islam is part of who they are. However, there are occasions when adherence to cultural ideals associated with Pakhtun identity can set in motion contradictions with ideals associated with Islam." Arshia said that according to Islamic law, she was entitled to half a share of her brothers' (from her father's) property. In addition, she was entitled to one-eighth of her husband's wealth. Her daughter was also entitled to inheritance under the same principles. When Arshia asked for it, her brothers and sons beat her and Parwaneh and chained them inside the house so that they could not file an Islamic case for their property inheritance in court.[27] Eventually the men threw them out of the house. Poetry had not worked for Arshia in the way it had for Neelam, even though she demonstrated poetic ability. She recited these verses when I asked her why she ended up at the khana-yi aman:

> I asked for a piece of land
> my name was written on it before you scratched it
>
> I am chained to this bedpost
> yet I own nothing in this room
>
> Can I catch my destiny running after it in sunshine?
> or patiently waiting for it by the river in the cold
>
> This dust is worth more than a hundred pounds of your gold
> My father and his father are buried in this ground
>
> I am but a tree with no leaves
> tomorrow, come and witness my shriveled soul

Arshia implies in her landay that she could do nothing about her destiny, even though she was aware of the injustice and of her Islamic rights of inheritance. She invoked the Pashto adage about the futility of running after her destiny. She knew her sons and brothers would not acquiesce. She missed her sons, but was wracked with grief from their betrayal. Majrouh (2003) wrote that Pashtun women often suffer physical violence at the hands of their sons while their husbands watch in silence. A response to this ultimate betrayal of a mother who gave him life is landay that "trap the man in his own value system" (15). They call on men to demonstrate honor in war before meriting the mother's love.

> Go first, my love, to avenge the martyrs' blood
> Before deserving the refuge of my breasts [28]

Neelam had indeed trapped her husband in his own value system by eliciting a certain response from him. Arshia, too, had called on honor and Islam to render intelligible her suffering. The fragments spoken by Arshia condensed a known history that was shared by many women. Gulalei would step in sometimes to elaborate: "Can you imagine being beaten by your son? Is this not the ultimate humiliation or shamelessness [bi-sharmi]?" Katiba stood outside listening, and Gulalei called to her,

"Would your son have done the same had he lived?" implying that her son's death had somehow benefited Katiba, which nobody in the room could negate. Neelam interjected this trajectory of thought: "A woman is nothing without a son." Becoming a mother, particularly of sons, invests Pashtun women with specific rights. A popular Pashto adage, repeated often to my sisters and me by our mother, is that a woman becomes a woman when she becomes a mother of sons. Here Neelam occupies the hegemonic discourse of patriarchy she challenged so well at the court. Even though Neelam is well aware of the disciplinary mechanisms that regulate the belief that women are nothing without sons, she nonetheless inhabits this subject position. If I had not witnessed Neelam's encounter at court earlier, I could not have grasped her struggle between living as an obedient woman and challenging social norms. Neelam, and indeed all the women at the khana-yi aman, navigate these contradictory and fragmented subject positions,[29] which become intelligible if one thinks of agency as a modality or capacity for action rather than as resistance to normative social conditions (Mahmood 2005, 157). Foucault's understanding of askesis, as a modality for action, has been fruitfully adapted by theorists of Islamic feminism such as Mahmood. This conception of agentive action not bound by the binaries of structure and resistance allows for a more nuanced understanding of agency. In Mahmood's conception, the devout women are working toward consolidation. In Butler's narration of the drag queen, the system is being destabilized. But at the khana-yi aman, women's words and actions provide a third possibility, in which they resist some norms and inhabit others.

Social Functions of Poetry

Islam and pashtunwali are interpretive frames of reference for understanding women's poetry, but the poems center around love, suffering, death, and violence. On one occasion, we were leaving to go to court with Naghmana, whose lover, Osman, claimed to have joined the Taliban. She had initially wanted to marry him without knowing much about him. While at the khana-yi aman, she was able to meet him a few times and learn more about him. As we headed out, a woman called out begrudgingly,

> When you meet your lover
> tell him you will kiss him tomorrow

Understanding the undertone of envy, Naghmana gave an immediate rejoinder.

> How will I meet him tomorrow, you fool?
> he will die on his way home today

> He ran away to become a talib
> now a recluse, I cross the city alone

> Who told you I was running away tonight?
> The liars are wagging their tongues in gossip

> Let us dig the graves now
> they say winter will end soon

Naghmana explained these verses to me that evening. She was referring to the incomprehensibility of her lover's decision, which would certainly lead to his death. Naghmana and other women whose husbands had joined the Taliban would often read the decision of the men joining the Taliban as their abandonment. When women invoked their suffering through the landay, resistance gained a new meaning not controlled by the Taliban. Other than through poetic expression, Pashtun women rarely disclose sentiments of envy, which is considered an evil. Through this short poem, the women drew my attention to the difficulty of endless waiting. Outside this context, they would retain a tolerant persona and not indulge in the frivolities of complaining. The other significant reference here is to winter ending, which was clear to those who knew that the Taliban often receded into the mountains in winter and emerged to fight in the summer. There were groans from other women who demonstrated their familiarity with this problem.

Getting a day in court was a source of great envy, as every woman at the khana-yi aman had to wait her turn to take her case in front of a judge. This could take a month or years. But going to court was not always fruitful, and facing the judge's interrogation was not easy. When

Naghmana came back in a gloomy mood, it was obvious that her lover had not given up his conviction to join the Taliban. Sadia, whose husband had joined the Taliban, tried to cheer Naghmana by offering these verses.

Will you abandon him when he becomes a talib?
Run far away from a madman

His grave calls him to Kajaki each night
Let's meet there with your new lover

At the family court, Naghmana had pleaded with Osman to reconsider his decision. He remained adamant. When she tried to say that it was his Islamic obligation to care for her, he said, "I will care for my wife in the way Allah intends." Whereas the older generations of the Taliban were not fully literate in canonical sources, the newer generation of Taliban has developed formal command over authoritative sources. What unfolded that evening was not a discussion about the fundamentalist ideology of the Taliban or how the people from outside viewed them. Rather, the women lamented the wretchedness of their love and abandonment. Both Sadia and Naghmana had lived through the Taliban rule. Here, the Taliban was not ensconced in its gruesome past but had become a specter in the present. Osman had not asked Naghmana to wait for him, nor did he promise to return. On our way back, Naghmana contemplated whether she should marry Osman before he disappeared. She interpreted his comments to mean that he was destined to join. Eventually she decided to marry him and leave the khana-yi aman. When I met her a few months later, she was pregnant and living with a distant aunt; and, as we had predicted, Osman had disappeared.

The lives of women were very unpredictable. Poetry made life meaningful and intelligible. Abu-Lughod (1986) outlines the three main functions of poetry for Bedouin women. She notes that poetry creates social intimacy, provides protection through anonymous and collective narration, and illustrates the hardship inherent in conforming to honor ideals (241–46). The poetry at the khana-yi aman, narrated by women from widely different backgrounds, shares some of these functional characteristics. It brings individuals together by bridging gender, cultural, social, and economic distance. Most women who sing landay are not literate. But many literate and powerful women, such as Safia Siddiqui, a famous Pashtun woman from Jalalabad, write and sing landay. Siddiqui was a delegate in the loya jirga of President Hamid Karzai's government. Her face is well known across Afghanistan, displayed on billboards during elections. Her landay are bold and explicit. She recites them fearlessly at large gatherings of men. Her formal education was reflected in her landay, which systematically and astutely take on historical and theoretical frameworks of honor.

> When I'm walking down the street, the people watch me
> Disrespectfully and surprisingly
> Watch me,
> They are talking and saying
> "Who is this lout?
> Who is she?
> Whose daughter is she?
> Whose sister is she?
> Whose wife is she?"
> Oh! Allah, is it honor? (Rubin 2005, 54)

Afghan women revere Siddiqui. Despite her sexually explicit poems and bold stance on honor, she is extremely popular. The Taliban attacked her in 2005, opening fire on her while she was canvassing during election days (Gall 2005). She was neither wounded nor deterred from writing against gender inequality in honor and Islam. In this poem, she inhabits a male spectator confounded by the boldness she exhibits as she walks down the street. Frivolous walking in public is frowned on in Pashtun areas. The Taliban banned women's presence in public arenas by forbidding them to laugh or use public restrooms. Taliban fatawa would often hold the male guardian, husband, father, son, or landlord responsible for women's comportment in public arenas. Sanctions included lashes and imprisonment. The last verse questions the honor of the men whose ward she is, who have obviously failed in their duty to constrain her actions. Her writing demonstrates that she is well aware of the anxiety and moral panic that her public presence provokes in men.

Siddiqui's poem shows how women's lives are endangered when their fathers, husbands, sons, brothers, and lovers join the Taliban. By poetically inhabiting the position of a Talib who was objectifying her through his speech and male gaze, Siddiqui eloquently upsets the gender hierarchy, which also implicates her despite her fame and privilege. When Siddiqui asks whose daughter, wife, or sister she is, she inhabits the voice of the Talib male who may be a woman's father, husband, or brother. Siddiqui is a powerful, well-known politician from an influential family, whose life could not be further from Neelam's obscure world. Yet they share a common risk when they remark on an abstract notion of honor and willfully situate themselves against it. Although anonymous and collective, landay do not provide protection to their deliverer in the way described by Abu-Lughod. This is because landay are deliberately defiant in challenging the honor code. Women like Siddiqui and Neelam expose themselves to tangible threats of violence when narrating landay, which has led to actual deaths of women, such as Zarmina, who lit herself on fire (Griswold 2014). Death here is not a hypothetical concept. Siddiqui and Neelam incite the normative structure toward different ends, and in doing so resituate their worlds.

Landay: Modern or Traditional?

Landay provide a vocabulary in Pashto for female sexual promiscuity. When a senior professor of Afghanistan's history read an earlier version of this work, he wrote in the margins, "Landay in theory, khana-yi aman in practice,"[30] which was a perfect encapsulation of the connection between the theory and practice of resistance and rebellion, piety and promiscuity in Afghan communities. Do public expressions of promiscuity render women modern in the same way that public expressions of piety make them traditional? What does it mean to be modern or traditional in this context?

In Afghanistan, notions of modernity and tradition, as they relate to piety and promiscuity, are entwined in complicated ways. The conditions of gender inequality affect almost all Afghan women. Although marginalized, the women at the khana-yi aman were not completely outside the patriarchal discourse, because they also lived in accordance with most Islamic and pashtunwali precepts. The women clearly saw themselves as Muslim. In many of our conversations, they described themselves as adherents of Islam, which they did not view as incompatible with being a Pashtun woman. Even though they deemed themselves as Muslim and Pashtun, their families, who also defined them as such, had ostracized them. What had made their ostracization possible? The women did not want to become secular, nor did they want to emigrate to the West or think of themselves as Western. They had discomfort with their system of oppression, which they voiced and performed in a variety of ways, all of which led them to the shelter. In the Western imagination, leaving a family is an exercise of autonomous will toward a form of individuation. Yet the women here are embedded in collective obligations of pashtun-wali and Islam. The possibility of inhabiting contradictory and complementary positions shows how the promiscuous self is dialogical and in a continuous process of becoming rather than fixed into a solid identity.

Recent works in anthropology on Islamic feminism have reverted to Aristotelian notions of habitus that differ from modern incarnations of this concept (Mahmood 2005, 138). For Bourdieu (1992, 67), habitus "produces and endlessly reproduces, thereby reproducing the conditions of its own perpetuation."[31] Habitus operates through structured predispositions that precondition and limit actions (53). However, within this structure is the possibility for calculated risk and regulated improvisation (57). In its Aristotelian understanding, as read by Mahmood (2005), habitus entails a pedagogical process in which habituation of virtues is undertaken with the paradoxical aim of rendering them redundant (139). For Mahmood, the possibility of agentive action for Muslim women is better formulated in Aristotle than in Bourdieu. Abu-Lughod's work (2013; see also 1986, 1993) shows also the productivity of "writing against culture" rather than using categories of religion and culture as paradigmatic explanatory frameworks for the actions of Muslim women and labeling the women as nonmodern or traditional.[32] Asad's work (1993, 2003) has us consider that the category of religion is a precondition for modernity, for without religion, modernity cannot exist.[33] In this sense, he shows the futility of constructing modernity and tradition in binary opposition to each other. Following Asad and Timothy Mitchell (1991, 2000), Lara Deeb (2006) disenchants modernity by connecting it to traditional piety and introduces the concept of the "pious modern," which provides a cogent framework for understanding how piety and promiscuity are rendered intelligible in Afghanistan. Her work shows two notions of progress, one embedded in modernization and the other in piety. She writes, "public piety is the key to the pious modern" (33–34). This idea of pious modernity pivots on visible piety and publicly authenticated Islam.[34] Afghans are conversant in issues of public demonstrations of piety because the Taliban made public piety mandatory for men and women. Women had to demonstrate their inner virtue through public acts of proper veiling and bodily comportment. Men, too, were implicated either through being held accountable for women's comportment or through pious bodily expressions of their own; for example, the Taliban mandated a particular length for men's beards. In this sense, public piety became a public good. The Taliban connected outer demonstrations of piety with inner moral disposition. Juan Cole (2008) notes that, for the Taliban, the "public display of soberness is felt to indicate a private, inner piety, whereas public frivolity [demonstrated through laughing or kite flying] suggest iniquity in one's inner moral life" (137). In this moral formation, self-discipline and personal ethic become communally mandated.

Not unlike Mahmood's conception of piety, in which reiterative acts of inhabiting normative discourse are read as a modality of agency, Deeb's conception (2006) of piety is untethered from passivity, and modernity is untethered from the West. Public piety and authenticated Islam entwine to form the entangled pious modern, or what Deeb has called the "enchanted modern." Deeb's work underscores the importance of understanding "how Islamists and pious Muslims themselves grapple with what it means to be modern, without assuming the nature of links between modern-ness and the West" (15). An argument often advanced about Afghan women is that they are passive recipients of patriarchal discourses and, if given the freedom, would abandon all tradition.[35] Even their protests are futile in their ability to refashion their circumstances.

But a closer look shows that ordinary Afghan women do not live within the binary oppositions between tradition and modernity, Islam and secularism, through which we envision them. Neelam did not see herself as modern or secular. Her idea of promiscuity was deeply embedded in traditional notions of piety in pashtunwali and Islam. Her landay did not invoke Western ideals of progress and did not render her wretchedness intelligible through Western ideals. She is not familiar with the feminist theories of Julia Kristeva or Judith Butler, nor did she emulate Elizabeth Bennett from Jane Austen, a character popular among well-educated Afghan women. She spoke about Shirin and the rivalry between Farhad and Khusru. Similarly, other women, such as Arshia and Parwaneh, did not call on Western concepts of inheritance. Arshia had no notion of what her inheritance entitlement would be in a Western country. Rather, their idea of property ownership is embedded in hadith and a Quranic understanding of women's rights. They invoked the examples of influential women in Islamic history, such as Khadija and 'Aisha. Naghmana was grappling with how to convince her lover not to join the Taliban, but her motivation to do this cannot be explained through an understanding of the Taliban as Islamic fundamentalists. Rather, she was concerned about the disruption to her world caused by losing someone she loved. Most men who joined the Taliban, like Sadia's husband, were eventually killed or kidnapped, leaving behind the women who depended on them for love or sustenance. Becoming a Talib had significantly different meaning for the lives of these women than it would in the West. The Taliban did not evoke a sense of fear in Sadia and Naghmana, as it had in the past, but rather distress about abandonment. Katiba was raped by her father-in-law. Her landay tried to make sense of a world in which her protector became her abuser. In all these landay, women are making sense of their world through a rooted understanding of their past as exemplified in Islamic and pashtunwali precepts. Running away was not an abandonment of tradition but rather an embrace of it toward a different end. Parwaneh and Arshia, for instance, wanted to lay claims to a world in which their inheritance was given to them, a world that was possible in a nostalgic Islamic past, rather than a secular future. In all these cases, binaries of tradition and modernity, Islam and secularism, fall apart as women inhabit multiple subject positions, sometimes contradictory and sometimes complementary.

The scholarship on Islamic feminism discussed earlier has taught us that secularism cannot neatly bracket religion in the public. Juxtaposing

Neelam's and Katiba's lyrics with the words of some of the secular-minded women who ran the khana-yi aman shows the contested terrain of Islam and modernity on which these landay are narrated. On the surface, it may seem that the managers were educated and modern, whereas the women living in the khana-yi aman were uneducated and backward. Yet a closer look reveals that categories of religion or modernity cannot easily be mapped onto feminine decisions about piety or promiscuity. Pious devotion is not necessarily a measure of religious disposition; equally, displays of promiscuity are not a measure of modernity. The displays of both piety and promiscuity unfold within the tapestry of modernity. Mitchell (2000) writes eloquently about the possibility of difference and modernity: "Every performance of the modern is the producing of . . . difference, and each such difference represents the possibility of some shift, displacement, or contamination" (xiv). Mitchell's call is to disentangle modernity from its Western origins and open the possibility of alternative and different modernities, which necessitates an understanding of different forms of subjectivities not encapsulated by Western notions of freedom and autonomy. The notion of the subaltern is connected to this notion of modernity. Are Afghan women subalterns attempting to voice their subjugation through poetry? It is insufficient to say that landay give voice to the suffering of Afghan women. Gayatri Spivak (1988, 2010 [in Morris]) has demonstrated the violence and futility inherent in modern projects that seek to render vocal the subaltern. One must consider how these landay reveal the complexities of power relations that subjugate the women in the first place.

What conditions make landay necessary? The landay illuminate the emancipatory and regulatory mechanisms that undergird systems of honor and patriarchy.[36] Ostensibly the women accessed some notion of freedom at the khana-yi aman. By running away from home, a decision not supported by their communities, they demonstrate a subversive will. Yet, on arrival, they are imprisoned within the shelter's walls. It is not specific to Pashtun women to use poetry as a subversive discourse. Landay may be understood as the poetry of subversion, but without the protection accorded to other poetic forms. The particularity of landay is that, while they inhere risk and danger, they provide the women with a capacity for action or a modality of agency to effect change in their lives. When used astutely, landay have the potential to change the trajectory of women's lives. For Neelam, her landay interrupted how she inhabited her present world. In contrast to a repetition of the norms of piety in Mahmood and Deeb, which are meant to solidify the referential system, Neelam's rendition shows her engagement with the task of repetition in a way that does not consolidate the system. Yet her landay rely on the honor system to be legible to her father-in-law and husband. She is clearly not standing outside the interpretive grid that renders honor intelligible. The notion of the promiscuous self clarifies how women inhabit complementary and contradictory positions simultaneously, and how these are not reducible to a secular or Islamic formation of tradition or modernity.

CHAPTER FOUR

Taliban's Women

"Wake up, it is almost time." As I woke up and sleepily rubbed my eyes, Gulalei was standing right above my head looking down at me grimly. Gulalei and I slept in a small room upstairs, and the rest of the women slept in a large room on the first floor, which had thick blankets that covered the carpet.[1] Gulalei and I slowly made our way downstairs to the other women. Gulalei's son had woken up from the noise and followed us down the steps. "It is almost time," she repeated to the sleeping women downstairs, shaking her head disapprovingly, "All of you should be jumping up for *sahri* [the meal eaten before beginning each day of the fast of Ramazan]."

Ramazan was in the month of August this year of 2011. Every day, Gulalei would wake everyone for sahri, an hour before *namaz-e fajr* (first prayer of the day at dawn). There was nothing unusual about this day. The women assigned to prepare sahri brought in the freshly prepared dishes, and a clean sheet was placed on the floor to serve the food. We sat down and talked about the difficulty of fasting in the month of August. The hot weather and the long days were wearing everyone down. Sohaila commented that the heat probably increased the religious blessings associated with each fast, considering the increased difficulty the fasting person endures, which no one disputed. After sahri and fajr prayers, we cleaned up and went back to sleep in our designated places.

Just as I had drifted off to sleep, I awoke to the sound of a loud thud and breaking glass. I looked over to Gulalei, who motioned me to go back to sleep. "It is nothing," she said. I looked at the broken glass from one of the door panels scattered on the floor and thought, "It is not nothing." As I rose to protest, we heard several banging noises as the floors began to shake. This was followed by hurried, nervous footsteps climbing up the stairs. Two terrified young women entered the room. "Are we under attack?" one of them said fearfully. Gulalei, who seemed more annoyed by our response than by the loud noises, finally sat up and said, "I told you, it is probably nothing." For the next few hours, we could hear shooting and loud bangs, but had no explanation of what was happening. The small television offered little information.

Later in the morning, one of the guards came into the main office and described the incident. The British consulate, which was not far from our undisclosed location, had been attacked by the Taliban. The attack was ongoing, we were told. As we gathered together in the living area, everyone had something to say about it. The entire day was spent evaluating the pros and cons of a Taliban government, and whether this attack was in the interest of ordinary Afghans, particularly women. The bravery of the women in the face of a proximate attack was admirable. No one spoke of leaving the khana-yi aman. As the mystery surrounding the incident faded, so did the fear. The violence, which was ever present, receded into the distance as we returned to our daily tasks of sweeping the living area, preparing for iftar, and washing clothes. In the afternoon, the blast came up again in conversation. Many women at the khana-yi aman were current or former wives of the Taliban, and some had run away after their husbands had joined the Taliban. For others, their husbands had become ghaib (absent or missing) after joining the Taliban.

Gulalei: What has changed since the fall of the Taliban regime in 2001? How have our lives changed? To tell you the truth, nothing has changed. It has become worse.

Sadia: Nothing has changed in our daily lives. We still live in fear of our husbands every day. The Taliban have gained more power now. Look at this broken glass.

Author: This is a shocking thing to say. How could the Taliban have gained power since their government fell in 2001?

Gulalei (amidst laughter): The Taliban government fell? When?

Sadia: All our local politicians do their bidding. The best kind of power is when you are invisible.

Gulalei: We are taught to guard our virtue ['*iffat*] to get respect ['*iz-zat*]. This is ingrained in us when we are young. Whether the Taliban see us or not, we are the protectors of our own morality.

Sadia: If we are so virtuous, how have we ended up here? Is this place not for the refuse of Afghanistan? Are we not hidden behind walls so no one can see us? Is the society not ashamed of us? We are sent here because we have transgressed. What have we transgressed? Islam? pashtunwali? Some other law? Are we seen as threatening? Who are we threatening? What are we threatening?

Zainab: My husband joined the Taliban and abandoned me. There are many women who are abandoned by their husbands when they join the Taliban. The men do not even bother letting us know where they went. I waited for many weeks. I was not safe in my neighborhood. When people perceived I was alone, I was abducted by a group of men and taken to a house. The men took turns to use force [*zabardasti*] upon me. I was blindfolded the whole time. They played loud music so the neighbors could not hear my cries. I ran away from there and ended up here.

Gulalei: We all have different stories. Look at Zainab. Her husband did not become a threat to her even after joining the Taliban. Mine did. But both of us are here now. Both of us cannot go back. Both of our husbands are in the Taliban. What do you make of this?

The fall of the Taliban in 2001 was greeted with global jubilation. Worldwide anticipation surrounded the end of an era of authoritarian totalitarianism and the beginning of a notionally secular democratic state.[2] The promise of saving and protecting ordinary Afghan women was central to the justification for the war in Afghanistan and toppling the Taliban (Abu-Lughod 2013; Coburn 2016).[3] With a view to gaining an understanding of the present Taliban, this chapter focuses on the narrative microhistories of their wives and children. The stories of women are often told through the lives of men. But how do women shape their own worlds? The post-Taliban state affords new potentialities of selfhood to women, but it simultaneously limits and marginalizes them. Within this political framework, women find means to resignify and subvert the hegemonic order. This chapter is motivated by the following fundamental ethnographic questions: What has changed in the everyday lives of ordinary Afghan women since the celebrated fall of the Taliban and the installation of a secular democratic government? How have changes at the state level informed the micropractices of everyday familial life? What different modalities of gendered resistance and feminine agency operate in the negotiations between women's rights organizations and the wives and daughters of the Taliban? How do these gendered capacities for action condition notions of state and shadow state, power and marginality, governance and citizenship?

Much has been written about how the Taliban have become the most formidable force to reckon with in Afghanistan (see, e.g., Cole 2008, Crews 2015). The ethnographic vignettes from the wives and children of the Taliban at the khana-yi aman provide evidence that the Taliban remain dominant social actors who wield tremendous authority in shaping public discourse on morality. This chapter is focused primarily on the narrative life-worlds of the women within the immediate context of the Taliban. It also draws on primary Taliban publications and circulations to demonstrate its views on family, women, secularism, and Islam. The Taliban newspaper, *Shariat*, published in Pashto and Dari, became well known across Afghanistan. This and similar publications demonstrate the self-conception of the Taliban from the early 1990s until today. The *Taliban Official Gazette* is a collection of their fatawa published by their Ministry of Promotion of Virtue and Prevention of Vice (Vizarat-e amr bil ma'ruf va nahi 'anil munkar).[4] The ethnographic, literary, and archival sources demonstrate that the Taliban plays a major role in the ethical fashioning of the everyday private lives of ordinary Afghan women, especially in Pashtun-dominated provinces where the Taliban exist as a parallel government. Such influence is not limited to the provinces, because the peripheries are fundamental to the center, and Taliban influence is, likewise, evident in political and administrative networks in Kabul. This chapter argues that within the complex inner workings of the center and its peripheries, between the state and its shadow, reside new possibilities of womanhood and feminine citizenship.

The Taliban has come to be known as the most powerful authority on

Islam in Afghanistan. Does the Taliban conceive of itself as the guardian of Islam? Does its governing strategy originate in Islam, and is this the reason for its success? The Taliban conquered Kabul with a concrete political ideology supplemented by tactical maneuvers to implement their ideological vision. Portraying themselves as humble men of God was a strategic maneuver that allowed many to underestimate the political acuity of this group. Although primarily recruited as outcasts with an intense hatred for bourgeois ideals, many Taliban members were also ordinary Afghans representing conventional principles. Cole (2008, 124) has called Taliban's Islam idiosyncratic in that they sporadically used Islamic law toward the sole goal of solidifying their power. The Taliban movement may also be described as an ideological caravan whose fluidity allows widespread membership.[5] Although the Islam practiced by the Taliban is a variegated tapestry of different Islamic traditions, all those traditions conflate on issues of gender and sexuality in the service of oppressing women.

Most descriptions of the Taliban in the West describe their antisociality and nonnormativity; however, such descriptions cannot explain their immense popularity, especially in the early years. The Taliban have been characterized as rural outsiders untainted by Kabul life, who have nothing in common with the urban dwellers of the cities. To some extent this characterization is accurate and, indeed, self-consciously perpetuated by the Taliban. Nevertheless, it misses important characteristics that coalesce their governance into a dominant force rather than a radically marginal one. At its peak, the Taliban controlled two-thirds of Afghanistan. Local scholars have long underscored the popularity of the Taliban in the Pashtun regions of Afghanistan and northern Pakistan. Nazif Shahrani (2008) notes that Pashtuns are likely to support the Taliban. He calls this support a form of Talibanism. For Shahrani, such Pashtun Talibanism explains why non-Pashtun communities mounted fierce resistance against the rise of the Taliban, while Pashtun areas such as Kandahar resisted very little. In this scholarship, the Taliban's success is directly attributed to their ability to organize the Pashtuns, which has marginalized other communities such as the Hazaras, who are reluctant to support this form of Talibanism (Shahrani 2008). In this vein, Abdulkader Sinno (2008,

59) states, "If history is any guide, whoever mobilizes the Pashtuns rules Afghanistan, and Afghanistan cannot be ruled without their consent." In these analyses, which highlight the historical dominance of the Pashtuns, the role of Pashtun women is almost never addressed. Do Pashtun women support the Taliban?

Virtue and Vice

"Let's do the story of Bibi 'Aisha's lost necklace," said Gulalei after I returned with Khwaga and her infant son from family court. Khwaga's husband, Razaq, had joined the Taliban in a high-ranking position. Before her marriage, she had been in love with a cousin who, for unclear reasons, had not been able to marry her. Khwaga was married to Raza when she turned fourteen years old, and one year later had a child. Her beloved cousin died in a tragic car accident three years after her marriage, and while she had not been in communication with him, his death devastated her nonetheless. Khwaga became extremely depressed and almost immobile. When her in-laws demanded an explanation, she was not able to articulate the reason for her misery. She asked her family to take her back until she was ready to return to her husband, but they refused. With no place to go, she arrived at the shelter.

Khwaga came from an affluent, well-known family who, with her in-laws, had monthly meetings with her to convince her to go back to her husband. In the court visit on this particular day, the judge told her that she was tarnishing the good name of her relatives, and her own lawyer agreed with the judge. Khwaga answered by saying that she did not want her infant son to grow up with a Talib father. When I recounted the court visit to Gulalei, she was not surprised. She motioned us to join everyone on the floor, and as we sat in a circle, Gulalei proceeded with a familiar account, a favorite Ramazan narration. 'Aisha, Prophet Mohammad's wife, was said to have lost her necklace while traveling with him. Upon realizing that her necklace was missing, she went in search of it while the Prophet's caravan left without her. A member of the Prophet's group brought her back the next day. Given that she had spent the night alone with a man, her absence raised suspicions of adultery. Surah 24 of the Quran, an-Nur (The Light), was revealed soon after. This surah pertains to the rules regarding adultery and fornication and has been foundational to gender laws in many Muslim countries. Most women at the shelter would recite surah 24 and other Quranic verses verbatim in Arabic and thought it protected them from false accusations of adultery. The requirement of four witness testimonies for raped women is a common misreading of this surah, Gulalei told me. Ironically, the Taliban used the same verses to establish stoning and flogging for adultery. Gulalei recited the verse that mandates that a false accuser be flogged if his testimony is established as fabricated:

> And those who accuse chaste women and then do not produce four witnesses—lash them with eighty lashes and do not accept from them testimony ever after.

She continued:

> Bibi 'Aisha, the Prophet's wife, was like any of us. She was suspected of adultery with such conviction by the people in the caravan that even the Prophet became suspicious. There was gossip about her. And then Allah saved her from punishment by intervening with surah an-Nur. And Allah admonished the Prophet for becoming suspicious of his loyal wife because of idle gossip. Can you imagine? The Prophet himself was admonished by Allah for suspecting his virtuous wife.

Khwaga interjected, "But what if the accusation of adultery cannot be established to be untrue. What happens then? How should we protect ourselves when we have no evidence? And Allah will not make an intervention on our behalf." Gulalei waved her hand and continued:

> Let me finish. Let me finish. "But it will prevent punishment from her if she gives four testimonies [swearing] by Allah that indeed, he is of the liars."

The women gasped. Khwaga asked, "*He is of the liars?* Does the Quran actually hold the man responsible for misaccusations?" Gulalei nodded and said, "Not only that, but a woman can give four testimonies herself to prove her innocence. She does not need additional witnesses." During my stay at the shelter, this became a favorite activity. Gulalei would recite these verses and recount the story upon request from the women. That evening, Khwaga lamented that she would eventually have to return to her husband, and her infant son would grow up in the shadow of a Taliban fighter. "I am helpless in changing my destiny," she said mournfully. Gulalei addressed Khwaga with the words of the Quran again: "Khwaga Jan, when you complain to Allah about your hardship, He will ask: 'Was my world not big enough so you could escape your suffering?'"[6] This was a reference to one of the verses of surah an-Nisa (The Women). Gulalei interpreted this verse to mean that Islam condoned running away from difficult situations. "Why else would Allah ask us if his earth is not spacious enough for us to move away from cruelty and injustice?" But Khwaga replied by saying that she had not faced abuse, which is what this verse ostensibly was about. She had left her husband because she had been in love with someone else and because she wanted to protect her infant son. Sohaila chimed in, "This is not exactly the model of Umm-al-Muminin [Mothers of Believers]." In our next visit to family court, I met with Khwaga's husband, Nadeem. He told me that he was studying Islam and wanted to follow Quranic examples. He said:

> Prophet Ibrahim followed Allah's will. His wife did not stand in his way when he was ordered to sacrifice his son. This is the Islamic obedience to your husband. She did not question him. She did not stop him. She trusted his judgment. He was ordained by Allah to do this. Such should be the faith in your husband's decisions. Why question him when he knows what is best for you and your sons? Look at Bibi Hajra. Her husband left her in the middle of the desert with an infant son, Ishmael, who was suckling her breast. She had no water and no food. Imagine her desperation. Bibi Hajra ran between the hills of as-Safa and al-Marwa seven times in search of water for her infant son. In her seventh run, she found water. Praise be to Allah. Her obedience to her husband made her eternal. To this day, Muslims commemorate her by following her path during Hajj.[7]

The lawyer Farooqa asked Nadeem how these examples were relevant today. "These examples are relevant for today's Afghanistan. The Communists brought women in skirts into the public and dug their own graveyards. Women dancing on the street is not progress. Following the example of the prophets is progress." The conceptualization of progress as a continuation of past events is a common belief among Muslims, as exemplified in adherence to hadith and sunnah. Growing up in a Muslim family in Peshawar, I was familiar with Hajra's story. But this was the first time I heard the story interpreted as one of wifely devotion. The story is usually narrated to demonstrate the power of maternal love, Hajra's love for Ishmael. It is also a story of Hajra's strong faith in God. But Nadeem's views are corroborated by the Taliban's publications and their views on the role of women. A reading of the Pashto and Persian prose and poetry inside the Taliban newspaper *Shariat* (Islamic Law), which was in circulation during the 1990s, provides a glimpse into their philosophical and moral world.

This newspaper was one of the primary sources of communication between the Taliban and their literate public. Taliban newspapers are interspersed with references to an Islamic past, especially about the role of women in an Islamic notion of the family. In a 1995 edition of *Shariat*, the Pashto column by Abdul Hakim Mujahid, "Become Attentive to the Dangers of Secularism to Islamic Shariat," elaborates in detail the impending threat of a secular democracy, described as an ideology devoid of religion, being perpetuated by Western [Soviet] interests into all Muslim countries. It notes that secularism may seem providential with its promise of parliamentary democracy, but the end results would be comically zero.[8] Other columns map democratic secularism onto communism and differentiate Islam from both ideologies. For example, "Who Are the Taliban?" (Pashto: Taliban *sok di?*) by Abu Ihsaan, published in *Shariat* December 18, 1995, outlines the important characteristics of this group:

> Taliban are the real children of this country. Taliban are the guardians of God's commands, God's laws and rule. Taliban are soldiers fighting against cruelty, tyranny, and injustice. Taliban are the seekers of justice and equality for all humans. (3)

This column tells the story of the fight between Islam and communism fought by the mujahideen. The column conflates the Taliban with the mujahideen in their struggle against the Soviet Union, referencing the Islamic jihad by the mujahideen (1979–89), the Taliban's predecessors, against the communist ideology of the Soviet Union. Here the Taliban link Western communism to secularism and democracy, whereas in the United States, communist ideologies are viewed as anathema to Western capitalism. Reading this column in Pashto makes it obvious that the Taliban deem partaking in secularist processes as potentiating havoc in this world and the hereafter.

The writings claim that the Taliban are the guardians of Islam in Afghanistan. In fact, the Taliban often situate themselves as local communal leaders fighting against corrupting outsiders. Within this Islamic ethical formation, many columns note the centrality of the familial unit, at the center of which is mother and wife. Taliban newspapers frequently promoted such an Islamic ethos. Yama Lahma's May 28, 1997, column in *Shariat* titled "Pattern of the Family in Islam" (Naqsh khanuwada dar Islam), which I have translated from Persian, outlines the model Islamic family:

> If sincerity [*simimiat*] and love [*mahabbat*] did not exist among the family members of the Prophet of Islam, would the Prophet (S) have been able to transmit and distribute [*pakhsh v nashr*] his religion of freedom and salvation [*din-e rihayi-e bakhsh*] with comfort and ease? Indeed not. Prophet of Islam endowed Bibi Khadija (R) with sincerity and love so that she acquired self-assurance [*qaut-e qalb*], and this enabled the collaboration [*hamkari*] and cooperation [*hamyari*] between Bibi Khadija (R) and other wives of the Prophet (S). Bibi 'Aisha's (R) role in transmission and distribution of religion of Islam [*pakhsh v nashr din-e Islam*] renders this point evident to everyone that the Prophet of Islam regarded his family members with sincerity, love, awareness [*agahi*], and consciousness [*bidari*]. Thus in no book is there an account of difficulties and headaches among the Prophet's family members despite the Prophet having multiple wives. Each wife has her unique ability and faculty to aid and assist the Prophet of Islam in the propagation of religion.

It is for this reason that the Prophet said, "Half of your religion is from 'Aisha (R)." And after the departure of the Prophet, we see that for the resolution of many religious problems, Muslims take advice from 'Aisha (R). This wisdom and intellect of Bibi 'Aisha's (R) is a result of the Prophet's attention toward her.[9]

In a later paragraph, the author continues by giving a specific example about Fatima and 'Ali:

Hazrat Bibi Fatima (R) was the offspring of Hazrat Bibi Khadija (S) and the great Prophet of Islam. Born in this family, she benefited from all the material [*maddi*], meaningful [*ma'navi*], and spiritual [*ruhi*] benefits and a strong upbringing by the mutual effort of her father and mother. She was brought up with a magnificent [*'ali*] Islamic spirit, and when she reached adulthood, she became a friend and supporter of her father, the great Prophet of Islam, in a variety of life affairs. When the great Prophet of Islam betrothed his daughter, he chose 'Ali, the son of his uncle [*kaka*, or father's brother], who was also raised in his own hands. A new upright family was created.

This column gives the example of three important women in Islamic history—Khadija, 'Aisha, and Fatima—to centralize the role of wife and mother and underscore the importance of proper upbringing of children by women. Umm al-Muminin are the Mothers of Believers, the wives and daughters of the Prophet Mohammad. I was often told that Umm al-Muminin are role models for all Muslim women. As pupils in Peshawar, my schoolmates and I memorized the lives of these women and used them in everyday examples not just of piety but also of courage and strength. As noted in other chapters, Afghan intellectuals such as Khadim and Tarzi also mention these women as role models in their writings. In this sense, there is a continuity of thought, and Taliban ideology regarding motherhood is hardly marginal to Afghan or Islamic historical discourse.

In addition to didactic columns about Islamic family configurations, Taliban newspapers include literary references meaningful to a Pashto- and Persian-reading Afghan audience. In the same December 18, 1995, edition, a few months before the Taliban occupied Kabul, the works of

Saadi (1210–92) and Khushal Khan Khattak (1613–89) appeared in adjacent columns. Saadi's *Bustan* and *Gulistan* are classic works of worldly ethics that have a history of use in Persianate Islamic state building. The poem by Khattak, the revered Afghan poet, is titled "Nasihat," which is also a historic form of public advice directed toward a Muslim ruler (Messick 2018, 35–36; see also 1993). Specifically, the newspaper printed a poem emphasizing the importance of simple living and not getting caught up in the riches of life. Here, I translate a few verses from the Pashto poem, which invokes important ethical ideals of battle (*jihad*) and creation of selfhood (*nafs*).

> Life travels like the wind
> Death must always be remembered by every person;
>
> This life's foundation is on air
> Such a life cannot be trusted
>
> Prophets and Friends of God have left for their graves
> Even they did not find here a foundation
>
> Always, I say to you, develop a desire
> Always, in your life, fight a battle [*jihad*] with your self [*nafs*];
>
> Come Khushal, leave the strangers of the heart
> Fill your heart with His desire.

An excerpt from Saadi's *Bustan* is juxtaposed with Khushal Khan Khattak's poem in this edition of *Shariat*. This is a demonstration that Taliban were conversant in both Pashto and Persian, which is not surprising given that most Afghan Pashtuns today are also fluent in Persian.

> I heard about a righteous king
> In a coat with two sided lining
> One said to him—"O Auspicious King
> Obtain a cloak of Chinese silk"
>
> He replied, "This is enough for covering and comfort
> Exceeding this is embellishment and exhibition

I do not acquire taxes from my subjects
To decorate my person, throne, and crown

If I wear the shrouds of a woman
As a man could I defend against an adversary?

I too have yearnings and fancies, a hundred and more
However the treasury is not for me alone

The treasury is filled but for the army's sake
Not for ornament's and jewelry's purchase."

In this ethical conception of the world, jihad is an ethical obligation pertaining to the spiritual growth of the individual. Devji (2005) has noted how Afghan jihad became an individual ethical performance rather than a political struggle, by using the notion of selflessness (102). In the preceding poem, jihad is defined as "battle with oneself." By individualizing and domesticating jihad, Taliban newspapers centralize the family as the proper site of jihad. After the Taliban captured Kabul, the May 28, 1997, *Shariat* published the following poem, "The Taliban (Pashto: Talibano), written by Gul Agha Ahmad Wardak, a part of which I have translated:

My dear young brothers mujahid Talibano
Islam's stars, pillars, and intellectuals

You ended dark nights of cruelty by lighting lanterns of mercy
You ended storms of cruelty delivering salvation

You demolished the power that did not belong here
You wrecked their plan that was not apt here

You bloomed flowers, you brought spring
You lighted lanterns, you brought spring

Your blood sacrifices brought freedom to this homeland [*vatan*]
You sacrificed your heads and brought independence to your homeland

You are a source of pride and courage
In harsh moments of history, you are the guardians of unity

Congratulations on the freedom you brought to this land
Congratulations on the prosperity you brought to this garden [*gulshan*]

Ahmadi sends his salutations [*salam*] to these youngsters
Families who have such courage, I send my greetings.

This poem underlines the social responsibility of the Taliban toward their homeland (vatan). Taliban newspapers refer to the Taliban as children welcomed by Afghanistan because of their sacrifices to rid the country of the evil forces of secularism and communism. Here the social obligation of jihad becomes central. After the Taliban established their governance, they published the *Taliban Official Gazette*, which emphasized their role in moral policing and establishing a proper Islamic ethos through social jihad. The *Gazette* situates the Ministry of the Promotion of Virtue and Prevention of Vice as "a central department of the Emirate, which is charged with the duty of increasing virtue and preventing vice in the country, according to the jurisprudence of the resplendent Sharia and Hanafi." Articles 2 and 3 (p. 22) regarding organizing the ministry outlines the social and individual obligation related to this tenet. They state:

> [T]he Promotion of Virtue and Prevention of Vice is "fard kifaya" (a religious duty that, discharged by one, will relieve others thereof). However, if someone has the capacity to implement it, its implementation is then "fard ain" for such a person.

> If a person is appointed on behalf of the Emirate as an official of the Promotion of Virtue and Prevention of Vice, he shall be called a "Mohtaseb" and it shall be "fard ain" for him to discharge the duty.

Although Devji (2005) notes that jihad was individuated into an ethical struggle, Taliban newspapers and fatawa tell a slightly different story. Before the Taliban captured Kabul, the poetry and prose of their newspapers emphasized individual jihad, but after they conquered Kabul, the emphasis became both individual and social. In the tenet stated here, jihad is described as both a social obligation (*farz kifaya*) and an individual obligation (*farz ayn*). These individual and communal obligations for promoting virtue are linked to the Islamic concepts of *tahzib* (civilization), *akhlaq* (virtuous disposition or ethics), and *adab* (etiquette or literature). Together these undergird the moral ethos of an Islamic social formation for the Taliban.

Islamic historical tradition has a robust intellectual engagement with the conceptions of virtue and vice. Muslim ethical literature comprises various strands—for example, a religious and scriptural tradition based in the Quran, hadith, and sunnah; a literary and historical tradition consisting of fables and poems based in the genre of adab and *nasiha* (guidance) and philosophical works influenced primarily by the Greek ethical tradition. Muslim scholars such as Ibn Miskawayh (d. 1030), Ibn Rushd (d. 1198), Nasir al-Din al-Tusi (d. 1274), and Ibn Khaldun (d. 1406) developed an understanding of the Islamic moral formation embedded in a refinement of individual character (Mahmood 2005, 137). In the late nineteenth and early twentieth centuries, the akhlaq, tahzib, and adab genres were taken up by Syed Ahmad Khan, Iqbal, Khadim, and others to promote the cultivation of ethics. Contemporary Islamist governments are the most recent incarnation of this intellectual tradition.

The Taliban instituted the Ministry of Promotion of Virtue and Prevention of Vice for the purpose of enforcing proper moral conduct in public. This ministry sparked international outrage and disbelief. Cole (2008, 123) has noted that the activities of this ministry in Afghanistan were an epistemic shift from the governing techniques of other Muslim liberal and modern democratic governments.[10] However, the idea undergirding this ministry is not new. Saudi Arabia and Iran, with Sunni and Shia governments respectively, share analogous institutions called *hisba* and *mutawain* (both are forms of Islamic religious police mandating public comportment). At the center of these institutions is the regulation of public comportment of women. The Taliban, as either state or shadow state, represents continuity with other forms of modern Islamic governance in Iran, Pakistan, Saudi Arabia, and even older Afghan governments. The difference lies in the Taliban's wholesale rejection of a secular and democratic participatory system. However, the epistemic rupture comes not just in the form of the modalities of governance but also in the form of the promiscuous subjectivities at the khana-yi aman rendered possible as a reaction to the Taliban. Thus I argue that while the power formation of the Taliban is in some ways in sync with other totalitarianisms, the resistance in the form of runaway women is new.

Performativity and Precarity

Foucault describes the three major modes of power that shape modern governance: sovereignty, discipline, and biopower. These modes of power are not mutually exclusive but build on each other to form the modern subject. Sovereign power is exercised through coercive rules and punishments and is inscribed onto the bodies of individuals through public spectacles of corporal punishment. Foucault (1975) shows in *Discipline and Punish* how, through the spectacle of the scaffold, power is dispersed through the body of the condemned. The tortured body is the central locus of power through which power circulates into the social body. The Taliban regularly exercise this mode of governance to cement their sovereign power. Torture is hardly antithetical to modern governmentality, just as honor is not antithetical to modernity.[11]

The first public act of the Taliban was to hang the castrated bodies of President Najibullah and his brother in the city center. During the Taliban's rule, it was common to parade the corpses of wrongdoers and miscreants around the city. Women were to be thrashed in public for attending school, wearing white socks, laughing out loud, washing clothes outside, or using a public bathroom.[12] Men, too, would be beaten for flying kites, playing musical instruments, or shaving their beards.[13] Although prior governments had practiced stoning and flogging, the frequency of such public spectacles increased when the Taliban began their governance in 1996.[14] During my fieldwork, the Taliban ordered and carried out public stonings and floggings. For example, when a young couple, Khayam and Siddiqa, declared their illicit relationship in public in Kunduz province in 2010, two hundred locals carried out lashing and stoning at the behest of the Taliban (Nordland 2010). Family members and neighbors participated in the stoning and lashing, including Siddiqa's brother and Khayam's father and brother. Video recordings show the accused man standing stoically as he is lashed. Spectators captured the stoning on mobile videos, which show Siddiqa buried vertically in a hole with only her head above the ground. Several men surround her as she is stoned to death, after which Khayyam also dies. Such public spectacles continue. In 2015, Rokhshana, a young woman from Ghor province, was buried in a hole in the ground and stoned to death; her lover was flogged and then released (BBC 2015). The accounts say that during the stoning, she was proclaiming her Islamic faith through a recitation of holy verses in an attempt to demonstrate her piety.

Two important issues are worth considering in Rokhshana's stoning. The first is the voluntary participation of the audience, demonstrating the influence of the Taliban. People of religious significance such as members of the Ulema Council tend to agree with the Taliban both out of fear of violent reprisal and because no one wants to give the impression of taking a lenient position on issues of illicit sexual relations. The moral authority of the Taliban is evident from the statement given by Malwi Abdul Yaqub, head of the Ulema Council in Kunduz province, who agreed that stoning was the appropriate punishment for sexual relations outside marriage (BBC 2015). The stonings are not new or surprising and only contribute to the Taliban's complex power network, which brings almost all Afghan Islamic scholars within its fold, at least on issues of sexual promiscuity. For example, in August 2010, the Ulema Council in Afghanistan brought together 350 religious leaders to demand an increase in corporal punishments like stonings and floggings for illicit sexual relations (Nordland 2010). The runaway women are aware that their lives could end similarly.

Another aspect worth noting is Rokhshana's failed attempt to perform a pious self by reciting Quranic verses as she was stoned to death. Why would Rokhshana ground her plea in Islam at the very moment she is being stoned to death because of an ostensible transgression of Islam's precepts? Was recitation of these verses giving her solace, comfort, and the courage to face imminent death? Even women activists do not dispute the appropriateness of stoning as penance for illicit sexual activity and, instead, focus on how to avoid stoning by demonstrating chastity through proper sexual comportment. In Gulalei's statements discussed earlier, she does not disagree with the punishment of stoning as proper retribution for illicit sexual relations. Rather, her perspective is to use the same Quranic verses to thwart the possibility of stoning by becoming a four-time witness for one's own chastity. At the heart of all these discussions is the chastity of women, as defined within a historical and discursive system.

When such video recordings emerge, about which I spoke at length with my Afghan friends, they cause concern among feminists. From my own knowledge of Islam's strict rules regarding murder, I know that killing someone is worse than adultery. So why then does not a single member of the crowd try to mitigate the violence? Why the willful participation? I asked a friend, Ameena, if she thought the Islamic precept of "promotion of virtue and prevention of vice" discussed earlier obligated the audience to participate in the killing or to stop it. Does this precept make stoning a communal obligation that must be performed by all those in attendance? Ameena explained that such killings make society more peaceful by lessening the frequency of violence. I asked her how they reduce violence when the killing itself is a violent act. She replied, "The issue is not the frequency of violence but the frequency of transgressions. If the transgressions lessen, so would the corresponding violence." Although this logic sounds circular, this depiction is not uncommon. Transgression in this case is sexual infringement on one's own chastity, which calls for communal retribution. If sexual transgression is understood as an Islam-sanctioned precursor to violence, then it follows that the precursor must be stopped. In this sense, participation in these killings is rendered intelligible by the participants. Legitimate sexual acts—primarily defined through Quranic verses, hadith sources, and exegetical precedence—occur between specific sanctioned actors and are promoted as conducive to individual and communal well-being. Illegitimate sexual acts are referenced by the identity of the sexual actors involved in the sexual event. Thus, deviant bodies are labeled as such not because of what they *do* to their own bodies but what they are willing to engage in *with* others, rendering deviance an essentially social act, which then stipulates social and communal responses.

The Taliban reading of Islamic theology consecrates sexual propriety as the critical referent for a moral ethos. By making public the punishment associated with adultery, the Taliban render promiscuity (i.e., any unsanctioned sex act) a crime against the social formation. Whereas previous regulatory apparatuses sought to localize and contain adultery, the Taliban optimized the circulation of signs of promiscuity. The body of the whore is constructed as pathologically promiscuous and potentially dangerous and, thus, conceived as the object par excellence for torture attended by moral outrage and public condemnation. Moral outrage overshadows the absence of accountability for murdering promiscuous bodies and obstructs and distracts from the importance of proving culpability and due process. Thus such communal moral outrage leads to the absence of the need for accountability and demonstrates the meaning of "moral panic."

Taliban law becomes more intelligible when Afghanistan is understood as a postcolonial state with a history of imperial encounters. In postcolonial states, arbitrary violence finds its origination in colonial rule (Mbembe 2001; Mamdani 1996, 2004). Cole (2003) has argued that the Taliban present a model of governance considerably different from liberal modernity. I agree that the Taliban are an epistemic rupture from the past, but not for the reasons outlined by Cole. A more apt description of the nature of their power comes from Achille Mbembe, who proposes the concept of *necropower* to "account for the various ways in which, in our contemporary world, weapons are deployed in the interest of maximum destruction of persons and the creation of *death-worlds*, new and unique forms of social existence in which vast populations are subjected to conditions of life conferring upon them the status of *living dead*" (Mbembe 2003, 40). The concept of necropolitics builds on the Foucauldian model of biopolitics and introduces the critical role of imperialism into the workings of modern societies. Biopower is not mutually exclusive with discipline and sovereignty but embeds and orients the older forms of governance in sophisticated ways. Mbembe presents necropower as an alternative to biopower, a different form of power that operates in colonized spaces (Mbembe 2003). In Afghanistan, necropower pivots on disciplinary mechanisms and employs specific techniques for surveillance, management, and the production of life, particularly honorable life, and, by extension, the production of dishonorable modes of being. Chandra Mohanty (2003) elaborates the discursive dimension of colonialism as it relates to the production of knowledge around feminist interests in colonized spaces: "Women are not only mobilized in the 'service' of the nation, but they also become the ground on which discourses of morality and nationalism are written" (133).[15] Violence is thus intimately tied to the production of gendered subjectivities in colonial spaces.

Judith Butler's theoretical intervention in feminist analytical frameworks has taught us that gender is always already performative. Gender is "real" only to the extent that it is performed through repetitive bodily actions (Butler 1990).[16] She invests the system of normative repetition itself with the possibility of difference. Each reiterative repetition allows for a disruptive crisis because it may exceed the normative structure that undergirds that repetition. In her recent work, Butler develops the concept of precarity as a critique of US imperialism. This concept can be usefully applied to Taliban rule. Precarity, more than performativity, is a useful lens for understanding sexual promiscuity as resistance to the Taliban because precarity encompasses lives that are not legible in public. Butler observes that "[performativity was] an account of agency, and precarity seems to focus on conditions that threaten life in ways that appear to be outside of one's control" (2009, i). Precarity is underpinned by gender because "people who do not live their genders in intelligible ways are at heightened risk for harassment and violence" (ii). Precarity is predicated on how gender is performed in public and private, and takes into account "differential allocation of recognizability" (iii). In other words, there is a hierarchy in the recognition of suffering. It is in this sense that the runaway women at the shelters live precarious lives.

Butler's theoretical framework is illuminating for the study of gender in Afghanistan. However, in her principled effort to critique US imperialism, she writes that "destruction of the burka, as if it were a sign of repression, backwardness or . . . a resistance to cultural modernity itself, would result in a serious decimation of Islamic culture and the extension of U.S. assumptions about how sexuality and agency ought to be organized and represented" (2004, 142). Butler is arguing against claims of the oppressive nature of Islam substantiated by the circulation of images of Afghan women in formless blue burqas.[17] However, by linking "Islamic culture" to the burqa, she also creates a monolithic Islamic culture rooted in a certain permutation of pious performance (the burqa). Many women in urban Afghanistan, not to mention across the Islamic world, do not don the familiar blue burqa. The burqa is popular among certain working-class Pashtun women in rural and urban areas. It gives them access to the public while maintaining anonymity. Thus the burqa is as linked to urban modernity as it is to Islam. In Afghanistan, veiling has been practiced in multifold ways that differ greatly according to class, geography (urban, rural), and social status. The blue burqa is commonly used in my birthplace of Peshawar where, prior to Taliban rule, women wore it in a variety of ways, some behind their backs, some folded up the front. Others held it in their hands without wearing it, and some wore it in full. There was no hard-and-fast rule. Before the Taliban came to power in 1996, I never saw any woman penalized for not wearing the burqa properly. Women controlled how and when to wear it. A monolithic Islam indexed by the burqa is linked more with the region's encounter with colonialism, whereby decades of Western intervention in the form of funneling capital to fundamentalist elements created homogenous religious subjectivities that now seem almost "natural" to Afghanistan. Yet the women at the khana-yi aman demonstrate that there is no "natural" way of being an Afghan woman. These women did not deliberately intend to destabilize the normative structure that undergirds the stigma attached to sexual promiscuity, although they certainly had knowledge that their actions would be perceived as promiscuous and thus would make trouble. The issue that we often pondered was how to inhabit the wretchedness of one's social position, which was taken as given. How do we live our precarity? And why was our way of life deemed promiscuous?

Both Butler and Mahmood are writing within societal formations and societies that have clear political structures. In Mahmood's work, the mosque women are resisting a secular-liberal social formation in Egypt. In Butler's work, the power formations against which resistance is differentiated are Western liberal democracies. But what are the women at the khana-yi aman resisting? At the very least, they are resisting the wretchedness of their past, present, and future. Moreover, liberalism and secularism cannot be mapped onto each other as Mahmood has done for Egypt. In Afghanistan, although the Taliban situated themselves against secularism, which they linked to Soviet communism, liberalism (as exemplified in the logic of market capitalism) was not antithetical to their interests. Thus the power networks in Afghanistan are far more complex, given the nontangibility of the Taliban (they are difficult to locate and negotiate with) despite their permeation across all institutional frameworks. How do we institute female citizenship in a shadow state?

Governing in the Shadows

In his key essay "Politics as Vocation," Max Weber ([1918] 1946) defines the state in terms of its use of physical force: "[A] state is a human community that (successfully) claims the monopoly of the legitimate use of physical force within a given territory." He notes the "territory" as a defining characteristic of the state and that "the right to use physical force is ascribed to other institutions or to individuals only to the extent to which the state permits it." Although this is considered a classical definition of the modern state, not all state forms are captured within this definition. For example, William Reno (1995) developed the concept of the shadow state for the study of political structures in Sierra Leone. The shadow state exists in parallel to the political institutions and is capable of utilizing physical force not sanctioned by the official state. In addition to using physical force, the shadow state participates in the political economy by rendering services and distributing resources. My ethnographic data corroborate that the Taliban is a shadow state. In a June 2018 report titled *Life under the Taliban Shadow Government*, published by the Overseas Development Institute, Ashley Jackson states:

> The reach of Taliban governance demonstrates that they do not have to formally occupy territory to control what happens within it. Governance does not come after the capture of territory, but precedes it. The Taliban's influence on services and everyday life extends far beyond areas they can be said to control or contest. That the Taliban set the rules in vast swathes of the country is a reality with which few in the international community are willing to engage. (Jackson 2018, 5)

Jackson's report shows the astute political strategy of the Taliban, which combines coercive power with sporadic violence: "There is no need to capture a city if atmospheric coercion, punctuated by occasional violence, is enough to ensure the population submits to Taliban authority" (2018, 25). The sporadic instances of public stonings serve the purpose of "occasional violence" to solidify the Taliban's influence. Service delivery; taxation; and the appointment of sympathetic public officials, from judges to bureaucrats, completes the system of shadow governance.

The Taliban indeed acts as a powerful shadow state with "a sophisticated system of parallel governance across Afghanistan" (Jackson 2018, 6). The group is viewed as the most influential moral actor in Afghanistan. Jackson's report also notes that even though the Ministry for Promotion of Virtue and Prevention of Vice has officially been dismantled, a well-instituted social organization in the form of school officials, mullahs, and local Taliban enforce the same rules (20). Because the ethical and pedagogical architecture promoted by the Taliban is deeply imbricated within the social ethos, the Taliban continue to exercise influence on issues of morality in everyday life. In this sense, they act as the guardians of Islam and, through that legitimacy, co-opt other services and resources of the state. In fact, Taliban rhetoric is far more sophisticated today than it was when the Taliban took over Kabul in 1996. For example, Taliban advocate for girls' education and embrace technology. On issues of sexual transgression, however, their stance remains unchanged.

The Taliban ruled Afghanistan from 1996 to 2001. Since the American intervention in 2001, they retreated to the margins, but their political significance in Kabul has not diminished. Their influence emanates not only from fear of militia violence but also because they exert moral authority over all matters pertaining to Islam. From the time of their establishment, the origin myth of the Taliban positions them as arbiters of sexual and social justice embedded in fundamentalist Islam. The mythical story of their origin, little known in the West, is often recited at the khana-yi aman and other places in Afghanistan. The origin story states that in 1994, Mullah Omar sent armed scholars to rescue two young women abducted by warlords in Kandahar. The alleged abductors were hanged in public.[18] Since their inception, the Taliban frequently fashioned themselves as pioneers of social justice, rooting out the economic and political corruption that had taken hold in Afghanistan. As noted earlier, when the Taliban took over Kabul on September 27, 1997, they castrated and then hanged the corpse of former president Najibullah in public as retribution for his corruption.[19] The public spectacles of corporal punishment were meant to consolidate Taliban power and inscribe fear onto the bodies of Afghans. But Taliban rule was substantiated by more than terror. Despite their lack of Islamic knowledge, they are to this day influential authorities on Islam, and in particular on issues of gender and sexual propriety (Ahsan 2018).[20] By extension, the Taliban are a major influence in how sexual impropriety or promiscuity is conceived in the public domain. Women who run away threaten the influence of the Taliban and consolidation of Taliban power.[21] The runaways show schisms in the Taliban's efforts to consolidate power. They articulate their resistance within new and different interpretations of the Quranic verses used against them. The knowledge and context of these verses are pivotal in mounting a resistance to Taliban ideology.

Taliban recruits are mostly Pashtun men whose social status is a complex interplay of their roles as Pashtun men and as supporters of militant Islam. Although it may seem that the Taliban focused on a particular political aspect such as religion, honor, pashtunwali, or gender to govern, the prowess of the Taliban resides in an impressive ability to co-opt religious charisma and ethnic status in the service of social domination. Because Islam is a binding force that unites Afghans across ethnic, communal, and class divides, every political program must appeal to Islam to be successful.[22] At the beginning of their rule, the Taliban did not have the intellectual or scholarly training comparable to the Iranian Shia ayatollahs or Sunni mullahs. Yet, to this day, long after the fall of the Taliban government, every Islamic law related to gender requires an approving nod from the Taliban. And since 2001, they have become more sophisticated in their understanding of Islam and how to temper their rhetoric for public consumption. Local Afghan governments are in constant negotiations with the Taliban, and women's rights groups are often sidelined.[23] As one prominent feminist activist said to me, "We are always worried about the deals happening between the government and the Taliban arbitrated by international actors like the United States. These deals overshadow our work and render us invisible." When women's rights activists *are* afforded a seat at the table, they are cognizant of how far they can stretch their demands regarding Islam, because it is considered Taliban domain. As Cole notes, "Mullah Omar and the Taliban claimed legitimacy as the

guarantors of sharia, and said that it was their duty to conform the bodies of Afghans to its strictures" (2008, 129). To this end, Mullah Omar
claimed himself to be Amir al-Muminin (Commander of the Faithful),
inscribing himself with the powers of the historical caliph Omar.[24] A caliph or khalifa is God's representative on earth invested with the authority
to speak on his behalf. Even today, the Taliban supreme leader is called
Amir.[25] It is almost impossible for Afghan feminists to compete with such
self-serving claims to divine legitimacy.

Mahmood notes that the Western focus on emancipatory politics in
Afghanistan ignores the connection between extremist elements and US
intervention (Hirschkind and Mahmood 2002, 341). Americans directly
funded the Taliban's predecessors, the mujahideen, in their war against
the Soviet army. In the struggle between capitalism and communism, all
sides conveniently abandoned women's rights. Academic debates in the
West are based on the false assumption that the United States "liberated"
Afghan women from a form of extremist Islam, or that this liberation was
at least the US intention. Even well-intentioned rigorous academic debate
about how US intervention configured both the secular and the religious
domains of Afghanistan to open space for autonomy and freedom obscures what actually transpired in the lives of women inside Afghanistan.
To present the Taliban as a resistance to liberal modernity is to erase the
historical roots of this movement. As noted earlier, economic liberalism,
exemplified in the logic of market capitalism, is not antithetical to fundamentalist Islamism, as the cases of United Arab Emirates, Pakistan,
and Saudi Arabia demonstrate. In fact, Pakistan and UAE were the only
ones to recognize the Taliban government (BBC 2020).[26] In Gulf states,
the capitalist citizen must also be a Muslim.[27] Thus capitalism, liberalism,
and Islamic governance grow in tandem with one another.

Although Mahmood's work has been pivotal in explaining piety movements that situate themselves against Western ideologies, her conflation
of secularism with liberalism is problematic.[28] Capitalism and liberalism
are not the same as secularism. During the decades of Soviet occupation
and the creation of the mujahideen—who, like the Taliban, were predominantly Pashtun—the tribal code of pashtunwali, especially those precepts
that intersected with Islam, was excessively deployed by the Americans in

the fight against the Soviet occupation.[29] The Taliban situate themselves against secularism, which they link with Soviet communism.

Given that the Taliban are predominantly Pashtun, many have grown up with more pashtunwali than with any official Islamic, Hanafi, or Wahhabi education. Hanafi is the predominant school of Islamic thought in Afghanistan, upon which the Afghan constitution is based.[30] The Taliban put forth a political ideology in which a good Pashtun became synonymous with a good Afghan, which became synonymous with a good Muslim, all of which became synonymous with heroic fighters against the Soviets.[31] Very much as in India and other colonial spaces, subject categories were created by imperialists and became linked to indigenous group identities such as Pashtuns, Hazaras, and Tajiks, which were then mapped onto religious affiliations: Muslim, non-Muslim, good Muslim, bad Muslim.[32] These distinctions were then reified through Afghanistan's multiple colonial encounters. I argue that the techniques of violence and instruments of brutality were embodied by the Pashtuns and then later perpetuated against their own and other societies inside Afghanistan, as Fanon (1963, [1952] 1967) has demonstrated for Algeria.

In the Cold War era from 1979 to 1989, fundamentalist Islamist elements were funded by the United States, Pakistan, and Saudi Arabia to fight against the Soviet Union. In his book *Islam in Liberalism*, Joseph Massad (2015) demonstrates that Islam is central to the liberal discourse on Western feminism, and indeed creates Western liberalism's very condition of possibility. Every ideology needs a binary opposite to coalesce and permeate successfully in the social sphere. Massad notes that Islam as a religion has been central to Western ideologies of liberalism and secularism as their polar opposite. Islam is often conceived as a homogenous all-encompassing category. In this sense, Western secularism and liberalism need Islam in order to define themselves. The other side of this coin in Afghanistan is that the Taliban and other fundamentalist ideologies often situate themselves in opposition to Western liberalism and secularism. The very condition that made the Taliban and its predecessors, the mujahideen, possible was the struggle between communism and capitalism as represented by the war between the Soviet Union and the United States fought on Afghan soil.

Taliban publications explicitly position the Taliban in a fight against communism, which is linked to secularism. More recently, in 2019, US president Donald Trump announced a plan for a peace deal with the Taliban, which raised concerns among prominent Afghan activists. Sima Samar, well-known activist for women's rights, a medical doctor by training, and chairperson of the human rights commission, said in an April 2019 interview with the *New Yorker*,

> I am very much concerned, because, of course, they keep saying that women will be included, but, in all the negotiations going on these days, in the talks between different groups, including the special envoy of the U.S., there are no women. The day before yesterday, there was a meeting that included Gulbuddin Hekmatyar. A year ago, or a year and a half ago, he was fighting against the people of Afghanistan and fighting against the U.S. He was in the meeting, and women were not. (Chotiner 2019)

How do we locate the citizenship of women in the context of Taliban governance? To start, it is necessary to disentangle the various strands of imperialism, particularly how imperialist rhetoric functions for its Western audience versus how colonial violence is perpetrated inside colonized spaces. These are vastly different imperatives that must not be conflated.

In the West, de-veiling Afghan woman may have been a pleasurable pastime, but such measures inside Afghanistan resulted in massively disagreeable consequences.[33] During my fieldwork, I often observed tense exchanges between women's rights activists and foreign diplomats. Against the backdrop of constant bargaining between the Taliban and the US government, the story that Americans were "liberating" or "saving" Afghan women seemed almost ludicrous inside Afghanistan. The khana-yi aman was often under direct threat from the Taliban, not least because it houses women who have run away from their families. Funding for the khana-yi aman was extremely limited, as it was the first bargaining chip used to appease fundamentalist Islamist elements. There was a constant fear of imminent shutdown. The Taliban exert public influence not through expertise in statecraft but through clever maneuvers that create a shadow system of governance, with which women's rights activists must grapple. As Samar's comments demonstrate, the Taliban is almost always guaranteed a seat at every negotiation table. Nagamine (2015) describes in detail the complex three-stage process of social infiltration by the Taliban. The first stage consists of building support in villages through incentives and intimidation. In the second stage, elaborate institutional legal and military frameworks are built to shadow the state. Permanent courts and taxation are set up in the third stage. In this way, the Taliban permeate all institutions of power; therefore, any feminist movement inside Afghanistan must reach an agreement with the Taliban to effect any measurable change.

Taliban rule is not without paradox. Some women deem themselves safer under Taliban rule. Draconian punishments for sexual crimes resulted in reduced numbers of rapes and other forms of sexual violence.[34] At the same time, girls were banned from attending school, and mandatory head-to-toe veiling was established across the country. Although most Afghan women already dressed modestly and many donned the full burqa, veiling now became the official business of the state. And although rape was severely punished, the Taliban also used it as an instrument of power, claiming divine piety nonetheless. Scholars of Islam have disputed the legitimacy of Taliban claims to divine authority and Islamic piety. For example, Cole (2008) has argued that public spectacles of grotesque punishment were staged by the Taliban to create a modern public that he shows is a form of "counter-modernity" (118).[35] Cole argues that public spectacle is related more to power than to piety. I argue that piety is sutured into the seams of the Taliban power dynamic. Indeed, the anchor of Taliban power is the rigidly defined and violently controlled sexual piety of women. Afghan feminists, well aware of the power of the Taliban, contend with these issues in their daily negotiations by asking, How do we form the female citizen in a cryptocolonial state within which a powerful shadow permeates all institutional frameworks?[36] To this day, the future of feminist movements remains uncertain, with no clear answers.

Wanton Subjectivities

Modern governments in Muslim-majority countries are increasingly declaring themselves Islamic.[37] The Islamist political agenda includes economic and social reforms and an adoption of Islamic ways of life. Although broad variation exists in what constitutes "Islamic," there is a definite trend toward some form of pious sociality and increasing Islamization of the public sphere and popular political movements, as evidenced through the works on Islamic feminism across various Muslim societies (see Ahmed 2012; Deeb 2006; Mahmood 2005; Scott 2010). This means that while there is impetus for revolutionary movements to create historical and epistemic ruptures, their agenda is not without nostalgia for the past.[38] Despite this forward-looking nostalgia, almost all Islamic governments and populist Islamic movements, such as Hamas, Hizbollah, and Tablighi Jama'at, declare some allegiance to the principles of secular and modern democracy. By "forward-looking nostalgia," I refer to the desire for progress from within the historical constraints of Islam as demonstrated through the deeds of the Prophet. The Taliban represent a unique form of Islamist government because secular democracy is not part of their political agenda.[39] In this sense, the Taliban represent an epistemic rupture from a past that conditioned the possibility for radically new gendered subjectivities and feminism in Afghanistan. The Taliban imposed a clear vision of a totalitarian government that did not allow for the possibility of democratic participation and articulated women's citizenship through historical models of piety, motherhood, and wifely devotion. However, these notions of women's citizenship are neither marginal nor unfamiliar to Afghan Muslims. In this sense, while the Taliban ideology represents a political and epistemic rupture, generally their policies toward Afghan women do not. As noted in the conversation at the beginning of this chapter, the Taliban continue to be a force to reckon with in Afghanistan. It is my contention that alternative life trajectories demonstrated through the stories of women who run away provide a glimpse into a politics of difference. While the runaway women do not represent mainstream feminism, they do shine a light on the struggles of women who want to live a life of independence and piety.

This chapter began with the question, What has changed in the lives of ordinary women after the fall of the Taliban? As far as moral policing and disciplining of female bodies is concerned, perhaps not much at all. The comments by Zainab, Gulalei, and others at the shelter indicate that their lived experiences continue to be conditioned by structures of patriarchy. Androcentric production of knowledge existed before the Taliban and continues after. The cunning of the Taliban lies in its reorganizing of the body of knowledge toward a mass audience and, in doing so, creating a new and modern public.[40] To perpetuate their rule, the Taliban created a fantastical homogenous category of women, especially Pashtun women. Their fatawa and publications assumed the existence of a coherent group of obedient women who abide by their rules, which created a binary between the Taliban and women, who had to be understood in oppositional terms. By defining women's public comportment through very narrow interpretations of Islam, the Taliban robbed women of their complex histories and plural subjectivities. Ironically, it is within this old-fashioned, totalitarian public shaped by the Taliban that new radical subjectivities of women are rendered possible. In the wise words of Thomas Barfield (2010), the Afghan past informs but does not limit the possibilities of the present. To put it directly, it is my contention and my hope that the stronger the oppression, the greater the possibility of resistance. The women at the khana-yi aman live that resistance daily through subtle and surprising social maneuvers.

Thus far, the largest women's rights organizations have attempted to use appeals to Islam to negotiate with the Taliban. In formalized negotiations between the Taliban and women's rights activists, the rules of decorum limit the scripts available to women. But ordinary women like Hangama, Gulalei, Sadia, and Neelam show tremendous dexterity in challenging the Taliban, who are often their next of kin. Can we ask of the ordinary Pashtun women the question that Simone de Beauvoir asked of French women: Why do women not dispute the sovereignty of men? In the introduction to de Beauvoir's *Second Sex* ([1949] 2011), Judith Thurman states that the woman "is determined and differentiated in relation to man, while he is not in relation to her; she is the inessential in front of the essential. He is the Subject; he is the Absolute. She is the Other" (6). Thurman states, "Humanity is male, and man defines woman, not in herself, but in relation to himself; she is not considered an autonomous being" (5). The khana-yi aman demonstrates that Pashtun women do contest their situation in the world, even as they inadvertently become implicated in networks of power beyond their control. While not completely autonomous in relation to the male domains of power, they use social maneuvers to navigate their lives toward a world they want to inhabit: a world not limited by the Taliban creed.

CHAPTER FIVE

Pedagogies of Womanhood

When Sadaf from Jalalabad decided to become the second wife of Habib, a man from her neighborhood, her parents were concerned.[1] They wanted her to marry someone else, so she ran away with the help of Habib and his first wife, Suha. Suha would often accompany Habib to the family court to support her husband in his second marriage. Suha and Sadaf were friends. When I came to court with Sadaf, Suha would often be there with home-baked bread. On one of the court dates, the following exchange took place between Suha, Sadaf, Habib, the judge, and the khana-yi aman lawyer Farooqa. The judge asked how Sadaf could forget her parents for a man she had just met. As Sadaf began to answer, Suha interrupted:

> Suha: Esteemed judge. My father arranged my marriage with Habib. It was fifteen years ago. We met for the first time on our wedding night. This is common, very common. All my sisters and friends were married this way. Even though I had never met him, nor did I know him, I fell in love with Habib. We have four children. He is very kind and sensitive. I am very happy with him. Last year, he came to me, he said: "Suha, I love this woman. If you love me, you will love her too?" He asked it as a question. I said, "I love you Habib, and I love her too." Dear judge, love comes in all forms and shapes. I love Habib. I love my children. And I love Sadaf too.
>
> Habib: Sadaf was my neighbor. I did not intend to fall in love with her. This happened to me. I did not make it happen. She would often walk up to the balcony, and I would see her putting up washed clothes on the clothing line. Slowly she began noticing me. We started meeting in secret. I knew she had dignity [*sharafat*], honor [*namus*],

and was from an honorable family. Suha knew from the beginning. When Sadaf's family found out, they were livid. I am a Pashtun man. I will take care of my Pashtun woman. Now she is my honor.

Sadaf: I proposed to Habib just like Hazrat Khadija did to Hazrat Muhammad. Do you know the story of the great male and female companions [loey as-sahabah]? Hazrat Khadija was older than Hazrat Muhammad. Twenty years older. People said it would not work. But history speaks for itself. When I told my family, they said that they had arranged a marriage for me. I decided to run away. They had someone in mind. They asked me how I could be so stupid to marry an already married man. "Is this how we raised you?" my mother asked. "You will become someone's second wife? Is this your value in your own eyes?" I tried to explain to them. Islam permits four wives, so why should I not become a second wife? Who are my parents to tell me I cannot? I can and I will. I am a modern Pashtun woman who knows and embraces Islam. Do you think my parents own me? This is my homeland [vatan] too. I can live here as I wish, with whom I wish. We are all Muslims here.

After we left the judge's chambers, we sat outside in the court garden. I asked Suha and Sadaf how they envisioned their future lives. They replied, "akhpal kor ke, vatan ke khushal." (We will be happy in our home and our homeland.)

Sadaf's and Suha's positions are predicated on modern and secular notions of willful independence and freedom, which nonetheless pivot on Islamic and Pashtun conceptions of family, honor, gender, and sexuality. This chapter explores this cultural paradox to historicize modern Afghan womanhood. It argues that the modern Afghan woman of the twentieth and twenty-first centuries is crafted through both disciplinary and emancipatory mechanisms that gendered the Afghan homeland as a beloved mother.[2] The emancipatory reforms pertaining to gender in the twentieth century regulated heteronormative and hierarchical roles for women in public. Thus, while public accessibility for women increased, a concomitant obligation of chastity and virtue was placed on them. A consequence was that women became central to the cultural work of producing the modern homeland (vatan), which, in turn, reified their position as mothers, wives, and daughters of this new nation (millat). The foremost of these mechanisms were (1) pedagogical Islamic texts; (2) transnational ethical and political pan-Islamism of the subcontinent, in which Muhammad Iqbal (1877–1938) was a key figure; and (3) literacy and secularism campaigns that gendered the conceptions of vatan (homeland) and millat (nation).

This chapter shows how Afghan women—with surprising maneuverability—understand, live, and become subject to a historical system of gender differentiation. The cultural work of the new nationalism in the twentieth century produced and reified categories related to gender and sexuality. In Pashto, the notion of woman is synonymous with that of wife. Both are called *khaza* in Pashto. In Persian, *zan* means both woman and wife. The words *khaza* and *zan* represent the double bind of womanhood. When this ambiguous conception was deployed in the service of modern state-building, a new womanhood that had both emancipatory and disciplinary characteristics was imagined. The nationalistic discourse in the writings of Qiamuddin Khadim, Mahmud Tarzi, and Muhammad Iqbal depended on heteronormative gender differentiation with well-defined roles for the mothers and wives of the nation. Promising women emancipation through work and education in the new secular nation was intrinsically linked to maintaining the regulatory Islamic order of gender and sexuality, which centered on chastity and female piety.[3]

The homeland, *vatan mor* (mother nation), was to be protected by men, husbands, and sons. The men who could not protect their homeland because of traits such as cowardliness and pusillanimity were called "womanly men" (Khadim 1937b). Motherhood was mapped onto nationhood, and an honorable woman was a virtuous mother who was self-sacrificing, pious, affectionate, and benevolent (Khadim 1938). The way for women to acquire honor in pashtunwali was through the traits of *surritowb* and *nurrtowb* (both meaning "manliness," or a gentility typically ascribed to men) and through motherhood and wifehood. Pashtunwali society authorizes the relationship between vatan (homeland) as female, which forms the basis of the sexual contract, and millat (nation) as male, which forms the basis of the social contract. Relegating the possibility of

homosexuality outside Pashtunwali created a heteronormative conception of the world. Khadim (1937b) notes in the chapter "Paki v 'Iffat"
(Cleanliness and Virtue) in his book *Pashtunwali* that "Pashtuns [specifi-
cally Kochis] are unaware of the possibility that men can have sex with
men. This [apparent] unfamiliarity defines their courageous masculinity.
This virtue gives them a strong physique and good health" (112). In this
chapter (which I translated from Pashto), honor of the nation is linked
to the sexual honor of women defined through heteronormative chastity
and maternal piety.

Where did Khadim's disavowal of homosexuality originate? His conception of a modern Pashtun nation hinged on pashtunwali traits that
promulgated a compulsory heteronormative masculinity. The disavowal
of homosexuality is linked to such a heteronormative notion of the Islamic
family in its Pashtun incarnation. Afsaneh Najmabadi (2005) has shown
that in Iran the heterosexualization of love with the arrival of modernity
in the last two centuries reimagined the marital contract as romantic
rather than procreative. She links this heterosexualization of the marital
contract to a heterosociality of the public that, in turn, necessitated the
unveiling of the Muslim woman to render her modern and available to
the modern Muslim man. Prior to the encounter with modernity, gender
and sexuality were more fluid and did not preclude the possibility of homoeroticism and homosexuality "behind the veil." However, the encounter with modernity under the Western gaze promulgated a heterosocial
Iranian public in which Muslim women were unveiled and ushered into
the public realm. Najmabadi observes, "For Iranian modernists, viewing European women as educated and cultured, the veil became a sign of
backwardness. Its removal, in their view, was essential to the advance-
ment of Iran and its dissociation from Arab-Islamic culture" (133). By
connecting the veil to backwardness (in the European view), the Muslim
woman was liberated from Islam and brought into the service of the state
to work in modern institutions. Concomitant to this, however, was the
ever-present threat of the unveiled woman as seductress, condemned by
Islamists and secularists alike. The unveiled Muslim woman brought with
her into the public the possibility of trouble or chaos (*fitna*) and was thus
condemned as "superwesternized" (154).

Thomas Wide (2012) notes that with the rise of Pashto written literature in Afghanistan at this particular historical moment in the early twentieth century, the governing apparatus was able to use it "to formulate a burgeoning Pashto ethno-nationalism and to reinforce normative ideals of independence and resistance to outside powers" (94).[4] Another normative ideal formulated and reified through Pashto consolidation is heterosexuality, which had different significance before the hegemonic perpetuation of Pashto. Although female chastity was important before this moment, the heteronormative ideal of marriage that protected such chastity and that was based on a modern notion of romantic love was promulgated through a modern Pashtun ethic of sexual propriety. The heteronormative concepts of motherhood, femininity, masculinity, love, and courage are repeatedly expressed in Khadim's book *Pashtunwali*, in opposition to a Persianate ethic of sexuality. Khadim was preoccupied with the production of the perfect Pashtun woman, reconfigured as a mother and a lover who produces courageous Pashtun men unafraid to die in battle. A pious Pashtun mother is a woman who is unafraid to bury her sons. Khadim writes at length, in the poem shown in his first chapter, about the moral imperative of women to send their lovers and sons into battle. In a similar vein, the renowned Pashto poet Khushal Khattak (2016) writes famously:

Ma sultanat ghwara ma daulat ghwara
Banhai te waya 'ismat 'iffat ghwara

Do not yearn for empire, nor for wealth
O woman yearn for chastity and virtue[5]

The Persian words for chastity and virtue, *'ismat* and *'iffat*, used by the eminent intellectual and politician Mahmud Tarzi, are used here in Pashto. Tarzi's daughter, Queen Soraya, and her husband, King Amanullah, provided a model for Afghans, in which heteronormative romantic love became central to the marital union. Their appearances in public as a modern monogamous couple popularized a modern notion of marriage in which romance triumphed over other reasons for marriage, such as procreation. Amanullah departed from his predecessor's example of having multiple wives by marrying only Soraya. Furthermore, he departed from the normal tradition of sequestering wives by bringing his wife into the public realm. Soraya was audible and visible in the public domain, and openly advocated for women's education and gender egalitarianism.

Vatan Mor, Vatan Kor: Motherland and Homeland

Contrary to popular expectations, the production and dissemination of Islamic socioethical literature across the Muslim world have remained steady or have increased with modern secular projects (Ahmadi 2008; Eickelman and Anderson 1999; Messick 1993; Schulze 1998; Starrett 1998; Doumato and Starrett 2007). Mahmood (2005) has shown that Egyptian secularism was accompanied by a widespread interest in Islamic knowledge and pious conduct in the twentieth century.[6] Within this modern framework, the Afghan woman, fashioned through the literacy and secularism campaigns during the reign of Queen Soraya was paradoxically adept in arguments of Islamic jurisprudence. An appeal to Islam was fundamental to this new secular feminism. Queen Soraya wrote about educating women according to the model of the early years of Islam (Burki, 2013, 104). The modernization projects of the twentieth century led to an increase in female literacy and access to the public, while simultaneously propagating the ideal of the pious and chaste Afghan woman.

Soraya Tarzi, born in Syria, was the only wife of King Amanullah and daughter of a pioneering figure of Afghan literary modernity, Mahmud Tarzi. She was a significant influence in the gender reformations of King Amanullah's reign.[7] Through her literary programs, Queen Soraya made women's rights and feminism a popular project. Her social reforms were directed at the ordinary Afghan woman rather than at scholars and *ulama* (religious scholars).[8] The production, presentation, and dissemination of lucid and accessible feminist materials from literary outlets such as *Irshad al-Nisvan* (Guide for Women) began in 1921. Queen Soraya's mother, Asma Rasmiyah Tarzi, edited this state-run magazine, whose goal was to promote awareness of women's rights and provide guidance on domestic matters, such as cooking and housekeeping (Burki 2013, 103; see also Skaine 2002; Emadi 2002). Queen Soraya's project lasted only a decade, but the resonance of such Islamic-secular programs that train women to become proper housekeepers persists within the social formation to this day.

As school-age students in Peshawar from fairly secular families, my sisters, friends, and I were enrolled in the *mujahida* academy when we turned fifteen years old. *Mujahid* means one who does jihad, and mujahida is its female permutation. At the mujahida academy we learned how to cook, bake, sew, and "make a home" for our future husbands. Suha, Habib's wife, had spent time in Peshawar and had also been a student at the mujahida academy. We became friends. In one of my visits to Suha and Habib's home in Jalalabad, I asked Suha whether she felt that it would be difficult to share Habib's attention with Sadaf. Suha laughed and motioned for me to follow her upstairs. She had refurbished and decorated the second floor of her house in anticipation of Sadaf's arrival: "I am looking forward to have her join me." I asked her whether she anticipated challenges in the form of jealous feelings or the monetary strain of distributing Habib's income over two families. She answered by narrating the example of the wives of the Prophet: "'Aisha was much younger than Sawda, but Sawda was benevolent in accepting 'Aisha. If Sawda had created a problem for 'Aisha, we would not have our hadith tradition. 'Aisha was a scholar who collected thousands of hadith. Sawda was not a scholar, but she supported 'Aisha. 'Aisha was young. Sawda was old. They all had a place in the Prophet's heart." She continued, "Habib is not a Prophet. But we all learn from the Prophet's example."

Pedagogical materials related to pious and virtuous conduct are widely circulated across Afghanistan. These literary materials are readily available in the form of pamphlets, books, newspapers, and other publications. Knowledge of literary texts permeates far beyond its literate audience through oral narratives commonly recited among women in social gatherings. In school, in mandatory Islamic education, all girls are taught the example of Umm al-Muminin (Mothers of Believers), the wives and daughters of the Prophet. Suha's understanding is not surprising, for Afghans take great pride in the Prophet's pedagogy. Although pashtunwali is not particularly an Islamic discourse, it was used in state-building processes for ethical and moral purposes, especially to construct the notion of pious womanhood. Pashtunwali, both the written text and oral discourse, refers to itself as Islamic and Pashtuns as Muslims. Although most have not read Khadim's *Pashtunwali*, references to oral customs of pashtunwali abound among Pashtun women. Growing up in Peshawar, I was well aware of many pashtunwali precepts without any knowledge of the written text. During my research for this book, I found the text of Khadim's *Pashtunwali* and was not surprised at its content, especially the references to female chastity, which had been taught to me through oral transmission. In fact I was familiar with almost all of the written text. This is the case for most Afghan women, especially those at the khana-yi aman. Pashtunwali, in its oral and literary form, is a primary source of morality. However, there are many other books, novels, and oral and written narratives that complement pashtunwali texts. Khadim wrote the text in the twentieth century, but the values and practices were entrenched prior to and beyond his written text. Many, like myself, had knowledge of the traits outlined by Khadim without having read the text.

For example, in his book published by Pashto Tolana (the Pashto Literary Society), *Nawai Rana: Ijtimai Afkar* (New Light: Social Thinkers), Khadim (1937a) wrote a chapter on vatan mor (mother homeland) in which he explicitly compared the homeland to a mother. Vatan (homeland), he says, has a nurturing relationship to its people, just as a mother (mor) has with her children. He compares a homeland (vatan) to a home (kor), and mothers build a home. Khadim asks, "Why do we call homeland a mother?" He answers by describing the *shafqat* (affection), *mehrabani* (benevolence), *qurbani* (sacrifice), *zehmat* (effort), and *fadakari* (dedication) of the mother. He goes on to say that the mother is a more apt comparison for homeland than the father (*plar*) because the upbringing (*tarbiat*) and birth (*paidayish*) of children is the domain of motherhood.[9] He says, "Homeland is a mother and even more than a mother." He ends the chapter with a verse from the Quran, which he writes in Arabic and then translates as, "From the earth we created you, and into the earth shall we return you. And from the earth we shall bring you out once again."[10] As in his book *Pashtunwali*, here, too, Khadim makes an appeal to Islam to ground his gendered nationalism. Vatan takes on a definite female religious connotation. Khadim also elaborates on the role of the mother in the nation in *Da Mor Mina* (Mother's Love), which maps patriotic love onto the love of the mother. The nation's sons would protect their homeland's honor, just as sons would protect their mother's honor. It is remarkable that this relationship can then become so distorted that sons may beat or even kill their mothers.

As noted in Chapter Four, motherhood as performed through proper upbringing of children, encapsulated in the popular notions of parvarish and tarbiat, which both generally mean "bringing up," was central to an ethical social formation. Taliban newspapers are interspersed with references to vatan in which the woman/mother has a central role. These references, like Khadim's texts, use the example of the Prophet's wives, who lived without discord to support their husband and were foundational to an Islamic social formation. Habib and Khwaga's husband, Nadeem, spoke about their fear of Westernization, which for them was the threat of Soviet secularism. The decade of the Afghan Civil War with the Soviet Union (1979–89) brought women out in the streets. Women could wear skirts and work outside their homes. The Taliban movement was, in part, a reaction to these measures and an effort to reestablish the Pashtun and Islamic foundations of Afghanistan. As noted earlier, the concept of vatan and its relation to honor (namus) has a well-documented history in Perso-Islamic texts (Najmabadi 2005; Kashani-Sabet 2011). In poetic literature, vatan refers to a territorial conception of a home or birthplace (Najmabadi 2005, 98). Mahmud Tarzi published his views on Islamic social ethos in a series of articles from 1911 to 1919 in his column "Akhlaqiat" (ethics) in the newspaper *Siraj al-Akhbar*: "Din" (Religion), "Vatan" (Homeland), "Daulat" (State), and "Millat" (Nation).[11] In a remarkably similar typology to Khadim's Pashto notion of vatan mor, Tarzi depicted vatan as a fruit-bearing tree, a vessel, or a mother of which the nation was offspring. These conceptions of nation and homeland were intimately tied to an Islamic conception of an *ummah* or *millat-i-Islamia* (a pan-Islamic nation), in which chastity and honor had fundamental religious value. Tarzi often highlighted the role of women in the modern nation through a litany of vocabulary on honor. He wrote, "Siraj al-Akhbar is a Muslim newspaper . . . and solely Afghan. The songs it sings and the music it plays amplify the attitude of the Afghan and the dignity [*moqamat-i-'olwiyat*] and honor [*sharafat*] of the Afghan nation."[12]

In his book *Modern Persian Literature in Afghanistan*, Ahmadi (2008) demonstrates that the encounter with modernity resulted in a mapping of the cultural and literary aesthetic subject onto the ethicopolitical subject through a deliberate project led by the cultural theories of Tarzi and other modernist thinkers (37). The ethical self in Afghanistan became synonymous with the political self through modern literacy and culture campaigns. In this era, the pursuit of literature and literary etiquette (*adab*) and ethics (*akhlaqiat*) was undertaken as a project of the modern state (*daulat*). Although the modernization process preceded King Amanullah, having begun during the reigns of his grandfather, Amir 'Abdur Rahman, and his father, Amir Habibullah (r. 1901–19), it was only during Amanullah's reign that gender reforms became an official state political project. The new literary nationalism of the twentieth century, in its simultaneous appeal to Islam and secularism, was intrinsically linked to the question of feminism. Tarzi tirelessly promoted his version of gender equality in which both men and women contributed to the nation. His views on women were progressive for his time and, like his Egyptian, Iranian, and Turkish contemporaries—Lufti el-Sayid (1872–1963), Qasim Amin (1865–1908), Reza Shah Pehlavi (r. 1925–41), and Mustafa Kemal Atatürk (1881–1938)—he, too, was motivated by his vision of women's rights and feminism (Nawid 1999). In 1924, Amanullah introduced Nizamnamah-e Arusi (Laws Regarding Marriage); his wife, Soraya, and her sister Siraj ul-Bannat, daughters of Tarzi, wielded tremendous influence in shaping gender relations at this time. Secular and coeducational schools were opened, and hospitals for women were constructed. Some of these reforms were met with public disbelief and even outrage. In 1928, Amanullah held a *loya jirga* (grand assembly of tribal elders) in which he asked Queen Soraya and a hundred other women, mostly wives of public officials, to take off their veils (Burki 2013, 104). Despite these seemingly outrageous measures, this feminism was based on the notion of a moral and ethical woman who understood her foundational responsibilities of constructing a successful "home" and "homeland."

Cultivating a National Honorable Ethic in Pedagogical Texts

Najmabadi (2005) explores the Iranian history of gender and sexuality to demonstrate how concepts related to nationalism and patriotism became gendered in the first half of the twentieth century. She states:

> Until the first decade of the twentieth century, when women began to claim their place as sisters-in-the-nation, nation was largely conceived and visualized as a brotherhood, and homeland as female, a beloved, and a mother. Closely linked to the maleness of nation and the femaleness of homeland was the concept of *namus* (honor). *Namus*, transported from its religious affiliation (*namus-i Islam*), was reclaimed as a national concern (*namus-i Iran*), like *millat*, which also changed from a religious to a national community. Its meaning embraces the idea of a woman's purity (*'ismat*) and the integrity of the nation, *namus* was constituted as subject to male possession and protection in both domains; gender honor and national honor intimately informed each other. (Najmabadi 2005, 1–2)

An analogous history unfolded in Afghanistan. In the second decade of the twentieth century, Tarzi published a poem (which I have translated and included here) on 'ismat and namus in a special edition on women in the newspaper *Siraj al-Akhbar*. This special edition was to provide models of famous women from around the world for Afghan women to emulate. The edition was called *Namvaran Zanan-e Jahan* (Famous Women of the World), in which he emphasized the need for modernization that nevertheless centered around the purity of the Afghan woman.[13] The text began with an explanation of the importance of women in the world. The introductory editorial emphasized the role of women in giving birth, thus situating them as important contributors to society. The newspaper then listed a wide range of women from across the world and throughout history, from Asiya bint Muzahim to Xanthippe, wife of Socrates. (Xanthippe, known for her bad temper and harshness, is destined to lament her behavior after the death of Socrates.) Each woman's name was followed by a short introductory paragraph, which emphasized their physical beauty, agreeability, and, in some cases, intelligence.

Almost all the women derived their significance through a male patron, father, husband, or brother.

The stories of the women were written in accessible Persian and are reminiscent of Khadim's Pashto chapters on the Prophet's wives. These writings were directed toward ordinary people and their everyday lives. While advocating for female access to the public domain, Tarzi simultaneously promulgated a certain vision of a pious, compliant, and chaste woman. The modern Afghan woman was always a virtuous woman, and a virtuous woman was one who protected her namus in public. The following is my translation of Tarzi's poem, with special attention to the vocabulary related to honor and chastity.

> A woman who has honor [*namus*] and esteem ['*arz*]
> Acquires the respect of all those who come close to her
>
> Esteem and honor are the spirit of the family
> Life, wealth, fame become honor and esteem
>
> Esteem pertains to the man, and woman is its protector
> Life of a man is from honor and esteem
>
> Virtue ['*iffat*], and chastity ['*ismat*], modesty [*haya*], shyness [*nang*], and faith [*din*]
> Are the jewels of every woman's honor and esteem
>
> Beauty and wealth, lineage and a hundred skills
> Are nothing without honor and esteem
>
> Such a woman is not from this mankind, is an angel and light
> Who has honor and esteem
>
> The value of such a woman [to Mahmud] is more than the world
> Who has honor and esteem.

In the sophisticated political discourse surrounding honor, such as in Tarzi's poem, the focus is on living an honorable and ethical life. Subjects of honor are motivated by social rewards for living felicitous and honorable lives. Women are incentivized to embrace their pious and virtuous roles, protecting their namus (honor) in public, and men are encouraged to become the protectors of the female namus. Women are pious mothers and wives of the nation, and men are their sons and husbands. The notion of homeland itself is gendered to mean mother or female beloved, which is to be protected by its (male) offspring.

Khadim's book on pashtunwali shifts from describing living an honorable life to a discussion of deaths related to honor, or honor killings.[14] Honorable conduct in most societies has historically been enforced in the public realm by the threat of death for deviant behavior. For instance, a wife's adultery is conceived as a threat to a man's masculinity, and in many literary and cultural depictions leads to death of the woman or the couple. Pashtunwali has its own specific interpretation of this honor logic. In his book *Pashtunwali,* in "Chapter on Women" (Da Khazo Pa bab), Khadim (1937b) states that women are to be divided into three categories: *mirokha* (married), *kondah* (widow), and *pighla* (unmarried or maiden). Honor rules vary based on the marital status of a woman. For instance, for an already married woman who becomes implicated in an illicit sexual affair, Khadim elaborates:

Mirokha: If someone kidnaps a married woman and is not killed, he must pay a debt of one blood and equal to that amount to buy his own life. If a woman becomes ill-reputed [*badnam*] with a man and they are caught at the time of crime, then according to Pashtun laws, they are killed and no debt is owed. In the case that they run away, then there are two options:

1.If they leave evidence—for example, a turban, shawl, or other thing behind—then in that case regardless of how they are caught, they are to be publicly killed.

2.If there is no evidence left behind, then no one has the right to publicly kill them. Yes. This is the case when there is no evidence left behind.

And the same rules apply to those friends and relatives [*khpal v khpalowan*] who give sanctuary [*panah*] to the fugitive. Pashtun laws allow for their killing because in this case Pashtuns consider people who give shelter to criminals as criminals. (190–191)

Here the killing is given as a prescriptive corrective for adulterous behavior. By "prescriptive," I mean that the killing is mandated rather than being given as descriptive narration of what may occur among Pashtuns. This reads as a simple quid pro quo: a sexually promiscuous action leads to a deadly response. Khadim, like Tarzi, is writing as an emissary of the state; however, his work demonstrates a regulatory imperative. Here, failure to comply with the proper rules of sexual comportment will lead to death. Tarzi's poem demonstrates the emancipatory imperative of the state, which has an interest in promoting ethics related to sexuality for maintaining both public order and its sphere of influence.

In these works, women are encouraged to behave properly for the good of the community. While the texts differ in their methods—one is emancipatory and the other regulatory—both discipline the chastity of women in the public sphere. Sadaf's decision to run away demonstrates individual will, which, embedded in emancipatory ideals of freedom, brought her to the shelter and thus relegated her to the ambiguous domain of the promiscuous woman. Still, the reason for her running away—to become a second wife to Habib—is a decision entrenched in Islamic conceptions of chastity and piety. Although Sadaf and Suha had not read Tarzi or Khadim, their actions are nonetheless oriented by notions of piety that originate in the intellectual traditions of pious womanhood.

In another passage in the chapter "Cleanliness and Chastity," Khadim (1937b) states: "Pashtuns regard the honor [*namus*] of their women so much that they kill their women even on the basis of a minor suspicion. Nor will they spare the man involved in this suspicion. If the man escapes, he cannot live in the same place any more or walk around openly, no matter whether he is a powerful or a common Pashtun. These issues are not subject to reconciliation. This is called *ghayrat* [honor or righteousness] or women's honor" (113). In the same chapter, Khadim narrates the story of the king of Kandahar, Amir Sher Ali Khan, and his brother Muhammad Ameen Khan.[15] In a battle, the king's son and brother were killed. The courtiers find a beautiful and reputable young Pashtun woman to entertain and distract the king from his sorrow. When the king approaches her the first night, she weeps and tells him that her parents have betrothed her to a man who is lost in Hindustan. The king then calls her his daughter and sends her back with her parents. Khadim ends the chapter by telling readers, "This is how much the Pashtuns regard honesty [*diyanat*], piety [*taqva*], virtue ['*iffat*], and pashtunwali" (117). Here, the young woman is let go by the king because she has already been betrothed to another man. The text entrenches the notion of sexual propriety of women as manifest through their fidelity to a husband. Would the king have let her go if she had not been named to a man? This question is neither asked nor answered by Khadim. But it is clear that sleeping with another man's bethrothed would disrupt the proper honor relations between men, who must abide by the rules of respecting each other's women (114–117).

Khadim was a prolific writer who wrote abundantly in Pashto, often highlighting the role of Islam and pashtunwali in the construction of an ethical social formation. He was an important public intellectual who pioneered the literary reorientation from Persian to Pashto through his role in the Pashto Tolana, formerly known as Anjuman-e Adabi Kabul (Kabul Literary Society). In his book *Loey as-Sahabah* (The Great Companions), Khadim (1936) narrates the lives of twenty-five important companions of the Prophet Mohammad. Three chapters of this book are devoted to two wives of Muhammad, Khadija and 'Aisha, and daughter Fatima. These three women derive their significance in Islamic history through their relational status and intimacy with the Prophet Muhammad. Khadim emphasizes their supportive roles as wives and daughter. In the chapter on 'Aisha (the third and youngest wife), he writes in detail how she conducted the affairs of the household with resilience and patience (*sabr*). The three women are noted for their exemplary ethics and morality. The idea of patience and fortitude often arose among the shelter women. Despite their obvious defiance through the act of running away, they nonetheless had reverence for or at least aspired to emulate these notable women in Islamic history. Many were named after the Umm al-Muminin (Mothers of Believers) and took great pride in their heritage.

The cultivation of an Islamic ethic pertaining to gender and sexuality dominated the twentieth-century Muslim world especially with the rise of nationalist movements. *Bihishti Zewar*, translated as the Ornaments of Heaven, is a series of texts that outline the Islamic ways of gendered life that should condition the moral ethos of women.[16] These texts remain popular across Muslim societies. *Bishishti Zewar* was written by Maulana Ashraf 'Ali Thanawi (1864–1943), a Deobandi reformist who was interested in writing an instructive text for the ethical Muslim woman. The Tablighi Jama'at was a later derivative of the Deobandi movement, in which the Taliban were indoctrinated.[17] In these ethicodidactic scripts, women must struggle through physical pain and emotional conflict to weave together families and homes. A woman is responsible for her husband's well-being, including his sexual fulfillment, emotional stability, and economic prosperity. These texts articulate that female sexual ethics are responsible for elevating the moral character of the family and rendering it worthy of entering heaven. The way this rhetorical stance is expressed in the micropolitics of everyday life at the khana-yi aman is symbolized in the adage the women used to describe their own place in their community: statements such as, "Behind the success of every man is a woman" abound with local variations in Afghanistan and circulate as "The bride brings the economic prosperity of her husband with her fate." Such statements place the burden of prosperity for entire families onto the shoulders of women. In this view, it must surely be the bride's ill-fated destiny or lack of morality that results in the financial and emotional woes of the husband. Upon marriage, a man's economic success is deemed a testament to a woman's kismet (destiny).

Bihishti Zewar, more than other texts, is embedded in the sharia norms and teachings, which place female sexual chastity at the center (Metcalf 1990, 6–7). It includes women in its audience and, ostensibly, integrates women into the fold of respectable morality by situating them as agentive subjects in charge of their destiny.[18] However, it does not challenge or question the gender differential between men and women, which is assumed as given. The text is divided into ten books and first presents the fundamental issues that undergird the relationship between the believer and creator, called *'ibadat*. Then it discusses the relations between humans, *mu'amlat* (Metcalf 1990, 31), including the concept of akhlaq (ethics), which, in Islam, is part of mu'amlat.[19] Akhlaq and mu'amlat condition the social relations between believers to form the core of Islamic ethical formations. Although Thanawi posits the sharia as having emancipatory potential for women, the texts are replete with disciplinary and regulatory material. The chastity of women is central to the proper functioning of mu'amlat.

For Thanawi, social customs had become an alternate path to sharia and had to be disassembled from a pure form of Islam to preserve the order and harmony of the Muslim world. That is, Islam had to be purified of customs. It is worthwhile noting that the Taliban movement, influenced by the Deobandi school, calls for a purist form of Islam devoid of custom. Nevertheless, the Taliban prioritized pashtunwali in many instances, which is customary law related to honor.[20] While many of their draconian laws targeting women had dubious connections to Islam, their interpretations were heavily influenced by local custom. For instance, the practice of exchanging women for debt (baad and badal) is blatantly un-Islamic and yet practiced in Taliban strongholds.

Thanawi explicates an extensive vocabulary of words related to honor in book six, where he takes up the issue of the remarriage of widows: "The only effort that will be effective is to rid your heart of undue concerns with honor [*nang v namus*]" (Metcalf 1990, 83, 144–45). He also lists *sharafat* and *'izzat*, correlated terms for honor, as obstacles to Islamic conduct. Proper Islamic comportment necessitates remarriage to widows in emulation of the Prophet and his companions. Thanawi declares:

> Will you call these women [remarried widows] evil? Repent, repent! Has your respectability [*sharafat*] risen above theirs [the Prophet's companions], so that your honor ['*izzat*] is spoiled by doing what they did and what God and the Messenger ordered? Will this cast a slur upon your honor [*abru*]? Will your nose be cut off? Just say outright that in your opinion it is dishonorable to be a Muslim. (144)

This passage emphasizes the sunnah of the Prophet to encourage widows to become integrated into society through remarriage. Although this passage concerns the rights of the widows, its audience is clearly men who are being encouraged to reintegrate widows into society by marrying them. Here Thanawi sets up a dichotomy between honor and Islam, between being honorable and being Muslim. Thanawi notes that marrying a widow is seen as dishonorable in many societies, including Muslim ones, but it is clearly authorized within Islamic practice and accords with the example of the Prophet. Here, Islam is imbued with emancipatory potential to subvert the confines of honor, which prohibit widows from remarrying.[21] However, Thanawi does not reject the categories of honor (namus, nang, 'izzat, sharafat, abru). Rather, he Islamicizes these categories in his attempt to purify them of un-Islamic concerns. Here, Islamic remarriage is set up as a desirable and necessary social outcome for widows, making it the condition for their reintegration into Islamic society. There is no possibility of living without a male patron. Thus, regardless of ideological priority, whether pashtunwali or sharia, custom or Islam, honor or religion, women bear the social burden of conformity and morality, and the entrenched gender hierarchies remain neither dismantled nor questioned.

Islamic knowledge, produced through didactic moral texts such as *Bihishti Zewar*, condition the sexual vocabularies that organize gender relations and render intelligible the related conceptions of promiscuity and piety. The didactic texts are reproduced as a function of power and are inextricably, even if indirectly, linked to the state. They organize the grid of intelligibility through which sexual relations are understood in Afghanistan and across the Muslim world, and are a modality of discipline and regulation (see Mani 1998).[22] These pedagogical texts originate from divine moral codes embodied in Islamic exegetical literature such as the Quran and sunnah. Even though there is no central authority for the dissemination and production of these texts, there are consistent themes across this scholarship, such as sexual chastity and modest comportment in public. The ascetic practices outlined have both individuating and socializing components, and, in some cases, there are clear penalties for transgression. The emphasis is on an individual, ethical self-fashioning, whereby failure in proper comportment leads to social consequences. Similar to other piety movements across the Muslim world and Europe—for example, in France, Morocco, Egypt, Turkey, Iran, and Pakistan—here, too, is a pedagogical concern with bodily comportment, sartorial conduct, and so on (Ahmed 2012; Göle 1997; Mahmood 2005; Scott 2010). The authors of these texts center and place the onus on the female body for realizing a corporal form of morality. The female body is the locus that connects inner states (desires and thoughts) to outward conduct (gestures, speech) (Mahmood 2005, 31).

In the sociocultural world of the early twentieth century in Islamic South Asia, notwithstanding the emphasis on egalitarianism and emancipation through state-sanctioned discourse, gender hierarchies embedded within a particular permutation of a heterosexual family became normative. Texts like *Bihishti Zewar* reinforce gender distinctions and hierarchies by bringing women into the fold of honorable social etiquette. In a significant departure from other religious texts, *Bihishti Zewar* addresses women directly and calls them to action to protect their own chastity ('izzat, abru). One story, narrated in book eight, is about the wife of the apostle Ibrahim, Hazrat Sara, who becomes the object of lust by a tyrannical king, but manages to ward off his lascivious sexual advances through prayer. The following describes the moral of the story:

> Moral: O women, look at the blessed power of chastity and see how Almighty God guards a chaste person. Also remember that the canonical prayer averts trouble and lets our supplications be heard. When you are worried, apply yourself to prayers (*namaz*) of supererogation and make continuous supplications (*du'a*). (Metcalf 1990, 259)

In another story, the wife of a bad-tempered husband bears his abuse through patience. That a wife could slowly modify her husband's behavior through sabr (patience) remains a popular narrative across Afghanistan. *Bihishti Zewar* concludes the story with the following moral for Muslim women to emulate:

> Moral: What a patient wife she was to continue to serve her husband under circumstances such as these! The story of the oath taken when he was ill shows that he had become very bad-tempered. She bore that also. The blessed power of such patience and service was that our Lord and Master saved her from the beating, tempering the judgment on her because she was so dear. . . . O women, obey your

husbands and patiently endure their bad temper. You then will be as dear as Rahmat was. (Metcalf 1990, 263)

These texts demonstrate a certain ethos that imposes Islamic morality and piety on women. How are these didactic texts linked to everyday morality? Suha had received part of her schooling in Peshawar and had been gifted a copy of *Bihishti Zewar* on her wedding, which is unsurprising. Our house in Peshawar had all volumes of *Bihishti Zewar*. We had not been forced to read these, but stories about pious womanhood originating from these texts, such as the story of Rahmat, circulated among women. Promiscuity, as seen through this pedagogical lens, is outside the purview of ethical conduct. One reason the women at the khana-yi aman were called promiscuous, which has the connotation of being immoral, was that they chose not to live with abusive husbands. In a sort of double bind and following the precepts of Islam, women who chose to be second wives also ended up at the shelter. In all cases, the issue is one of women exercising individual will, whether such will is grounded in Islam or in some other notion of freedom. An exercise of autonomy that defied their families brought them to the shelter and rendered them marginal. By running away and becoming marginal to their families, they had also been labeled promiscuous, which cast a shadow of dishonor on their families and, thus, activated the regulatory apparatuses of honor.

Thanawi was writing these texts to purify a Muslim ethos from customary influences, the foremost of which for him was Hinduism, which ostensibly did not allow remarriage of widows.[23] Regardless of Thanawi's intentions, the stories from these texts influenced the decisions of women like Sadaf and Suha in becoming peaceful co-wives to a Muslim man. In one of our court visits, I had the opportunity to speak to Habib and ask how he explained his decision to enter into a second marriage:

I am a Muslim and consider my duty to marry more than one woman if I am physically, mentally, and economically able to do so. The chaos [*fitna*] in society comes not from men marrying multiple women but from women not finding husbands. This is a known fact. This is why there is prevalent promiscuity in the West. Men are not allowed to take more wives and be responsible for them, so they have a good time with women and leave them. Is this what you call morality [*akhlaq*]? What is wrong with taking on the responsibility of Sadaf? Islam does not require me to ask Suha, but I did. Islam allows me four wives. Progress [*taraqqi*] is following the example of the Prophet and his companions [*loey as-sahabah*]. Progress is not dancing in the streets or wearing skirts.

Habib's conception of progress is remarkably similar to Nadeem's, described in Chapter Four, who narrated his decision not to divorce his wife, Khwaga, in similar words. Social progress was often linked to past events, especially the life of the Prophet and his companions. This nostalgic world was almost always depicted in opposition to a Western, secular conception of progress, represented by both capitalist and communist societies. In these accounts, promiscuity is linked to social chaos originating from an abandonment of Islam, with oblique references to secularism and communism. There is also a call to notions of Islamic piety espoused in the deeds and examples of the Prophet and his companions, all of whom had multiple wives. Could this cultural construct of promiscuity exist without the historical conception of the pious and virtuous self embedded within and emergent from an Islamic past? In other words, to understand how promiscuity is conceptualized in this ethical world, one must understand the literary and cultural mechanisms through which the virtuous self is enacted as an evocation of the Islamic past. Honor is well anchored in the images of the threat of promiscuity, and preserving the chastity of women is central to the business of the social.

Written in the thirteenth century, *Akhlaq-e Nasiri* is an influential text of Islamic ethics read by twentieth-century Muslim reformers such as Thanawi, Iqbal, Khadim, and Tarzi. The author, Nasir al-Din al-Tusi (1201–74), wrote this book in response to the text *Tahzib al-Akhlaq v Tathir al-'Araq* (The Refinement of Character and Cleansing of Ethics), written by Ibn Miskawayh (932–1030). Tusi's book is divided into sections on ethics, economy, and politics. He also discusses sexual comportment, chastity, women, and marriage, as in this passage:

The best of wives is the wife adorned with intelligence, piety, continence, shrewdness, modesty, tenderness, a loving disposition, control of her tongue, obedience to her husband, self-devotion in his service and a preference for his pleasure, gravity, and respect of her own family. (Wickens 1964, 161)

Tusi further elaborates the virtues of a suitable wife: "A virgin is preferable to one who is not, for she will be more likely to accept discipline, and to assimilate herself to the husband in disposition and custom, and to follow and obey him" (Wickens 1964, 162). Syed Ahmed Khan (1817–98), Muhammad Iqbal, and other intellectuals of the subcontinent revisited this concept of akhlaq in their twentieth-century efforts to cultivate a pan-Islamic social ethos. Akhlaq, or cultivation of ethics, was central to Iqbal's vision of a separate Islamic homeland, a notion further taken up in the Taliban newspaper *Shariat* under the Islamic rubric of *nasihat* or *nasiha* (guidance).

Another important text worth mentioning with regard to ethics and morals is *Sirāj al-Tawārīkh* (Torch of Histories). The series of texts, written and compiled by Fayz Muhammad Katib (1862–1931), published between 1913 and 1919 in Kabul during the reign of Habibullah (r. 1901–19), mentions adultery, sodomy, homosexuality, and homoerotic infatuation as indecent acts that, in some cases, result in a killing. For example, in volume three of *Sirāj al-Tawārīkh*, several instances are mentioned in which indecent and promiscuous sexual actions result in state-sanctioned consequences. Adultery is often mentioned together with the crime of murder, both of which result in capital punishment. In short, adultery leads to death (McChesney and Khorammi 2012, 3:743–45, 767).

> Rule 31: For anyone who entices or forces by threats the wife or daughter of another man to run away with him and is arrested through the efforts of the governor and the subjects, the governor must arrest that crafter of evil and send him to the capital . . . [where] he may be appropriately punished in accordance with divine ordinances and royal justice (*siyāsat-i pādshāhii*) as a warning to others (3:743).

> Rule 38: [L]et it be recorded that should a man with a wife and a woman with a husband within the jurisdiction of any governor com-

mit adultery or commit intentional homicide and that is proven before a qazi [officiator or Islamic cleric] and the qazi issues an order of
capital punishment, it is incumbent upon the governor to send a full
account of the case along with the shackled defendant to the capital
so that after verification, (the culprit) can receive his (or her) just
deserts. (3:745)

Rule 39: When such persons arrive in the capital and are stoned to
death, it is forbidden to collect fines from their heirs and survivors.
The stoning and execution is sufficient. (3:745)[24]

In a later section of the same volume, Katib writes about how the *hadd*
punishments from the Quran were historically implemented. Hadd is a
concept originating from the Quran and translates as "the limit." This
concept defines the most serious crimes in Islamic jurisprudence, which
divides crimes into those against Allah and those against humans. Hadd
crimes are within the purview of the former and necessitate public penalties such as amputation and death by stoning or flogging. Illicit sexual
relations are hadd crimes, offences against Allah and thus punishable
by death. Katib elaborates, "If, for example someone should murder another or commit adultery then he would be subject by the Shari ah law
to retaliation and (in the latter case) by "God's limit" (ḥadd) to be killed
as is required (the Qur'anic punishment)." (McChesney and Khorammi,
2012, 3:1012).

The first volume of *Sirāj al-Tawārīkh* narrates the events of 1840–41,
during which some immoral women publicly exhibited their disgraceful
actions through licentious bodily comportment, marking themselves as
whores. The text says, "Some immoral women had found their way to
the English camp [d]isplaying all the signs of being adulterous women"
(1:263). The well-wishers of the shah wrote to the Englishmen warning
them of social chaos if these women's actions were not curtailed.

These indecent women have adorned themselves and are going to the
English camp. It's unknown whether they are from noble families or
are simply whores (*fusaq*). Although the perpetrators are impudent
and godless, still, they give the regime a bad name and in the end

such unworthy goings-on will provoke people of honor and pride into a great uproar. (1:263)

Katib notes that the English ignored these pleas from well-wishers and used the women to intimidate the locals: "Dangerously flirting with the fire of sedition they even said, 'Your women do not belong to you'" (1:263). The stories of immoral and promiscuous women were foundational to historical writing about the threat of chaos and sedition in public. The inauguration of the social domain itself is embedded within the conception of promiscuity and female chastity, demonstrated by public comportment. Failure to present sexually righteous comportment—rendering the woman a temptress—threatens the righteous social contract between honorable men.[25] There is a clear connection between immorality and female sexual desire for someone other than the husband. There is also the presumption of godlessness, for God-fearing women surely would not behave in this way. Katib's question of whether the women are from noble families or "simply whores" outlines how promiscuity is rendered intelligible. Would they not be simply whores if they were from noble families? This question is not resolved by Katib, who moves on to the settlement of political affairs between men. In another section, the tale of a brave woman is narrated with attention to her purity and maternal prowess: "A woman braver than many men / Purer than a river-washed gem." Given her purity and courage, "It is fitting that this noble woman was the mother of brave warriors and bore men of honor and integrity" (McChesney and Khorammi 2012, 1:78).

In this socioethical world, women are either respectable mothers or simple whores. There is a clear connection between maternal purity and honor and, by extension, between sexual promiscuity and immorality. The threat that the whore presents is the threat of chaos and sedition. A woman's role in the social order is to produce legitimate and honorable sons whom she must be ready to bury in the event of war. Infidelity is an offence not just against humans but against God and society. It is for this reason that zina (adultery) necessitates public retribution.

Although some women are described in terms of their purity and maternity, others are rendered outside this ethical realm. In fact, as discussed in Katib's texts, sexual slavery was legitimate and common. The social issue was not the moral problematic underlying sexual slavery but sexual slavery's proper documentation authorized by the state. Sexual slaves are referred to in the Quran as women whom the "right hand possesses" and who have different obligations and duties from those of a wife. Given their dehumanization, they are not conceived as breaking any social rules. Katib's texts clearly state that Hazara (an ethnic group from the region of Hazarjat) women were forced into sexual slavery. He writes that the Hazara women were often subject to rape and coerced sexual encounters. The appalling treatment of Hazara women is demonstrated in the following exchange after the king discovers that one of his *sardars* (chieftains) has abducted the daughters of Hazara leaders as concubines.

> Concerning the virgins whom he and the other army officers had taken (as concubines) he wrote: Why are you perpetrating such a business? . . . The sardar who had been the (main) perpetrator of this business thoughtlessly replied, "What one observes about Hazarah girls is that they are nothing more than animals—ape-like and ursine. No human being would ever want to live with them whether as married women or as concubines." (McChesney and Khorammi 2012, 3:694)

Hazara women are referred to as slaves or what "the right hand possesses" (McChesney and Khorammi 2012, 3:1010).[26] In a later section, Katib further elaborates sexual slavery. He notes that royal soldiers would "intrude into the homes of the Hazarahs of Hajiristan, embrace the wives of those men, and commit indecent, loathsome, and prohibited acts which no one should do." In one such instance, the text narrates the story of a girl who is walking to her sister's house and is abducted by force. "They brought her [the young woman from Hazarajat] to Kabul according to the practice by which thousands of Hazarah women and girls were sold into slavery" (McChesney and Khorammi 2012, 3:1462). This story demonstrates how sexual slavery was officially sanctioned because the soldiers are asked to produce certified documents to show the purchase of the slave girl. Thus the issue is not sexual slavery but the proper documentation of it. This state of affairs reflects the dehumanization of non-Pashtun women, who were considered less than human in the Pashtun discourse of the state. Through this logic, Pashtun men were permitted to rape and steal the wives and daughters or non-Pashtun families.

Whereas heterosexual slavery is permitted, homosexuality is not. Homoerotic infatuation is mentioned a few times by Katib, wherein male objects of desire are portrayed as lovely, beardless, and moonfaced. This desire, like promiscuous heterosexual desire, is linked to the threat of social turmoil. Katib tells the story of three beardless men who inspired homoerotic infatuation in some soldiers, which led to the threat of sedition (McChesney and Khorammi 2012, 3:1618).[27] The beardless men had to be transferred to curtail this desire and prevent social chaos. There is another story of a master and his servant that results in what comes across as a righteous killing for homosexuality (McChesney and Khorammi 2012, 3:573–74).[28] Beardlessness and loveliness are well-documented character traits of non-manhood in Perso-Islamic texts (Najmabadi 2005, 16). For example, the portrait of Mullah Yar Muhammad Afghan is written about as such: "Though sixteen in age, in face he was as the moon of the fourteenth night."[29] Although Katib links homoeroticism to chaos and penalty, he allows for the possibility of such desire. There is a marked shift from the other writings in Pashto and Persian, such as Khadim's *Pashtunwali*, which relegates homosexuality completely outside the purview of sexual activity.

Islam as an Ethical and Political Ideal:
Muhammad Iqbal and the Mard-e-Mumin
In his presidential address in 2016, Ashraf Ghani invoked the poetry of Muhammad Iqbal as an appeal for peace in the region (Khan 2016). Iqbal was one of the most notable Muslim intellectuals of the twentieth century, who significantly influenced the formation of a Muslim ethos in the Indian subcontinent through his writings in Persian and Urdu. Khadim (1937b) pays homage to Iqbal in his book *Pashtunwali* by claiming that Iqbal had written favorably about Afghanistan in his poetry. On his official invited visits to Afghanistan, Iqbal was in conversation with King Amanullah, to whom he presented and dedicated his book *Payam-e-Mashraq* (Message of the East), and participated in conversations about the opening of Kabul

University. In his writings and poetry, Iqbal was primarily concerned with the creation of a new "Muslim man," whom he called *mard-e-mumin*. Central to the creation of this new Muslim was the idea of *khudi*, which can be understood as ethical selfhood. Although Iqbal sometimes alluded to the role of women in the new social ethos he was promoting, he did not write directly on the subject of gender until later in his life. In his poem "'*aurat* aur ta'līm" (Woman and Education), Iqbal states:

> The knowledge through the effect of which woman becomes
> non woman—
> *this* knowledge the possessors of insight call death[30]

Iqbal's poems are often used in Islamizing nationalist discourse in Pakistan to signal the dangers of specific forms of knowledge acquisition for women. In the verse quoted here, Iqbal is alluding to certain womanly traits that a woman may lose if she acquires a wrong form of education, which would lead to death of a society. The following is from another poem, "'Aurat" (Woman):

> I too am very sorrowful at the oppression of women
> but it's not possible, the opening of this difficult knot![31]

Iqbal laments the *mazlumi-e nisvan* (oppression of women), but presents it as an irreconcilable problem with no social solution. One must therefore accept the wretched condition of women as preordained. Like his contemporaries Khadim and Tarzi, Iqbal considered motherhood central to a woman's role in the nation, a rejection of which would lead her to become a nonwoman, causing social devastation. Thus, in Iqbal's view, the only way a woman could be woman qua woman was through motherhood. The other role for women was to provide inspiration as muses to great thinkers such as Plato. In "'Aurat," he continues:

> She was not able to write the dialogues of Plato, but
> from her flame burst out the spark of Plato![32]

Even in educated discourse, women are never seen as heads of households but as sexual or reproductive beings, either as pious mothers, loyal wives, or promiscuous seductresses and muses. The link between sexual purity and moral goodness has been naturalized in the marital institution, as spousal loyalty has become the archetypical permutation of ethical life wherein chastity and maternity are the only possibilities of womanhood. Scenarios in which sexual permissiveness threatens social cohesiveness are useful rhetorical devices that reiterate the dangers of unbridled sexual passion. In Afghanistan, as elsewhere, conservatives and liberals join hands in constraining female mobility and inciting righteous sexuality in the public. In all conversations about morality and social order, the problematic under scrutiny is sexual liberation for women as it manifests in the form of obtaining a divorce or the freedom to choose sexual partners.

Homogenizing taxonomies of chaste or licentious, virgin or whore, pious or promiscuous have long been developed to categorize Muslim women in classical texts, which are then inhabited by ordinary Muslims. "If I am not a virgin, then I must be a whore," many unmarried women at the shelter told me. Married women had to demonstrate chastity through monogamous loyalty to their husbands, who could take on multiple wives. Such homogenizing categories stifle potentialities, incite moral outrage toward difference, complicate gender relations, and condition the micropractices of everyday life. In Islam, as in many other religions, any semblance of sexual permissiveness is stifled by social sanctions. The khana-yi aman is the place where women can independently choose sexual partners in marriage or obtain a divorce. It is therefore a target of derision in the public domain. As noted throughout this book, the women who run away to the khana-yi aman do so at the risk of being called promiscuous. A wide range of nonsexual actions and attributes are subsumed under the ambiguous category of promiscuity, which functions through a historically rooted conception of pious womanhood.

Modernity of a Promiscuous Past

A question may be posed about the relevance of these historical texts to today's Afghanistan: What does the intellectual tradition of pious womanhood have to do with the self-conception of Afghan women in the present? In other words, why is it useful to historicize Afghan womanhood? What does it have to do with the actions of the women at the khana-yi aman? None of the women at the shelter were trafficked into sexual slavery.

They had all run away of their own volition. Of course, these women are temporally distant from the women described in historical texts. Yet the khana-yi aman women are well versed in many of these texts and debate them with each other. Thus the relevance of these historical texts derives from their importance to ordinary Afghan women in their everyday lives. The actions of the women at the khana-yi aman cannot be isolated from the historical context embedded within the rich canonical sources through which piety is established. Running away cannot be read as a wholesale rejection of her Muslim identity, nor can becoming a second wife be read as a complete consolidation of a Muslim identity. The binary of tradition (pious) and modernity (promiscuous) frequently used to render intelligible Afghan women in academic discourse falls apart through an ethnographic perspective on the shelter. Careful ethnographic work demonstrates the historical complexity of running away at the risk of "becoming promiscuous."

Asad's work (2009) on Islamic tradition as a discursive formation highlights the importance of refraining from employing a simplistic binary of modernity and tradition. Asad emphasizes not disregarding historical texts in understanding modern Muslims. He notes that Islamic discursive tradition, like all traditions, strives toward coherence through the actions of its adherents. Mahmood (2005), a student of Asad, adapts his work to the issues of Islamic feminism. For Mahmood, Islamic tradition is "a form of relation between the past and present predicated upon a system of rules that demarcate both the limits and possibility of what is sayable, doable, and recognizable as a comprehensible event in all its manifest forms" (114–15). Mahmood's work on the modernity of Islamic tradition is worth quoting at length, given its impact on studies of Islamic feminism:

> [A]n engagement with the founding texts of Islam is not limited to scholarly commentaries alone, but entails the practices of ordinary Muslims, such as when an unlettered Muslim invokes the authority of sacred texts to solve a practical problem, or a child argues with a parent about the correct (or incorrect) nature of an Islamic practice. (Mahmood 2005, 116)

Thus, the Islamic referential system is authorized not only through the theoretical knowledge of scholarly tradition, but the practical context through which non-scholarly Muslim women ground their everyday actions in their understanding of an exemplary and authoritative Islamic past. In this conception of Islamic tradition as discursive formation, "reflection upon the past is a constitutive condition for the understanding and reformulation of the present and future" and "the very ground through which subjectivity and self-understanding of a tradition's adherents is constituted" (Mahmood 2005, 115). To put this in Foucault's language, on which this understanding of Islamic authority as a discursive formation is based, subjects are historical effects of their power networks. The power networks are not entirely contained in notions of a consolidated state or macrosocial formation. Power permeates the microcapillaries of everyday practices and creates its subjects as well as the possibility of its resistance. Such resistance is not outside the power network but is its very product.[33] The possibility of difference comes from individual, ethical self-fashioning, a process Foucault calls askesis and which, as noted in Chapter Three, Mahmood translates as a capacity for action. Thus regulation and emancipation are intricately entwined by disciplinary mechanisms. Unlike most conceptions of agency and freedom that focus on resistance against the normative power formation, askesis is the process of inhabiting the normative structure toward emancipation.

Suha and Sadaf were clearly not standing outside the interpretive grids of honor and Islam. Yet running away and showing defiance labeled Sadaf promiscuous. Running away shows defiance and a demonstration of individual will, a move toward emancipation. Becoming co-wives to Habib, however, demonstrates a rootedness in regulatory frameworks of Islam. The subject positioning of Suha and Sadaf manifests through their decisions to simultaneously inhabit and resist normative structures.

CHAPTER SIX

Subject of Honor

Morals, Ethics, Politics

Power relations are central to studies of gender and sexuality. The question of how one becomes the subject of a power formation has been fundamental to recent feminist and anthropological scholarship (see, e.g., Das 2007; Mir-Hosseini 2001; Mir-Hosseini and Hamzi 2010; Najmabadi 2005, 2013; Osanloo 2009; Scott 2010). This chapter explicates how honorable subjectivity manifests for women seeking an emancipatory politics in Afghanistan; it does so by asking where their capacity for action lies within the historical formations of Islam and pashtunwali. The anthropology of feminism has taught us not to be limited by the vocabulary of structure and agency, oppression and resistance (Abu-Lughod 1986, 2013; Das 2007; Mahmood 2005). Within this scholarship, the subject is not predetermined; rather, the experience of suffering makes the subject (Butler 1990, 1993, 2009). We now understand agency not simply as subverting norms in an attempt to acquire freedom but as transformative work that leads to change. The capacity for action is acquired through deliberate ethical work to transform the historical and cultural conditions that situate us. In other words, the subjection itself is means to political action, which is why ethical self-fashioning is key to forming a politics of difference. The feminists in Afghanistan understand this because they call on Islamic tradition and pashtunwali to create an emancipatory politics. At the khana-yi aman, the women do not stop at enacting ethical practices that originate in the moral codes of pashtunwali, Quran, and sunnah. In fact, they go further in their ethical practice by employing strategic manipulation (Barfield 2010, 21) to navigate and circumvent the restrictions of their historical circumstances. Barfield's contribution to the anthropology of Afghanistan allows us to read moral codes as both prescriptive and descriptive, ideological but not definitive. The women build a capacity for action by putting to use the moral codes that have historically subjugated them. In this clever social maneuver lies the cunning of the khana-yi aman.

This chapter is situated within the conceptual architecture that conditioned the turn in feminist anthropology, which relies on the Foucauldian understanding of subjecthood, morality, and ethics (Asad 1993, 2003; Deeb 2006; Povinelli 2002; Taneja 2018). For Foucault, ethics is one aspect of morality, which is formed by a prescriptive moral code and the concrete actions of moral actors. In Afghanistan, the subject is historically and discursively produced within the regulatory and disciplinary apparatuses of honor and Islam, which may be read as the prescriptive moral codes that contribute to the ethical formation. The moral codes are encapsulated in pashtunwali, Quran, hadith, and sunnah, and are definitional and prescriptive, but not definitive.[1] Within this historical and discursive framework, I read promiscuity as the "capacity for action," which Foucault, based on the Aristotelian tradition, has called askesis.[2] Foucault's conception of a moral subject is particularly pertinent to the khana-yi aman because he is influenced by the Aristotelian tradition that also shaped Islamic pedagogical scripts on sexual ethics. Examples of such influence can be seen in the works of prominent Muslim philosophers such as Ibn Miskawayh and Nasir al-Din al-Tusi (Mahmood 2005, 28). Ethical work, self-discipline, and risk are at the core of acquiring freedom.

The condition of possibility of promiscuity is the ethical and moral circumstance that situates women in Afghanistan. In order to understand the cleverness of the khana-yi aman, we must first understand the history of pedagogical discourse on sexual ethics that situates the women in their moral worlds. In other words, the womanhood of Afghanistan must be historicized. The conception of promiscuity or immorality would not be possible without the particular historical and social conditioning surrounding honorable womanhood. The discursive and material practices, including invocations of textual traditions and interactional exchanges at the family courts, reveal the historical influence of honor discourses in everyday life. These court encounters close the gap between theoretical discourses and their application in the lives of ordinary Afghans. At the same time, they demonstrate that the historical conditions do not limit or completely explain the actions of the ordinary women at the khana-yi aman. For instance, Neelam's use of poetic verses to perform a promiscuous self, which did not actually exist but was manifested to anger her husband and prompt a speedy divorce, shows how misinhabiting honor might lead to unanticipated outcomes. Neelam's actions show how she was able to stand outside the historical honor formation, even if temporarily, and use it to influence her husband's decision because he was still trapped within the formation. As noted earlier in this book, her husband later said that Neelam had detached herself from his world. Paradoxically, Neelam demonstrated an astute understanding of this world of honor and, by risking a performance of promiscuity in public, was able to direct this world into a place where she wanted to live. These actions show how ethical work in combination with risk has emancipatory potential.

Because there are definite penalties for transgressive sexual conduct, the least of which is being called promiscuous, the social impetus is on developing individual honorable comportment. This means that the label of promiscuity is merely the first step in a protracted disciplinary regime that regulates sexual transgression. Not every woman will undergo each punitive step, but knowledge of the disciplinary system governs individual action. The fear surrounding promiscuity is not simply of being jailed or facing familial ostracization, although those are the immediate and tangible consequences. It is of suffering divine retribution. In comparison to other feminist movements in the Islamic world, the feminist movement motivating the institution of the khana-yi aman is unique in its support of sexual conduct that can be read as outrightly promiscuous and, thus, religiously immoral. Despite individual reservations, the shelter inhabitants and administrators tolerated, accommodated, and in some cases admired bold, sexually transgressive women. At the core of the khana-yi aman is a withholding of moral judgment for sexually promiscuous conduct. This is how it maintains a rhythm of everyday life. Indeed, this is how it survives.

Even so, the shelter is not without conflict. In many cases the runaway women do face condemnation by the shelter administrators, lawyers, and even fellow runaways, despite a stance of withholding moral judgment. Moreover, women are constantly judging their own actions against their interpretation of Islamic history and notable Muslim women such as the Umm al-Muminin (Mothers of Believers). At the khana-yi aman, women's morality is informed by a moral code that includes pashtunwali, Quran, and hadith. They are clearly practicing pashtunwali tenets in the form of hospitality (melmastia) and refuge (nanawatai) to form a community or guest house (hujra) in pursuit of justice ('adl) and independence (*azadi*). These are historically male domains, access to which females have been denied. The women are also proudly Muslim and practice Islamic precepts originating in Quran and hadith, such as *rozhay nival* (fasting) and namaz (prayer). In this sense, through their concrete moral actions, they show adherence to the moral codes of Islam and pashtunwali. As described earlier, within the framework of Foucauldian ethics, ethical work or askesis consists of forming a relation between a moral code and moral action. It is in these relations of ethical self-fashioning that the possibility of political transformation resides. The women inhabit some precepts of honor and Islam, but misinhabit others, by which they put themselves at risk. And this risk potentiates their moral actions with the emancipatory possibility of political transformation.

Marriage, Promiscuity, Risk

Many women at the khana-yi aman had escaped near-death experiences brought about by the discovery of their sexual indiscretions. If the woman was married, the husband might decide not to divorce her immediately, even when he has become cognizant of her sexual indiscretions. In this case, women run away of their own volition with fears of later and harsher reprisal than divorce. Palwasha was a strikingly bright woman who arrived at the khana-yi aman with her two-year-old daughter. Her husband suspected that she was having an affair with their neighbor and would regularly beat her. One day, she left. I met her at the khana-yi aman wearing a beautiful red dress. Before the women enter the khana-yi aman, they renounce all their worldly possessions, so I asked her where she got the dress. She had sewed it herself in the tailoring room on the second floor. I asked if she would share her story with me. She motioned for me to wait with her daughter as she brought two chairs. She sat across from me with her daughter on her lap and began her story.

I was ten when I got married. My husband was fifty, maybe sixty. Men do not keep track of their age. Why should they? They can bear children when they are ninety [laughs]. I did not want to have sex with my husband on the wedding night. *His* wedding night. I did not want to get married. It was not my wedding night. He tied my hands behind my back. [Her eyes watered.] It hurt. It hurt a lot in the beginning. After a while, it stopped hurting. Or I became numb [*yakh*].[3] One day, he started suspecting that I was having an affair with the neighbor. My neighbor and I. We were very friendly. He was handsome and kind. One day [my husband] saw me laughing with my neighbor. My husband beat me black and blue. I ran away. He kept my four-year-old son. I have my daughter.

I asked, "Were you having an affair with the neighbor?" Palwasha looked me straight in the eyes and answered, "Would it be immoral [*ghair akhlaqi*] if I did? Would you consider me a whore [*fashhash*] if I did?" I shook my head and asked how she would survive without her husband.

My father's house is empty. I would rent out the upper portion and live there with my daughter. I know how to do my work without re-sources. I make resources where there are none. I found out about the khana-yi aman through an indirect reference in a newspaper. I am literate. I read. I am not illiterate [*jahil*] like my husband.

I traveled a few times with Palwasha to the court to get a divorce from her husband. On one occasion, the lawyer informed us that her husband, Omar, would be there with his brother Tariq. Palwasha looked visibly upset. When we got to the courtroom, she found an empty room and sat there quietly. As people came in and out, she seemed uncharacteristically lost in her thoughts. We waited until the lawyer came to tell us that her husband had arrived outside. He had come for reconciliation. Palwasha asked me to join her in their meeting. I carried their daughter as she talk-ed to her husband. The brother stood on one side. Her husband asked her to come back. He said he missed her. The lawyer stood by, taking notes. Palwasha asked the terms and conditions of her return. He looked at his brother Tariq, who said, "Become kind to my mother. Keep my honor." Her husband looked at Palwasha and repeated the sentences. To the amazement of everyone there, Palwasha nodded quietly. The next day, she left with her daughter to return to her husband.

In order to understand why Palwasha may have chosen to go back with her husband, one must understand how womanhood is constructed through a discourse of honor and morality. Although revealed through particular institutional arrangements, honor may be understood as a strategy or a technique, rather than a particular structure or institution. For example, it is deployed for precise goals (e.g., honor deaths); appropriated through specific institutions (e.g., marriage or kinship); and used to reify existing authoritative structures (e.g., armies, religious schools, police). Honor functions through these instances, but it is not reducible to them. While it is distinct from other forms of power that exist in societies, it permeates throughout all, linking them together in complex strategic relations. It authorizes and invests systems of subjugation across all societies, more explicitly in some societies than in others. Even though honor may be read as an effect and functions in real ways as all institutional effects do, it has real consequences in the everyday lives of ordinary persons.[4] An analysis of honor formation explains why women return to their husbands, given their subject position in the honor formation, but it does not explain why they would risk running away, as Palwasha did. It also does not explain why Palwasha would become friends with her neighbor despite her husband's reservations. Why would she risk being called promiscuous?

In his book *Freedom, Equality and Justice in Islam*, Afghan legal scholar Mohammad Hashim Kamali (2002) discusses the concepts of *al-hurriyyah* (freedom) and *musawat* (equality) in Islamic jurisprudence, both of which have a communitarian and social aspect. He notes that women and men have equal status as it pertains to their moral worth and religious dignity (61–75). But the marital contract in Islam is hierarchical and gendered, with specific duties and obligations pertaining to husband and wife. The moral ethos of marriage in Islam positions men above women in that men are clearly the heads of the household. In pashtunwali, the analogy of women as property under the laws of marital contracts is clear: women, like property, form the basis of honor relations, and there are important parallels in social transactions with respect to women and property. Edwards (1996, 69) notes that claims to honor are entwined with claims to property and land, and failing to protect ancestral land and women is key to becoming *bi-ghayrat*, which translates as "dishonorable" or "cowardly."

The marital contract as an economic, sexual transaction between men and women is by no means unique to Afghanistan. However, the peculiarity emerges in how pashtunwali interacts with Islam and how this interaction creates the social matrix in which the marital contract is authorized in Afghanistan. This particular social matrix obligates men and women in significantly divergent ways. Islamic law obligates a woman to be sexually available to her husband and places her sexual obligation above other religious obligations, such as fasting for Ramazan. The sexual duties of the wife take precedence over duties to Allah so that a woman cannot engage in nonmandatory fasting or praying if it impedes her sexual obligation to her husband. Her sexual availability must not be compromised, as this destabilizes the marital contract. Kecia Ali (2010), in her book *Marriage and Slavery in Islam*, a rare gendered account of the intellectual and social history of Islamic jurisprudence, notes that almost all jurists "agreed that the husband supports his wife in exchange for her sexual availability to him" (194). Although women must be sexually available to their husbands, wives have little negotiating leverage in demanding reciprocal sexual accessibility from their husbands.

The social concerns surrounding adultery emanate from the perception that a woman is less sexually capable than a man and, therefore, cannot manage multiple sexual partners. If she takes on multiple sexual partners, it causes social havoc. Because men are allowed multiple wives, the sexual prowess of the male obviously trumps that of the female because it is assumed that men can fulfill multiple sexual relationships simultaneously. The woman is allowed only one husband at a time, to whom she is exclusively sexually devoted. Male polygamy is mandated through strict rules of engagement concerning resource allocation; a man may take on successive wives (no more than four) only if he has the temporal and fiscal capacity of fair distribution among them—that is, if he can distribute his money and time among them equally.[5] Nevertheless, polygamous

relationships are abundant in Afghanistan, and first wives play an important role in finding suitable future wives for their husbands.

The categories concerning sexual rights in Islamic thought are androcentric and mainly concern male entitlements toward women, and
not vice versa. Through an analysis of slave ownership by both male and
female Muslims, Ali (2010) shows that marital transactions were different from other social transactions in Islamic history (43).[6] As outlined by
Ali, the discourse of apportionment recognized female conjugal claims,
but was reluctant to interpret those claims as sexual. This discourse of
apportionment defined female conjugal claims in terms of companionship
and cohabitation, and conditioned the ambivalence surrounding sexual
claims by women (114–15). In Islam, she notes, a woman cannot initiate
her own marriage contract, and the transactional relationship situates her
differently than a man (43). Ali further notes that women's sexual agency
is not connected to her legal agency, which renders her intent irrelevant
in most cases, unless the intent is presumed favorable toward the husband. Therefore, if she were to attempt to leave her husband, she would
have no right to do so; however, if she were to make a sexual overture
toward him, this would signify a desire to return (141). Afghan law, in
accordance with standard Islamic precedence, stipulates that the husband's intent is paramount in divorce. And, as noted earlier in this book,
in divorces initiated by women (called *khula* divorces) based on missing
(ghaib) husbands, the woman must return to her husband if he wants a
reconciliation and reappears before the mandatory waiting period ('iddat)
is over.[7] In Hangama's khula case, the judge became annoyed when she
said she had met her husband a few weeks before, since a private visit is
construed as conjugal and signifies a desire to return to the husband. The
laws regarding divorce are not wholly clear in Afghanistan, and almost
all are decided on a case-by-case basis after significant negotiation among
the families, lawyers, and a judge. No two cases are alike. Outside Kabul,
these cases are decided among families. The khana-yi aman allows the
state to step into these historically private negotiations.

The designation of certain carnal behaviors as sexually proper and
essential to feminine morality is not an individuated ethical project. The
emphasis on sexual propriety through the cultivation of bodily chastity

is a political project, and disciplining the female body through didactic campaigns of morality is well situated in Islamic religiolegal doctrines. Didactic texts such as *Akhlaq-e Nasiri* (Nasirian Ethics) and *Bihishti Zewar* (Ornaments of Heaven) have long proliferated in the socioethical worlds of Afghan women. In this socioethical world, any notion of women's autonomy that locates agency in freedom-seeking is read as antithetical to Islamic history. Muslim female acceptance of Islamic values of modesty, and especially sexual virtue, is a precondition for women's involvement in public life. In this context, any political movement that denies affiliation with some strain of Islam delegitimizes itself. And this is especially the case for feminist movements. Labeling women as *khariji fahsha* (foreign whores) is commonplace in Afghanistan. "No one wants to be called a whore," I was told time and again. The repugnance that the word *whore* inspires in moral societies is universally understood. The social status and privileges associated with appropriate sexual behavior undergird the whore–virgin divide in most societies and condition the angst of those who, while defending the right of those in the former category to exist, are careful to self-identify as the latter. Those who were sympathetic to the women of the khana-yi aman would often say, "We have no right to judge them. Allah will be their final judge."[8]

One year after Palwasha had returned to her husband, I visited her house. Her husband's brother Tariq, who had been vocal at the court, was present. He was training to become an Islamic scholar. I asked him why it was important for him that Palwasha and her husband reach reconciliation and how he determined the terms for Palwasha's return, which were good behavior and keeping honor. Tariq answered by explaining the logic behind the marital contract in Islam and pashtunwali:

> In Islam, the marriage contract, and the obligations of wife toward husband and husband toward wife, are paramount. This relationship comes before anything else. The first question a man and woman will be asked on the Day of Judgment will be about marital relations. For a wife to greet her husband with a smile when he comes home is a form of jihad. One cannot overemphasize the importance of marital relations. This is the foundation of an Islamic society. Let me explain

why it is difficult for women to initiate a divorce [*khula*]. From the outside, it may seem this is because Islam oppresses women, but this is not the case. You have to understand the entire system [*nizam*], not parts of it. When a woman marries a man and then gets a divorce, she becomes forbidden [*haram*] to him. After a divorce, the couple cannot get married again. In order to get married again, the woman must marry another man and establish sexual relations with him. Only after the second man divorces her after having sex with her can she return to her first husband. This may seem oppressive [*zulm*] to you, but it actually protects the woman, not the man. In a system in which men can have four wives, women are always in demand. Please understand that Islam is a complete system [*mukammil nizam*], which must be followed in full. We cannot follow parts of it, because this leads to chaos [*fitna*]. So yes, the right to divorce is given to a man, but if he divorces his wife mindlessly, he will not be able to get her back easily. She will have to marry another man and establish sexual relations with him. This is to punish the man and discourage him from giving a thoughtless divorce. He will lose his wife.

Tariq explained that this was why Islam permitted divorce but called it a least favorable act. So if Palwasha and her husband had been divorced, she would not have been able to easily come back to him. It would have been a long, convoluted, and painful process. This is why thoughtless divorces are not permitted. He said he saw it as his moral obligation to intervene and protect his brother's marriage. "Alhumdulliah [praise be to Allah], as you see, now the family is together. What more can one want?" Later, I asked Palwasha if she was content with her decision to return. She said that she could not have lived without her son and that examples within her family had made her cautious. She said that Tariq's first wife had successfully obtained a khula from him. But then she missed her two sons and wanted to return. When the mufti (Islamic legal expert) had explained the process of return, the family realized that it was almost impossible. Tariq's wife would have to remarry, but she could not stipulate before her second marriage that it would be temporary. She would have to enter that marriage with a pure commitment toward her new husband. If, however, it failed on its own, only then could she return to her first husband, Tariq. After Palwasha had understood the consequences of her decision to obtain a divorce through khula, she decided to return to her husband. Tariq did not see the process of divorce as unfavorable to women. Rather, he explained the mechanisms inherent in the difficulty for women to obtain divorce, and then the difficulty to return to their husbands, as unfavorable for men. But what about Palwasha's neighbor? When I asked her about him, she shrugged and looked away: "I have not seen him again." I found out later from Palwasha's sister that the neighbor had moved after finding out about the difficulty his presence had caused in her life. She commented, "He knew the honorable thing to do was to leave."

Although female sexual desire is not denied in pashtunwali, it is placed in subordination to male desire and to women's maternal desire. In Islamic jurisprudence, as explicated by Ali (2010), here too is a definite hierarchy that privileges male sexual desire. However, the way that Tariq, Omar, and Palwasha lived these moral precepts did not reify such intended hierarchies, nor did they view the hierarchies as oppressive. Tariq had lost his wife and could not get her back easily. In his view, Islamic norms, in making reconciliation after divorce difficult, favored his wife. Tariq continued with his explanation:

> Please understand Islam and pashtunwali as a complete system. The problem is when we try to install these in bits and pieces. There are few occasions in which men and women become forbidden [*haram*] to each other. My divorcee is haram to me. If I become sexually attracted to a woman, her mother and daughter become haram to me forever until the Day of Judgment [*ta qayamat*]. This is why we have *parda* [veiling] as a foundation of pashtunwali. It is grounded in Islam. Why is parda important? Let's say I am married to a woman, and her mother is young and beautiful. I become attracted to her. Now her daughter, who is my wife, has become haram to me. You may think this would not happen. But it does. This is why there are strict rules of modesty [*haya*]. Again, you may think this is oppressive to women. But it protects women by keeping their men's sexual desire in check.

Tariq's explanation is undergirded by the notion that controlling miscreant sexual desire forms the basis of a moral ethos. Ethical work in Islam and pashtunwali creates an abiding relationship between moral codes and moral actions. In other words, to be a moral actor, one must ethically fashion oneself in accordance with the moral code. However, as we see in the actions of some runaway women, such as Neelam and Hangama, power cannot be neatly contained within a moral code and neither can its resistance. In subtle and manifest actions, women and men misinhabit honor codes, toward unintended consequences.

In Tariq's view, Palwasha had made a wise decision to return to her husband. If she had stayed at the shelter or acquired a lover or moved back to her father's house, she would have been called promiscuous, which would have jeopardized her life and that of her daughter. She protected herself and her daughter against such a threat. Leaving her husband would make Palwasha promiscuous even if she did not have sexual relations outside marriage. Becoming friends with her neighbor, without having sexual relations, had made her promiscuous and subject to beatings. However, if she married again and had sexual relations with her second husband, only to return to her first husband, this would not make her promiscuous. From Tariq's explanation, it became clear that as long as Palwasha was making an effort to conduct herself morally in accordance with Islamic and pashtunwali precepts, she would not be considered promiscuous. By contrast, defiance or running away is construed as immoral. What constituted risk was not merely having sexual relations. Risk involved a deliberate defiance of morality. Given Tariq's explanation, it made sense why Neelam would perform a promiscuous self and resist the moral formation to step outside it. It also made sense why Hangama would lie about having met her husband. Neelam and Hangama chose to misinhabit their moral positions because misinhabiting and taking a risk enabled them to reorient their worlds in intended ways. Palwasha, by contrast, chose to live in accordance with the moral precepts by strengthening the relation between her actions and the moral codes.

Gender Hierarchies and Independence

Pashtunwali, in its coimbrication with Islam, shapes a highly gendered world in which one must enter a binary division of male or female to find an intelligible existence. The compulsory, heteronormative bond conditions the basis of the social contract in this world. There is a historical absence of female modes of being in pashtunwali, as it focuses on androcentric ways of life. The ethic of pashtunwali is not addressed to female bodies. The ethical world constructed by pashtunwali is created for and inhabited by men. While love (*ishq* or *mina*) and various forms of courage (*tora*) are glorified in the ethic of pashtunwali, the social burden placed on women is toward conformity and adaptability. Too much sexual independence will inevitably lead to social disorder or chaos (fitna).[9] Women have a relational status to men in pashtunwali and are essentially mothers, lovers, and wives of men.

Khadim's book *Pashtunwali* (1937b) discusses in detail the gender precepts of pashtunwali. This text was published in Pashto during the reign of King Mohammed Zahir Shah to whom it is dedicated. It was supported by Pashto Tolana (the Pashto Literary Society), which Khadim references in the introduction with a prayer that Zahir Shah's era would contribute to the promotion of Pashto language and literature. The book is divided into chapters titled, for example, "Akhlaq v 'adat" (Ethics and Morals), "Da jang qawaneen" (Laws of War), "Khazay pa jang ke" (Women in War), "Mashrano mankhat" (Obedience of Elders), and "Badal akhistal" (Taking Revenge). I introduced this author and discussed the text in detail in Chapter Five. In the chapter "National Pride," the author narrates the story of a foreign researcher who asks a young, impoverished, desolate Pashtun man in Afghanistan, "Who are you?" The young man replies with great pride, "I am a Pashtun." Khadim notes that a Pashtun poet is narrated to have said, "After Islam, it is enough for me to be a Pashtun" (73). Khadim states that pashtunwali should be a source of pride for Pashtun men and women.

The world of pashtunwali portrayed by Khadim is hierarchal and gendered, and while hierarchical differentiation may not preclude fluidity, it does not promote egalitarianism. Masculinity and femininity may be acquired through certain character traits, but masculinity is distinctly structured above femininity. Khadim mentions the Islamic concept of *musawat* (equality), but only as it pertains to equality among men in relation to their ruler. He never approaches the issue of male and female equality. The path toward equality and honor for women is through acquiring the masculine attributes of *nurtowb* and *sarritowb* or producing brave Pashtun men. *Pashtunwali* describes the role of women in their relational status to men, as mothers, lovers, and wives. Women are mentioned in several portions of the text, and in some places, as noted later here, Khadim speaks *as* an ideal woman. *Pashtunwali* is given to idealized descriptions of the Muslim woman. It is assumed that an honorable Pashtun woman is always already Muslim. Freedom is mentioned tangentially in relation to obedience, in the chapter "Obedience to Elders," which suggests conformity through submission.

Lila Abu-Lughod's work on Muslim societies has been instrumental in shaping intellectual trajectories of gender analysis. While her work is a major challenge to universalist assumptions of teleological feminist consciousness, her call is to "respect everyday resistance" as an analytic to unravel "complex interworkings of historically changing structures of power" (1990, 53). Her work on Bedouin honor provides the most important model for the pashtunwali world. Abu-Lughod describes the coimbrication of Bedouin honor with Islam as it relates to gender and sexuality:

> [T]his negative attitude toward sexuality is identified with religion only because piety constitutes one of the standards of moral worth in a Muslim society. Insofar as Islamic belief and practice represent the highest ideals of Bedouin society, identification of the prevailing social system and status quo with Islam is inevitable—it accords the society legitimacy. But religious ideals are then confused with social ideals, and personal honor comes to depend on conformity to both. (Abu-Lughod 1986, 144)

In her work on the Bedouin group Awlad 'Ali, Abu-Lughod moves away from patriarchal codes of conduct by replacing them with parallel codes for women underwritten by modesty (*hasham*) instead of shame.[10] She argues against reductionist approaches to studies of honor that view ideals of honor-modesty and honor-shame as encapsulating entire representations of moral systems (1986, 144). Michael Herzfeld (1980, 1985) also rejected honor-shame complexes to describe moral codes for a more linguistically and socially contextualized understanding of honor as reputation or *egho-ismos* (Greek: aggressive self-regard), which is not entirely encompassed by the word *honor*. This kind of honor, which is completely social, is not exclusively explained as a male attribute, limited to and emanating from the male domain, but rather in "relation to male concerns" (49). Thus women can also possess and accumulate honor through social practices of hospitality. This is comparable to *khuruj* hospitality practices studied by Ann Meneley (1996) in Zabid city, an urban town in Yemen. *Khuruj* literally means "going out" or "visiting" (41).[11] Khuruj is enacted entirely by women as a means of ranking families through hospitality practices of exchange and competition. Meneley notes that embodied piety, performed through bodily gestures and religious comportment, conditions the basis of social status and familial identity. In these studies, the emphasis is on women acquiring honor by performing a moral personhood through various manipulations of the cultural systems. At the khana-yi aman, Pashtun women have found ways to enact honor through practices of melmastia (hospitality) and hujra (guest house or guest hosting).

In the chapter "Laws of War," Khadim (1937b) relates the story of a battle that his elders witnessed in 1897–98 (32–35).[12] The timeline suggests reference to the Anglo-Afghan wars. He narrates the tale of an English general observing a tall and stately Afridi Pashtun woman through a telescope. Wearing a black shawl, a bullet vest around her waist, and a rifle on her back, she enters the battlefield to walk among the dead bodies. She bends down and raises the head of each corpse in order to determine whether she recognizes it. She kisses the forehead of six, but throws down the seventh head and slaps the corpse's face. The general sends a messenger to ask the woman why she did this. The woman, after much convincing, replies that the first six are her sons who were killed with wounds in the front and who, evidently, died in active battle. The seventh was her husband, who had been killed from the back and must have fled the enemy, dying a coward's death. Khadim writes a note about how this is the spirit of a woman's pashtunwali, and, indeed, her responsibility is to bear brave sons who would die a courageous death in war. The story ends with the English general announcing a ceasefire because he decides that his side cannot defeat such maternal courage.

In the chapter "Ethics and Morals," Khadim (1937b, 15–24) writes simultaneously as a man and as a woman, a mother and her son, a lover and the beloved. My translation follows.

> A *qaum*'s national [*milli*] soul [*ruh*] is represented by its national literatures [*milli adbiat*]. The representation of a nation's soul [*milli ruh*] is the responsibility of that nation's literati [*qaum adbiano*]. Pashtun national literature is replete with epics of war and swordsmanship. Please note the following landay:

> When dancing swords are raised before war
> I have laughed much at my peers

> May you return with wounds of a black gun
> Not with tales of disgrace

> If my beloved shows gallantry in war
> Friends would thus venerate me with honor

> My beloved stepped back from the swords of war
> I regret giving him lips in vain last night

> Let your black kohl turn red with blood
> May your unharmed body not disgrace our love

> A war of swords I would have fought
> In a war of fate, I stand senselessly

> I heard my beloved returned safe to bed
> My heart feared that he may have wounds on his back

> I will sacrifice myself for my brave beloved
> Who stains his hands with enemy's blood

> Time has come for Pashtun youngsters
> Brave men must die for their homeland [*vatan*]

That he is not martyred at Maiwand
May God Almighty keep my beloved from such a disgrace

Young men are standing with swords on their backs
Ready to lay their heads for their homeland.

My beloved has laid his head for the homeland.
I will thread his shroud with locks of my hair

For the sake of the beautiful spear
that hangs around your neck, I will go beside you

Sisters of brave men weep
Sisters of cowardly men adorn their eyes

Beloved, do not turn back from war [*jang*]
Lest my friends taunt me

Victory comes with graceful courage
If not victorious, young men will die from disgrace

Why would my beloved not demonstrate bravery?
I accompany him halfway up to the battlefield

I am responsible for my beloved's death
As shots were fired, I went to the roof

I will make a mark with my beloved's blood
That shames the flowers and roses in Shinkai's garden

The warriors [*ghazi*] will reach high places
Where Gilan's girls visit (15–18)

A little later in the same chapter, we find one of the many references to Khushal Khan Khattak.

Khushal Khan is a warrior literate. He is a great aficionado of skill. He says:
    Those who demonstrate evident bravery
    I Khushal Khattak sacrifice myself for the sake of such ability.
(18)

Several passages elaborate women's participation in war alongside men. For example:

> At the time of war, women like men show up at the battlefield. For tribal [*qaum*] and homeland's [*vatan*] defence they take part in battles alongside men. For example, a female lover [*mashoqa*] said to her beloved ['*ashiq*].
>
> With you in the sunlit fields
> I Pakhtuna [Pashtun woman] am not afraid to use a sword for love.
>
> At the time of war, if someone runs away or turns their back to the enemy, Pashtuns calls him *daos* [coward]. This person cannot look his relatives ['*aziz*] and tribe [*qaum*] in the eyes for the rest of his life. If he dies with his back to the enemy, Pashtuns do not accept his corpse, nor bury him. (Khadim (1937b, 31)

Khadim's *Pashtunwali* posits a gendered world in which the domains of women are present only from the perspective of men. In this conception of the world, women are properly subordinate to their men within a righteously hierarchal society. To use Luce Irigaray's vocabulary, *Pashtunwali* has a "blind spot" when it comes to women (1985).[13] Khadim was writing as a Muslim and includes many references to Quran and sunnah. Like *Pashtunwali*, the Islamic texts mark men with varying degrees of sexual potency: from eunuchs to sexually viable beings (Ali 2010, 116). In the same vein, *Pashtunwali* addresses cowardly men as "womanly" and courageous women as "manly." In the chapter "Da jang qawaneen," Khadim (1937b) narrates a story about a cowardly soldier in Isfahan who tries to run away from battle. The commander sends him back to face the army and tells him, 'O womanly man [*khazunke*[14]], if your right hand is cut off, so what? You still have your left hand. If your left hand is cut, you still have your teeth to cut your enemy's flesh. Go. Fight your enemy until your last breath'" (26–27).

Courage is demonstrated through manliness and acts of bravery in war. Women can share these ideals, but when women perform feats of courage or bravery, the traits remain masculine and are not feminized. Chastity and modesty, as feminine traits, are additional virtues that complete the female repertoire of honor. This gendered world conditions the everyday experiences and constructs the frames of reference through which sexuality has come to be understood. At a young age, all Afghans, particularly Pashtun women, are instilled with some notions of honor, such as what has a proper place in an honorable existence and what does not if one is to have a felicitous life.[15] At the very beginning of life, feminine and masculine bodies are habituated to conform to certain social principles and ways of inhabiting the world. Ideals of honor are inculcated through disciplinary mechanisms to which honorable subjects must submit or transform themselves to successfully adapt. These mechanisms are constantly and regularly applied to manifest the subjects of honor, who, in turn, reify the very mechanisms that mark them. In any such power formations, deviations must regularly be contained, ostracized, or, at the very least, accounted for. For example, those who know themselves to be dishonorable, rather than asserting their status as such and potentially transforming the social matrixes, must instead constantly transform themselves to become acceptable to standard notions of honor. Perhaps this would explain why some women, such as Palwasha, would agree to go back to an abusive husband, despite enacting the labor of running away and reaching the khana-yi aman. In the end, her husband was able to convince her to accompany him back through an appeal to the namus of the family. This namus pivots on Islamic notions of marriage and divorce, which reifies the marital contract and makes separation difficult.

From a Politics to an Ethics of Honor
(from the Social to the Individual)

So what exactly is promiscuity in honorable contexts, and how does this label get associated with certain people, particularly women? Why does it cause moral panic and anxiety across most societies? Narratives of women's lives are spoken from the perspective of the dominant culture, whether the goal is to consolidate or change the social ethos. For instance, many books have been written about the Taliban, but almost none about the women who live with them. Rarely are the stories of miscreant women told or their life histories considered. Where else would we seek the traces of honor, morality, sexual violence, and promiscuity but within the gendered interstices of the everyday lives of ordinary women? I found in these everyday life stories the resonance of centuries-long histories of violence and conflict.[16]

Does pashtunwali account for individual difference? Must I always be described in conjunction with and through other Pashtuns and my Muslim brethren, without whom I cease to exist? Is my existence contingent on being part of a whole? David Edwards (2017) notes that Islam is embedded within the precepts of pashtunwali such as the jirga (tribal council), which, while prioritizing pashtunwali precedents (*nerkh*) over Islam, nevertheless includes religious figures to provide religious sanction (31). Too much independence would lead to a man being called *badmash* (troublemaker) and even *lewanai* (mad). There is a delicate social balance maintained by controlling irregular behavior. Louis Althusser, in his essay "Ideology and Ideological State Apparatuses" (1971), and Michel Foucault, in his book *Discipline and Punish* (1975), both hold that ideology (or "power" for Foucault) is not merely the "false-consciousness" of a subject, which can be corrected by arriving at a true understanding of his situation. Rather, ideology/power creates subjects, and, for Foucault, it differentially distributes these subjects over a statistical economy of life forms.[17] Pashtunwali is ideological, as it claims who the Pashtun people are, while its Pashtun audience is supposed to understand that this is who they are (ideology as identity) and that this is how things are done (ideology as normativity). It is ideological also insofar as it both constructs and reinforces social norms and society in general. The book *Pashtunwali* does include legal passages, but is in large measure given over to idealizing descriptions of what the Pashtuns are like and what they do. That is, most of *Pashtunwali* is descriptive, although regulatory sanctions do apply to the exceptional cases. Indeed, the frequent invocation of Quranic verses is toward this idealizing end of how Pashtuns *should be* as good Muslims and adherents of Islam. Punitive measures are reserved for occasions when Pashtuns fail to adhere to their own Islamic and Pashtun ideals.

As pashtunwali, historically a tribal code in rural areas, became co-opted by the state and involved in nation-building processes, particularly in the twentieth century, the modern issue of consent and consensus became central to ruling. Antonio Gramsci (1971) has noted that hegemony, insofar as it involves establishing consent through law, far exceeds the effectiveness of ideology. Along these same lines, Afghans were slowly co-erced into forming consensual social contracts.[18] Consent, in other words, can be manufactured.[19] In this sense, pashtunwali made its transition from an aspirational ideological code to a hegemonic one, which estab-lishes rules of behavior and orientation and also identifies and discourages transgression by establishing consent and consensus. This explains why Palwasha would go back to her husband, a decision she deemed good for herself and her family.

Foucault's distinction between ethics and morals, particularly in rela-tion to sexuality and embodied action, is useful in this regard. Mahmood (2005) has fruitfully applied this Foucauldian distinction to the Egyptian mosque movement. As Mahmood notes, embodied action should not be read within the binary logic of subversion-consolidation of norms; rather, embodied action "endows the self with certain kinds of capacities that provide the substance from which the world is acted upon" (27). Pash-tunwali constitutes honor subjects through moralistic injunctions read as a collection of rules, norms, and values. But does pashtunwali's honor have the potential to expand beyond moral obligations? Does this honor have the capacity to authorize ethical practices to instantiate transforma-tions of our social worlds?[20] Reading the honor subject through the his-torical and social matrices within which it is inevitably imbricated, and which condition its various modalities of action, enables us to ask about the possibility of difference. In practicing the precepts of pashtunwali, honor subjects are endowed with the potentiality to enact honorable ac-tions. But where in this honorable world is the potentiality for promiscu-ity or difference? The uniqueness of the khana-yi aman women is that their actions are in harmony with their principles. They are not just tak-ing a rhetorical position; they are enacting a risky, promiscuous position and endangering themselves in the process. The presence of the khana-yi aman itself is a risk.

Legal norms of pashtunwali materialize in the moments of sexual transgression. By announcing the sexual worlds that pashtunwali de-nounces, the promiscuous women of the khana-yi aman lay claim to a power configuration that had them condemned. The promiscuous women critique the honor systems by making decisions that differ from and dispute what is legitimate and authorized. In this very basic sense, they are making political actions. The women labeled *avara* (vagrant or wanderer), *badnam* (disgraced), or *fahsha* (whore) are persistently resituating themselves within the honor systems through a continuous critique of their own selves and the moral systems that implicate them. They practice Islam and pashtunwali by adhering to the concepts of fasting, veiling, praying, and hospitality, yet also participate in promiscuous lives explicitly forbidden in Islam and pashtunwali. While some have enacted promiscuous actions, others live promiscuous lives through no tangible actions, but are still construed as promiscuous. In this way the women both consolidate and resist the normative structures of Islam and pashtunwali.

Embodied Honor: Nanawatai as Shelter

Pashtunwali has an impressive repertoire of bodily conduct and comportment—narrated through practices of hospitality, camaraderie, shelter, friendship, and love—that socially define men and women as Pashtun. The women at the khana-yi aman accessed these practices to form communal bonds among themselves and, in doing so, simultaneously resisted and consolidated the discourse of pashtunwali. For example, some women, like Palwasha who had run away to get divorced and brought her two-year-old daughter with her, were not relinquishing their maternal responsibilities. Thus, while rejecting the role of the wife, these women still embraced the role of the mother. Disentangling the role of mother from that of wife is in itself a rebellious act. These roles are intimately entwined with pious womanhood in both Islamic and honor discourses, as seen in the Taliban publications, Khadim's writings, and women's own publications, all of which have an emphasis on birth (*paidayish*) and nurture or upbringing (tarbiat). In taking on seemingly contradictory positions that separated the role of wife from the role of mother, women like Palwasha invested pashtunwali and Islam with both emancipatory and disciplinary possibilities (Najmabadi 2005).

Women at the khana-yi aman participated in honor practices that were historically relegated to the male domain. For example, the hujra is a guest-hosting practice in a male-only space where men form homosocial

bonds to develop deep and lasting friendships. Here, the famous precept of Pashtun hospitality, melmastia, is enacted. Hospitality is shown
through elaborate mechanisms of hosting large gatherings. Every Pashtun
house has a hujra for male bonding, and women do not enter the hujra
except when called on as prostitutes or dancers to entertain men. Communal prayer is also a male-only domain and a religious obligation for
men. Men congregate in mosques to pray namaz, which is fundamental
to creating communal relations. Women are not obligated to pray at the
mosque, although in some cities, such as Istanbul, women may enter and
pray behind the men. In Kabul, the mosques do not have a space to ac-
commodate women, who pray at home. At the khana-yi aman, women
prayed in groups and enacted the precepts of hujra (guest house or guest
hosting), melmastia (hospitality), and especially nanawatai (refuge) and
'adl (justice).[21] Khadim (1937b) describes melmastia:

> Taking care of guests is a very ancient and embedded custom ['adaat]
> among the Pashtuns. Every Pashtun considers taking care of guests
> an essential part of their life. Pashtuns emphasize taking care of
> guests to such an extent that even if they are in a condition where
> they cannot host a guest, they still never send them away! If one stud-
> ies Pashto language, one sees the many proverbs for welcoming and
> meeting guests. These proverbs are ostensible evidence of hospitality.
> Kandahar Pashtuns say: "come well," "may God bring you." And
> the reply given is: "live prosperously," "may God make you flourish."
> The Southern and Eastern Pashtuns say, "may you never be tired,
> and safe travels." (90–91)

> Pashtuns usually live in villages. They do not prefer becoming
> residents of cities. Every village has a mosque inside or at the out-
> skirts. Each mosque has an attached guest house [hujra]. Every vil-
> lage, large or small, has many mosques and hujras. Every hujra has
> about twenty to thirty beds. (91–92)

> If they have nothing else, they still ask you to sit comfortably on a
> pillow and relax. They bring you hot water to wash your hands and
> face, and prepare tea. They insist upon the guest spending the after-
> noon with them, and try hard for the guest to spend the night. The

result of this genuine and sincere respect and regard is that a person thinks that he is in his own home. This humanity and brotherhood is not frequently seen or common outside Afghanistan. (96)

Gulalei explained how she saw pashtunwali precepts embedded in the khana-yi aman:

> Honor is inscribed on our bodies at a young age. We are told where to sit, how to stand, not to laugh too loudly. A good Pashtun woman does not draw attention to herself. We cover our bodies to protect ourselves from the sexual gaze of men. Veiling [*parda*] protects men from going astray. When we leave our villages, we leave behind our homes, but we take pashtunwali with us. We brought it here to Kabul with us. Can you see it here at the khana-yi aman? The idea of refuge is not foreign. It is at the core of pashtunwali principles. *Nanawatai* means giving sanctuary [*panah*] to anyone who asks for it, even if it puts your life at risk, and even if the person asking for refuge is an enemy. When a person becomes your guest, all rules of hospitality [*melmastia*] apply to them regardless of who they are. These are the principles of pashtunwali. Hospitality, refuge, friendship, love, courage, and justice. We live these principles at the khana-yi aman, but we do it on our own terms.

Gulalei had an astute understanding of the concepts undergirding pashtunwali, an understanding grounded in her personal life history. She had not read *Pashtunwali*, but she lived it nonetheless. This was true for most Pashtuns I met. Tariq explained pashtunwali in surprising detail, but was not aware of its written form. He explained parda (veiling) as a foundation of Islamic social formation that allowed men to conduct their social interactions smoothly without the distractions of sexual and promiscuous desires. As Gulalei noted, the idea of refuge or sanctuary is well known in Afghanistan. Nanawatai (refuge) is a central tenet of pashtunwali and is related to the notion of melmastia (hospitality) and hujra (guest house). Khadim describes these concepts of nanawatai, melmastia, and hujra in detail in *Pashtunwali* as a process of conflict resolution between two opposing sides enshrined in specific rules of engagement. It involves asking for forgiveness and a demonstration of repentance. A destitute person, even an enemy, is not turned away but given shelter even if it puts the host at risk of death. Decades of wars have made people distrustful, and, as a consequence, social etiquette has undergone significant transformations. Nevertheless, hospitality and sanctuary function as important markers of social status among Pashtuns and non-Pashtuns. When women willfully appropriate these male practices at the khana-yi aman, they put themselves and the system that undergirds and assigns these practices as masculine at risk.

Discursive Promiscuity

Some women at the khana-yi aman regard the social obligations of honor as constraining and express a desire to move away from sanctioned forms of inhabitation. Others express a will to inhabit honor obligations to their fullest. Most inhabited some honor precepts and misinhabited others. Through slight and significant deviations from authorized forms of being, new forms of being became possible. At the khana-yi aman, an expression of a different and promiscuous self, which was clearly not pious, became possible. For Foucault, power formations not only anticipate but rely on resistance to enhance their capacities. Any form of resistance is not only co-opted by the power formation but also its very product. The possibility of stepping outside power formations resides in individual ethical self-fashioning.[22] This ethical self-fashioning will not lead to a radical historical rupture, a clear break from the past; but in the slow and deliberate work of endurance and protest, women may lay claim to new and hitherto unimagined worlds.

Discursive promiscuity resides in an embodiment of honor that allows for the risk of misinhabiting honor. Women at the khana-yi aman are living their difference by inhabiting and performing a variety of promiscuous selves. Enacting promiscuity in public puts them at enormous risk. Running away is connected to promiscuity, even if one runs away to escape abuse. The all-encompassing category of promiscuity subsumes a wide range of runaway women, from those who run away from sexual abuse to those who run away for a lover. Historically speaking, landay sung by women are a poetic performance of sexual transgression without putting the women at risk for transgression. But when the khana-yi aman women sing the landay, they are transgressing in theory and practice. In his later work, Foucault introduces the concept of fearless speech or *parresia*, first known to the Greeks in Euripides [c. 484–407 BC]. Foucault describes this ancient form of courageous free speech as a way of expressing courage in the threat of imminent danger. Parresia entails a form of risk, threat, or danger to the teller; and, in its extreme form, telling the truth puts the truth teller at risk of death.[23]

The runaway women are playing that game of life or death in which the courage to speak the truth puts them at tremendous risk. *Fahhashat*, translated variously as sexual promiscuity, indecency, or obscenity, has the potential to subvert normative representations of female sexuality and contemporary understandings of female subjectivity. In the interactions at the khana-yi aman, these potentially radical effects of sexual promiscuity are represented and articulated. I interpret *fahhashat, fahhashi, avargi,* and *badnami*, all various local notions of promiscuity, as processes that contest the wholeness of the honorable subjectivity pashtunwali imposes on women. Women protest honorable subjectivity by willfully becoming marginal. In other words, they are deliberately casting themselves out from the discursive matrices that situate them as marginal.[24] The khana-yi aman is a space that thematizes and provides directionality to the fragmented chaos (fitna) and marginality of willful promiscuity.

Toward Promiscuous Futures

After my *khala* (mother's sister) was found dead in December 1985 at her husband's residence, her body was flown to our ancestral village, where my grandfather is known as a feudal khan, and which is now named after my mother's brother. My father woke us in the middle of the night at our house in Peshawar. It was a few days after my eighth birthday. A relative's family lived nearby. They came unannounced, yet there was certainty that they would come. It was as if the news of death had already been anticipated. I remember my mother and her cousin hugging and crying at the sudden departure of my aunt. That night, we embarked in two cars on a solemn four-hour journey to the village, during which my mother cried quietly the entire time. Following Islamic stipulations, the body had to be buried as soon as possible after her death. When I saw my aunt's face inside the wooden casket, she looked icy blue. The stillness of her body in her mid-thirties spoke in ways that could not be silenced. It revealed centuries-old stories. Soon after, the men in our family came to the women's portion of the house to give a shoulder to her casket and walk her to her grave. We stood silently as she was taken away by the men. Dressed in a white shroud, she was taken out of her casket and laid to rest in the family graveyard. My mother was not allowed to be present when her only sister was lowered into the ground. It is believed that women's uncontrollable emotions will cause a disruptive scene at a burial. In her life, Sophia Khala's father and brothers had turned their backs on her. Now they faced her in her death.

After Sophia Khala died, her enlarged photographs were placed in our grandfather's urban house, a historic British cottage once occupied by Sir James Abbott on several acres overlooking green hills. My

Sheffield-educated maternal grandfather, perhaps from heartbreak, died five months later from heart failure. Many tears have fallen for Sophia Khala, and many trips have been made to our village where her grave rests in a green valley between the majestic Himalayas. During each trip, her white marble grave is washed with great care, and garlands of red roses are placed on it. We stand around her grave and hold up our hands in prayer. We pray for her salvation. We pray for her soul. Sometimes the village women passing by will sing her a spontaneous song enunciating her free spirit that this world could not contain. Despite these performative theatrics, her death is not questioned. It is taken as inevitable. In her grave, she has reached her proper place. It is only in her death that her life can be celebrated. Why did Sophia Khala have to die?

I was raised on stories of how my aunt was the rebellious sister. Her birth name was Naseem, which rhymed with my mother's name Parveen, and their younger brothers' names Saleem, Naeem, and Rahim. She changed her name to Sophia because she thought it was different and nonconforming. She wanted to stand out. She refused to be like the others. She refused to comply. As a young girl, I gathered that Sophia Khala had to die. She was too senseless to have lived. She was too much of a troublemaker. Stories of her madness included some that have remained with me. Sophia Khala and my mother were a few years apart. They attended a convent boarding school for Muslim girls in a nearby hill station. The convent girls were not allowed to greet the nuns first. They had to wait to be addressed. I was told how Sophia Khala would yell a greeting, "Good morning, Sister," nonstop to the nuns until she would be disciplined by being locked in a room. At home, she played cards and smoked cigarettes. She would throw noisy tantrums when she lost in tennis or badminton with her brothers. My mother, by contrast, was sane, responsible, and mature. My mother does not smoke cigarettes, and she is content with the birth name given to her. My mother tells me that my khala named me Sonia, as it rhymed with her chosen name, Sophia. Both names are unusual for Pashtun and Muslim women. Perhaps my khala chose me to be different, and to tell her story.

What kind of world would have allowed my mother, who followed the rules, and her sister, who recklessly broke the rules, to survive together?

If my aunt was loved, then why was it difficult to give her a little space in the thousands of acres and several houses that the brothers inherited? Why could she not have come back to her father's home? Despite lengthy, emotional conversations with my uncles, these questions have not been answered. In fact, these are questions that I have been discouraged to ask.

Recently, as a thought experiment, I encouraged my mother to ask her brothers for her share of inheritance. Their initial shock was comical. First they absurdly questioned my mother whether my father had given his sisters their share. I intervened to tell them that he had, and that, re-gardless, my mother's share was not dependent on her husband's deal-ings with his sisters. Frantically they produced an old document that my mother and father had been forced to sign soon after my grandfather died. My mother says that she has no memory of signing it. After my persistent questioning, one of my uncles told me that the men, including my father, had gathered around my mother months after she lost her only sister and cherished father and coaxed her to sign away all her property rights. They insisted that she had willfully disclaimed her inheritance, and cast doubts on her present sensibility. My uncles claimed that my mother had now lost her senses and thus was asking for her share. "Everyone is very shocked. Even our mother is stunned," my uncle said. In another conversation, one of my uncles mentioned how lavish my mother's and Sophia Khala's weddings had been, stating that too much had already been wasted on the two sisters, despite the fact that their own three weddings, each of which I attended, were historically extravagant. My mother and her sis-ter had no say in the family's financial affairs, including planning their own weddings. The men handled all affairs, including deciding whom the women would marry and where and how much would be spent on wedding logistics. When I reminded my uncles about the lack of women's participation in financial affairs, and also that legally or Islamically the dowry or wedding expenses do not replace a woman's inheritance, they emphasized my father's signature on the document. When I told them that my father had no legal or Islamic right to sign away my mother's property, the oldest answered, "Ahsan Lala signed the document. Will you question your beloved father?" I noted that my relationship with my father was different than the one he had with his wife. Keeping his wife disenfranchised from her ancestral property worked in my father's favor, ensuring her compliance. My uncle ended the conversation by saying, "Stop thinking too much."

It is not uncommon for women to be forced to sign such fraudulent property documents by family members especially when they are distraught, even though these documents have no grounding in Islamic or state law. Women are often guilt-tripped into signing by being made to feel like a financial burden. I witnessed countless such cases in Kabul. It was only after conducting my ethnographic fieldwork that I gained the confidence to question my own family. For my mother, the shift from goodness to ungoodness was precipitated through the mere act of asking for a share in her inheritance. Soon after, my mother was unceremoniously told to leave her father's residence. As a widow in her seventies, she became detached from her brothers. My mother built her relationship back with her brothers after she again submitted to being disinherited. She also returned what remained of her dowry that her father had given her on her wedding. When I asked my mother why she did this, she answered, "The love for my brothers weighs more than the property and land." I noted that it was a truncated form of love in which her rights had been trampled. She shrugged and looked away.

It is almost impossible for women to fight such injustice in the courts. Even women like my sisters and me who are eminently educated, living abroad, independently financially secure, and conversant in Islamic and state law are unable to embark on these court battles. This is for emotional and practical reasons. My sisters told me they conducted a cost-benefit analysis, and the familial togetherness weighed more than the hassle of asking for their rights. My sisters, like my mother, do not want to create familial discord. I told them they were participating in their own disenfranchisement and oppression. No one is asking why giving a woman her Islamic legal rights will cause familial conflict, especially when everyone involved claims to be a pious Muslim. A daughter's share is guaranteed in Islam. When my family found out I was writing this book, one of my cousins called me. When I picked up the phone, he immediately quoted this familiar verse from the Quran, surah al-Baqarah: "They are your garments and you are their garments." When I replied that this verse was meant for husband and wife, he said that it could be extended to the entire family. I told him that he was quoting the Quran out of context. He insisted that given their strength, nobility, and courage, my mother and khala must have willfully sacrificed, and that we should protect each other as a family and not make these stories public. I told him that the men in the family do not own a woman's memory even if they are her sons, her brothers, or her father. He told me I was causing family fitna (chaos or family trouble). We ended the conversation.

Years after Sophia Khala's death, Samia Sarwar was killed. Her death too was followed by stories of her inability to conform and to be good. Unlike her younger sister, Samia was known to be defiant and reckless. Because her death made international news, family discretion became imperative. No one close to her spoke publicly about her life. My older sister had been Samia's classmate in Peshawar Convent. They had been best friends since sixth grade. She had lived a few houses away from us. I remember Samia's long, silky black straight hair and her free-spirited laughter. She shared comic books, romantic novels, and music cassettes with my sister and their friends. Outwardly she had a quiet demeanor, but sometimes she told bawdy jokes and laughed nonstop when we were shocked. She had decorated her room in disco lights, which she would turn on after making the room dark. She would then dance and sing with reckless abandon. Even in grade school she was unconventional. Before she turned sixteen, she was engaged to her cousin, whom she eventually wed. She ran away a few years after her marriage. When her family pressured her to go back to her husband, she ran to a shelter. Close to her thirtieth birthday, she died with a bullet wound, shot by her mother at the shelter. Why did Samia have to die?

Asna, my father's eldest brother's daughter, had wavy black hair that she loved to willfully bounce when she danced at weddings and social gatherings. One of my favorite memories of her is the beautiful dance she performed at our cousin's wedding to the song "Dafliwale." She was young, vivacious, and high spirited. A few months before I came to the United States to attend university, she visited me in Peshawar. We were first cousins of the same age and lifelong best friends. Our paths were now diverging. My father had agreed to send me to college in the States. I am the first woman on either side of the family to attend college abroad before marriage. She pleaded with me to speak to her family. Her wedding had been planned to her khala's son, and she did not want to get married. She wanted a way out. At the time, I thought she would compromise and be fine. A few years later, she too was dead, hung from a rope in her father's house. She had refused to conform to the rules of her husband and had come back to her father's house. She left behind two toddler daughters, and may have been pregnant with a third. Her dead body was covered in bruises. My paternal aunt described her as a "small bruised dead bird" when she bathed and readied her body for burial. Asna is buried next to my father in my father's familial village. Her photographs now hang from the walls of the house in which she died. Although she makes a visible and audible presence, only certain stories are authorized to be told about her. Why did Asna have to die?

I have revisited the life stories of Sophia Khala, Samia, and Asna innumerable times. I have spoken many times to those close to the women. No answer is sufficient for why these women died. Was it mere greed, to exclude them from their rightful share of inheritance? Was it because the young women had always been defiant? Was it their potential for causing trouble? Did the women choose to die so the rest of us can live? One attribute they all shared was their desire to run. They all died because they were literally or metaphorically running away. Runaway women are imperative to a conversation about the creation of a pluralistic politics. In occupying the margins of the Taliban and post-Taliban state, runaway women demand a rethinking of analytical frameworks through which questions of state, politics, social justice, equality, and democracy can be conceptualized. The interpretive grid through which Afghan women are rendered intelligible is piety and honor. The runaway women have fashioned a different world on the other side of honor and piety.

When I write these stories, I realize that they may be co-opted by those who want to wage wars through the bodies of Muslim women. I understand the global power dynamics that seize these stories as fodder for programs of imperialism. I write against all forms of violence, institutional and embodied, local and global. The analytical frameworks in all the chapters of this book originate from the words and gestures of the women on the ground. And I have not sought to contextualize these words through Western frameworks of universal feminism. The intellectual goal of this particular project has been to create an independent space in academia in which Muslim woman qua Muslim woman can have a conversation about difference, political change, and plurality. Is it possible for Muslim women to drive the narratives of our own struggles without the fear of co-optation?

My theoretical frameworks originate in the works of the women who wrote before me, such as Saba Mahmood, Leela Gandhi, Veena Das, Chandra Mohanty, Lara Deeb, Gayatri Spivak, and Lila Abu-Lughod. Spivak's famous essay "Can the Subaltern Speak?" demands that the female academic embrace her intellectual task of tracing the itineraries of power that situate the non-Western woman as a voiceless and passive victim of her circumstances. She ends this essay with these poignant words: "The female intellectual as intellectual has a circumscribed task which she must not disown with a flourish" (Spivak 2010 [in Morris], 283).[1] This essay has revolutionized feminist theory. The woman whose suicide conditioned the possibility of this remarkable essay was Bhubaneswari Bhaduri, Spivak's grandmother's sister. Bhaduri had written a letter that eventually reached Spivak. In her subsequent writings, Spivak reveals how this death and the letter were intricately connected to her intellectual journey. Spivak's essay is often misread as disallowing the subaltern woman a voice to speak. Rather, she is outlining the problematics of representation, even when women in close proximity write about one another. In a powerful paragraph, Spivak narrates how different women hear the same stories differently: "To begin with, then, an act of piety. The woman to whom Bhubaneswari wrote the letter that was forgotten was my mother's mother. The woman who told me the story was my mother. The woman who refused to understand what she had said was my first cousin. . . . She was quite like me in education, and yet it made no difference. She could not hear this woman" who had attempted suicide. "It was Bhubaneswari who could not be heard, even by her." She later states, "My point was not to say that [the subaltern] couldn't speak, but that, when someone did try to do something different, it could not be acknowledged because there was no institutional validation. . . . The point that I was trying to make was that if there was no valid institutional background for resistance, it could not be recognized" (Spivak 2010 [in Morris], 228).[2]

Careful ethnographic writing allows us to detail the intricacies of local gendered life, while remaining attentive to the problem of representation. This is not in an effort to represent or give voice to the subject, to speak for a woman. My concern has been to reveal the everyday struggles through which Afghan women create and inhabit their world, in which we are all implicated. This is an attempt to trace the gendered historical itineraries of friendship, refuge, shelter, and sanctuary, and how runaway women adapt to or transform these concepts. Refuge is not confined to the shelter either temporally or spatially. The idea of refuge precedes modern institutions of shelter. Nanawatai (refuge) and panah (sanctuary) are key concepts of sanctuary in pashtunwali. Pashtunwali has references to runaway women, and the nobility of allowing them refuge. Most Pashtun homes have a hujra (guesthouse) in which all guests, regardless of belief or creed, are welcome. Melmastia, variably translated as hospitality or friendship, is a key Pashtun concept. In appropriating these historical concepts at the shelter to create new and different friendships and alliances, the runaway women are transforming the power dynamics that situate them as oppressed.

The Taliban envision themselves as the arbiters of piety in Afghanistan. They have made attempts to codify piety through legal stipulations. How are margins to this coerced piety created through the words and gestures of the runaway women? Who occupies these margins, and why? The demarcation of peripheries works in tandem with the state. As Mohanty (2003) reminds us, "it is not the center that determines the periphery, but the periphery that, in its boundedness, determines the center" (42). In a similar vein, Asad (2004) concludes Veena Das's book on the margins of the state with the poignant reminder that "the entirety of the state is a margin" (287). In creating a space on the margins for runaway women, the shelter potentiates new solidarities not bound by the post-Taliban state.

Mohanty (2003) advocates for the urgency of connecting local gender struggles with universal commonalities to achieve solidarities across borders (226). How do we achieve these solidarities, a universal sisterhood if you will, without flattening difference?[3] The shelter does not promise a mature, utopian politics against the totalitarianism of the Taliban state. The work of the shelter is deliberately unfinished. It refuses the telos of certainty and will not conform to a program of universal feminism. In her book *Affective Communities*, Leela Gandhi (2006) explores the creation of solidarities by narrating a radical form of friendship that allows for unpredictable affiliations. She writes about a pluralistic political configuration in which "selves who make up a culture loosen themselves from the security and comfort of old affiliations and identifications to make an unexpected 'gesture' of friendship toward all those on the other side of the fence. There is no finality in this action, no easily discernible teleological satisfaction" (189). The concern here is with the process that makes difference visible, not with a definitive end goal. The politics itself is chaotic, immature, and incomplete. Allowing radical difference to thrive is fundamental to the survival of the shelter. The transitory friendships and alliances that develop inside the shelter are a microcosm of solidarities that are now emerging in Afghanistan. Could these fragmentary solidarities, which allow for a multiplicity of radically different subject positions to coexist alongside each other, become the grounds for a politics of change?

Hangama means "riot" or "chaos" in Pashto, and in many ways the women at the khana-yi aman saw themselves as disrupters or hangama.[4] Many Afghan women, especially Pashtun women, are named Hangama despite the fact that hangama means "disruption." This reflects the conflicts and paradoxes surrounding gender and power mechanisms in Afghanistan. The stories of Hangama, Neelam, and Arshia demonstrate that piety is conditional and generated through institutions and public exchanges. My work as an ethnographer has been to make visible these embedded institutional structures and historical matrixes that condition piety and, by extension, promiscuity. Promiscuity is fundamental to rendering relative the claims of generic piety. The khana-yi aman may be called an institutional form of a feminist movement, but the women inside embody noninstitutionalized forms of suffering.[5]

Twenty-six shelters in operation today are run by NGOs; most are run by the NGO Women for Afghan Women. All the shelters are in jeopardy of government takeover (Kramer 2018). Multiple attempts to take over the shelters by various post-Taliban Afghan governments demonstrate the precariousness with which they operate. There is an interest by some members of the Afghan government to control and surveil these spaces, which have been labeled as brothels that promote promiscuity. The future is as uncertain as the past.

Many people commenting on my work have suggested that I reconsider using the word *promiscuous*, in part because the deviant and immoral images evoked by the term do not fit the description of the women. However, a fundamental goal of this book is to argue against processes that conflate piety with morality and promiscuity with immorality. The women who run away demonstrate that such categories do not exist in simplistic binary expression. The Taliban did not introduce piety to Afghanistan, nor were they the first ones to make it compulsory in Afghan society. However, the newness of Taliban governance and the way they mandated piety created a public in which women like Gulalei and Neelam can exist alongside women like Sadia and Arshia. For these women, Taliban Islam is not an abstract and distant entity but a real experience that is lived together, and still this book is not about the Taliban. It is about the women who live with, give birth to, form bonds of affection with, run away from, and sometimes go back to the Taliban. The lives of these women are intrinsically tied to, but separate from, the Taliban. Whereas according to Western frameworks of feminism and autonomy, the women may not live radically in the present, in running away and taking the risk of being labeled as promiscuous, they create possibilities for radical change. They are building the ground on which differences, contradictions, and multiplicities of piety and promiscuity, morality and immorality, can coexist without eradicating the other.

Women are at the center of the conflict in Afghanistan, yet the stories about conflict are written by and for men. It is hard to overstate the importance of women's lives to the American intervention. But today the situation for women has not undergone considerable change despite massive human rights campaigns. Shifting the question from "Why are women killed?" to "Why do women choose to run away?" centers the lives of women. Some women choose to run; others stay. Both choices are marked with tremendous difficulties. Through nineteen years growing up in Peshawar followed by my ethnographic fieldwork, I learned that women do not run away impulsively. Each act of running away is more than a simple rejection of their communities and families; it is a call for everyone to be better, to do better. It is a thoughtful, strategic estimation of risk. Running away is more than a rejection of what is; it is an imagining of what could be, an inchoate creation of a new and better ethos that tolerates the once intolerable.

Writing this book has not been easy. How does one write a conclusion to a book that began by seeking to question the ultimate end one faces: death? This book has been a reflection on why women run away despite risks of death and disrepute. If the runaway women make it to the shelters, they form a community assembled around the values of inclusion and nonjudgment. Although all forms of life are present at the shelter, the public repertoire the women inhabit is around Islamic notions of womanhood. For example, the promiscuity of a woman who runs away is rendered intelligible through the vocabulary of the historical piety of the Umm al-Muminin (Mothers of Believers). Throughout these chapters, we have seen how performances of promiscuity in the present are embedded within historical constructions of gendered piety. The courageous, promiscuous self is a way of being in this world that emerges from a foundation of Islamic knowledge about a mythical historical past. This strategic maneuvering of a historical tradition enables women's agency, carving a path for resistance and difference. Taking control of the production of scriptural knowledge creates agentive action.

The women and the Taliban invoke the same historical narratives, but they do so toward different ends. When women run away, they become labeled as promiscuous. However, this does not stop them from deploying and inhabiting discourses of Islamic piety or from living as moral subjects in the world. Thus promiscuity in this sense is not the opposite of piety or morality. These multiple, often contradictory moral selves coexist to create a new and different world.

Notes

Introduction

1. Sometimes defined as an honor code, pashtunwali is a historical, discursive, and material practice that women embody through praying, fasting, poetry (landay), and participating in rituals of honor, piety, hospitality, refuge, and sanctuary.

2. Names of some women have been changed except when they are already well-known cases in the media.

3. *Randi* is used mostly in Pashto-speaking areas; the remainder of the words to signify promiscuity are shared across Pashto and Persian.

4. Rosi Bradiotti (2011, 2012) has developed a theory on nomadic subjectivity in which, following Foucault, she emphasizes the generative nature of power. Power relations are not only outside but also inside (2011, 17). She observes about her own work, "[O]ur own currently situated perspective in a globalized contest is the premise for my project of redesigning subjectivity as a process of becoming nomad (2011, 5).

5. A number of works on Islam and feminism have influenced my thinking through the years—for example, Abu-Lughod (1986); Ahmed (1992, 2011); Booth (2001); Hoodfar (1997); Kashani-Sabet (2011); Mahmood (2005); Mir-Hosseini (2001); Mir-Hosseini and Hamzić (2010); Najmabadi (2005, 2013); Osanloo (2009); and Scott (2010).

6. Scholarship on Afghan women has been prevalent in the West, in which they are often linked to piety, honor, and Islam. See, for example, Bezhan (2016), Billaud (2015), Coburn and Larson (2013), Grima (2004, 2005), and Olszewska (2015).

7. The relationship between subjecthood and power has been well appropriated in anthropology. See Asad (1993, 2003), Deeb (2006), and Taneja (2018). For the particular theoretical framework that extrapolates the politics of recognition, particularly the notion that marginalized peoples have to reify their marginalized position in order to obtain political recognition, see Povinelli (2002).

8. For a discussion of the constitutive relationship between power and sexuality, see Foucault (1978) and Bersani (1995). For a discussion of embodied capacities for action and their relationship to subjectivity, see Mahmood (2005).

9. A lot has been written on Pashtuns, but this literature either ignores the role of women or sees them as compliant within the bounds of convention. See, for example, Barth (1959), Nichols (2013), Lindholm (1982), and Tapper (1991).

10. Ewing (2008) describes stigmatization of honor in Turkish immigrants in Germany (see p. 93). She shows how the hegemonic liberal state intervenes in the intimate lives of minority Turkish Muslim immigrants through family court cases.

11. For an analogous work on how Muslims navigate belonging and refusal to belong, see Parla (2019).

12. See, for example, Mani (1998, 36). Mani criticizes British colonial apparatuses for misreading local Indian texts. Through a careful reading of historical colonial documents, she shows how the British misread and misinterpreted the descriptive and heterogeneous nature of Hindu texts as prescriptive and normative.

13. Mahmood (2005) adapts the Foucauldian notion of askesis, as a capacity for action, to the pious women in Egypt. She uses this notion as a consolidation of the normative structure of Islam through an embodiment of its practices demonstrated by praying, veiling, and fasting. She posits this in opposition to Butler's conception of the drag queen, whose excellence in imitating the normative structure shows the vulnerability of the patriarchal system.

14. Afghan women are among the last few Muslim women whose lives are narrated through honor frameworks. The ethnography in this book shows that honor frameworks are insufficient to explain the range of emotion and conflict in the lives of everyday Afghan women.

15. Asad (2009) notes, "Islam as the object of anthropological understanding should be approached as a discursive tradition that connects variously with the formation of moral selves, the manipulation of populations (or resistance to it), and the production of appropriate knowledges" (10). Also see Hallaq (2009) and Messick (1993, 2018).

16. Foucault (1972) explicates his notion of discursive formation in detail in his book *Archaeology of Knowledge: And the Discourse on Language.*

17. For a discussion of tradition as an effect, see Kogacioglu (2004).

18. *Millat* usually implies a nation with a structured state; *qaum* is a nation with or without a state.

19. See Appiah (2010) for a discussion of honor as a moral code.

20. Sunnah is a compilation of habits and traditions of the Prophet, and forms an important part of the repertoire of being Muslim.

21. By "epistemic rupture" I mean the significant changes that condition a clear break from the past. This is a break that shifts modes of knowledge production. For more on the notion of epistemological rupture (albeit in a different context), see Etienne Balibar (1978), who discusses this concept from Bachelard to Althusser. For more on knowledge production and its link to power mechanisms, especially with relation to governmentality, see the later lectures of Foucault (2003, 2007, 2008).

22. Fieldwork for this book was conducted between 2010 and 2012 at a shelter in Kabul.

23. The idea of "saving" Muslim women from the clutches of culture and Islam has been critiqued. See, for example, Abu-Lughod (2013), Kogacioglu (2004), and Siddiqui (2015).

Chapter One

1. Names and some biographical details have been changed to protect the subjects. In some cases that are already circulating in international news media, real names have been used.

2. This is a personal interview with a shelter official. All interviews were conducted in confidentiality, and the names of the interviewees are withheld to protect privacy.

3. The path to the shelter was not straightforward. Women arrived from a variety of places, including jails, relevant ministries, and various feminist organizations.

4. In my most recent correspondence with the deputy minister of MOWA, Nabila Musleh, she replied: "[T]here are 26 Women Protection Centers [WPCs] in 20 provinces of the country. We call it officially WPC, not shelters anymore. The donors supporting WPCs are INL/US, UN Women, and Columbo Plan. I don't have data on which year how many WPCs were available, but as you know, the number was gradually increased through the years. The laws that are being used for adjudicating cases of WPCs are the EVAW law and the Criminal Code" (email message to author, May 5, 2020). Although these place are now called Women Protection Centers, I use the original term *khana-yi aman*, or home of safety, in this book.

5. For example, some shelters are run by an analogous women's rights organization called Women for Afghan Women (WAW). The shelter where I stayed was not a WAW shelter. WAW is more organized and centralized, with a more concentrated mechanism of funding. It has an impressive website that describes its shelters in detail, and a strong international presence with an active office in New York. The WAW website gives a detailed breakdown of funding. It is registered with the US Internal Revenue Service, and is funded by European, American, and United Nations agencies, as well as private corporate and individual donors. Government grants constitute 86 percent of funding, individuals and foundations 9 percent, and special events 5 percent. The audited financial statements from 2018 show approximately USD 2.6 million in consolidated (Afghanistan and US) assets (https://womenforafghanwomen.org/financials).

6. Hashmi has conducted work on the category of "zina" and how it is variously interpreted in legal discourse inside Afghanistan. Zina becomes linked to both rape and adultery.

7. See also the United Nations Assistance Mission in Afghanistan and Office of the High Commissioner for Human Rights (2010) and Kfir (2014).

8. The version of the Civil Code most often referred to in court hearings is Civil Code of the Republic of Afghanistan of 1977 (Afghanistan Legal Education Project 1977).

9. As I show in my ethnography, the judges used a variety of sources to render their decisions. These include their own knowledge of Islamic law and of Afghanistan's constitution. During family disputes, family members would also occasionally invoke customary law. In all the cases I witnessed, I saw judges use a combination of their personal knowledge of Islamic law and the Afghan constitution to resolve disputes. For a detailed analysis of law in Afghanistan, see Barfield (2003). This report is based on Zadran (1977). See also Barfield (2008).

10. Taliban negotiations with the Afghan government are conducted through various international arbiters, including the United States. See, for example, Smith and Yusufzai (2020).

11. Sylvia Plath died a tragic death at a young age. She led a difficult life. Even as a brilliant writer who influenced many, she had little power in her personal life. Plath is revered across the Muslim world, particularly among Muslim women writers.

12. Moving away from deterministic theories of agency, many of which have a dual understanding of structure and agentival action, allows us to become attentive to local and non-Western permutations of agency.

13. Women express their agency in a variety of ways, not just as resistance or consolidation of normative structures.

Chapter Two

1. See Civil Code of the Republic of Afghanistan, article 131, topic 8, Dissolution of Marriage, 30. Afghanistan Legal Project. https://www-cdn.law.stanford.edu/wp-content/uploads/2015/10/Civil-Code-of-Afghanistan-ALEP-Translation.pdf.

2. Pashto dialects from various regions are transliterated vastly differently depending on pronunciation. I have tried to stay close to the way the women quoted were speaking.

3. For an analogous work in Germany, see Ewing (2008). She shows how Turkish immigrants negotiate their marginality by navigating their subject position as traditional or modern Muslims.

4. The words *tarbiat* and *parvarish* have a specific meaning for an Afghan audience. They are invoked frequently in everyday conversation either as praise (someone has been brought up well with *salim tarbiat*, or healthy upbringing) or insult (a person experienced *kharab tarbiat,* or faulty upbringing). Runaway women are often accused of not having sufficient tarbiat, causing their inability to conform. Runaway women at the shelter would often bring up the topic of how they were seen as troublemakers.

5. For Foucault's extensive discussion of power and subjectivation, see, for instance, Foucault (1978).

6. *Mahr* is often translated in the West as "Muslim alimony." This translation is not sufficient because it does not take into account the complex rules undergirding mahr in Islamic law. For example, mahr must be paid by the groom to the bride on wedding day. The amount of mahr is usually decided between the two marital parties in advance of the wedding.

7. The four lawyers were young graduates who had recently earned their degrees from the local university. The two female lawyers were allowed to enter the khana-yi aman; the two male lawyers stayed in the main office. On some occasions, many women would be taken for collective court dates in a minivan; at other times, only one woman would go with a specific lawyer. For court dates, the male lawyers would meet the women at the main office. There was no clear structure to how the cases were assigned a lawyer. In some ways, it was random. But if the woman spoke Pashto, chances were high that she would be assigned a Pashtun lawyer who could communicate with her.

8. Abu Lughod (2013) has narrated the story of Bibi 'Aisha as an example of gendered Orientalism, in which certain horrific images of Muslim women are circulated in the West to justify imperial projects.

9. I have used various words to describe the concept of promiscuity. One of them is *fahhashat,* which circulates as obscenity, lewdness, vulgarity, and so on.

10. For an analogous history of virginity testing in Turkey, see Parla (2001).

11. *Randi* is uncommon in non-Pashto-speaking Afghanistan, but is used in Kabul and Pashtun-dominated places. It is used in Kabul by some Pashto speakers. To my knowledge, this particular word does not exist in Persian, which has other ways of saying the same. While *randi* literally means a widowed woman, it is used for any woman without a male patron and has a very negative connotation. It is often used to refer to women conceived as prostitutes and whores. In my years of fieldwork, I have not seen it linked to a man except in a pejorative way, where he is being referred to as a woman—for example, a *khazunke,* a man who is like a woman (*khaza*). *Khazunke* is used by Khadim (1937b) in *Pashtunwali.*

12. There are many terms for women who do not conform, all of them pejorative; all of them imply a non-rootedness (*avargi,* which comes from the root *avara*). I have used various permutations of *fahashat* (*fahhashi, fahhash, fahsha*) as well as other terms, such

as avara (wanderer) and randi. A prostitute or doer of promiscuity is called *fahsha*, and the act of promiscuity is variably fahhashi, fahashat, or fahhash. *Avara* is a term linked to Afghan refugees in Pakistan and Iran because of their lack of rootedness, and when used for women, it means promiscuous. Promiscuity is clearly linked to a kind of nomadism or inability to find rootedness.

13. Wimpelmann (2017) discusses gender politics in Afghanistan.

14. *Jabr* is similar to *zabardasti* and implies force.

15. Siddiqui (2015) shows the complex ways in which the category of "rape" is invested with meaning in court documents in Bangladesh.

16. Baad and badal are pashtunwali concepts. Badal means exchange to compensate a debt, and may imply retaliation in some cases. See Barfield (2003).

17. Reading of the marital contract through an economic logic has been well studied by scholars. For historical studies, see, for example, Levi-Strauss ([1949] 1969) and Mauss ([1925] 1990). For analogous studies in contemporary Muslim societies, see Hoodfar (1997).

18. This understanding of piety and promiscuity is indebted to Saussure's understanding of language as a system of negative differentiation in which words gain meaning through linguistic differentiation. His lectures given between 1906 and 1911 were first published posthumously in 1916. See Saussure (1972).

19. See also Abu-Lughod (2010) for her plea for careful ethnographic work for Muslim women and Muslim societies.

Chapter Three

1. Legendary folklore in Persian and Pashto often depicts an ongoing argument of contradictory positions between a man and woman or God and a human. Many women in the shelter had not read classical literature, but had learned the literary tales through oral transmission. Some had received formal education in these texts or had acquired it through personal effort. "Shirin and Farhad" and "Laila and Majnun" were written by the Persian poet Nizami Ganjavi (1141–1209).

2. Andre Vélter's reading of how Majrouh understood Pashtun women is nuanced through ethnographic fieldwork.

3. For a slightly different perspective that nonetheless does not allow Pashtun women to escape the purported all-encompassing explanatory framework of honor, see Boesen (1980).

4. Andre Vélter notes that landay as collected by Majrouh are not influenced by Persian (Majrouh 2003, x). The reason for this could be that Majrouh collected landay in Peshawar, where most Afghan refugees were Pashto speaking. At the khana-yi aman, the verses were intertextual, with many cross-references between Pashto and Persian, not surprising given the constant interaction between the speakers of the two languages.

5. Embodiment and piety have been written about in the Islamic context in detail. For an understanding of piety and embodiment in the Muslim context, see, for example, Mahmood (2005), Deeb (2006), Scott (2010), and Ahmed (2011).

6. Cole's chapter on women's lives under the Taliban is one of the best theoretical engagements with this issue. He explicates how the Taliban reshaped the public and private divide through their gender policies. Here Cole (2008, 149–50) quotes Zoya from her book *Zoya's Story* (Follain and Cristofari 2002).

7. The *Taliban Official Gazette*, article 4, fatawa no. 12 and 13. These fatawa are promulgated by Vizarat-e amr bil ma'ruf va nahi 'anil munkar (Ministry of Promotion of Virtue and Prevention of Vice). The author retrieved the *Gazette* from the Library of Congress, and it is on file with her.

8. There is debate about the authenticity of these hadith, which circulate among women through oral transmission. These are not cited to specific sources, but are invoked in public and private conversation. Another popular hadith is that if Allah had allowed a woman to prostrate before anyone else but him, it would be her husband. Also, a hadith I heard narrated was that a wife did not have the right to refuse sexual intercourse with her husband. One woman told me, "Angels curse such a woman all night who has refused sexual intercourse with her husband." This complicates the understanding of what constitutes marital rape, or whether such a category exists, given the wife's sexual obligation toward her husband.

9. I explicate the ethical formations of honor and pashtunwali in Chapter Six and show how the realms of ethics, morals, and politics manifest in Afghanistan. Mahmood (2005) describes the Foucauldian incarnation of ethical formations "as particularly helpful for conceptualizing agency beyond the confines of the binary model of enacting and subverting norms" (29).

10. Abu-Lughod (1986) notes that ghinnawa "concerns the relationship between the Bedouin poetic discourse and the discourse of ordinary social life" (32). Her understanding of discourse is inspired by her reading of Foucault (275n23).

11. The notion of 'agl circulates in Persian as 'aql.

12. In Khattak's poetry, I have translated *nafs* as "self," which could be construed to signify one's desires or one's passions.

13. See Mahmood (2005) for a discussion of the concept of shyness or *al-haya* as an alternative path toward agentival action through embodiment. This alternative path toward agency depends on repetitive bodily gestures such as veiling or prayer (157–158). See also Abu-Lughod's (1986) description of the concept of *hasham* or modesty as an alternative path for women toward honor (105–108).

14. Mahmood (2005). In this section of her book, Mahmood builds on but also departs from Butler's theory of performativity and shows the difference between the drag queen and the veiled woman in inhabiting their respective normative structures (164).

15. Griswold (2014, 3) notes that landay commonly have twenty-two syllables.

16. Gulalei noted that surah 97, called al-Qadr (The Majesty) of the Quran, states that worship on the night of al-Qadr is better than a thousand months. However, she pointed out that the exact night on which it falls is not certain. Various traditions attribute certain nights with a higher likelihood of being al-Qadr. In Afghanistan it is popularly believed that this night falls on odd-numbered nights in the last ten days of Ramazan, of which the night of the twenty-seventh day has the highest likelihood. A belief that many women share is that on this night they have a higher chance of being heard by Allah.

17. For a particular permutation of subjecthood that inaugurates in violence or death, see the essay by Achille Mbembe (2003).

18. Majrouh (2003, 14–15) as adapted and introduced by Andre Vélter.

19. Singing is permitted because of gender segregation at weddings and other occasions. Women sit in their separate quarters and can sing and dance. Rarely would foreigners or men be allowed in these spaces.

20. Griswold (2014, 7) includes this popular landay but does not describe in detail the

significance of the cornstalk in relation to virility, perhaps to protect the narrator.

21. These Pashto curses are not different from their American variations, in which references are made to sexual intercourse with mothers and sisters.

22. Julia Kristeva (1980) adapted Bakhtin's ideas of dialogism to feminist literary studies specifically in her development of the idea of intertextuality.

23. Griswold (2014, 5) claims, "Women singers are viewed as prostitutes. Women get around this by singing in secret—in front of only close family or, say, a harmless-looking foreign woman." This is a rather harsh condemnation. Women do sing at weddings and other occasions, and it is too simple to say that singing is linked to prostitution. It depends on the occasion. Also, the specific singing witnessed by Griswold may have been purely a performance for a foreign white gaze.

24. Geertz's 1973 essay is integral to understanding the Geertzian notion of "thick description," which uses semiotics to analyze "deep play," a phrase that comes from Jeremy Bentham.

25. This Quranic verse is very popular among married couples, women, and families. It is often invoked in poetry, prose, and literature. The clothing is interpreted not just as a reference to sexual relations but to forming protection and support between couples and their families. Here is the relevant portion, in surah al-Baqarah (The Cow), 2:187. "It has been made permissible for you the night preceding fasting to go to your wives [for sexual relations]. They are clothing for you and you are clothing for them" (see the Quranic Arabic Corpus, http://corpus.quran.com/translation.jsp?chapter=2&verse=187). Various permutations of these verses circulate among ordinary Afghans.

26. Scholars dispute the authenticity of this popular hadith, but it circulates among women, who often call their husbands *majazi khuda* (God on earth).

27. The laws of inheritance originate in Quranic verses, but are interpreted and applied differently across various Muslim societies. For a detailed arithmetic of inheritance in Islamic law with special attention to women, see Ali (2010) and Khan (2008).

28. Majrouh (2003, 16). Here Majrouh is saying that men must become worthy of their mother's love by performing battles. This is similar to Khadim's understanding of motherhood in *Pashtunwali*.

29. Das (2007, 5) notes, "fragments allude to a particular way of inhabiting the world."

30. David B. Edwards noted on an earlier version of this chapter that landay must be included in a theory of promiscuity. I am grateful for his guidance and his own thoughtful writings on Afghanistan.

31. Pierre Bourdieu (1992) uses the analogy of a game that one is not born into but that one learns as one acquires a mother tongue.

32. Kogacioglu (2004) uses Foucaldian theory of power networks to show how tradition congeals as an effect of power post-killing in honor crimes in Turkey.

33. Talal Asad's work is the most comprehensive analysis of tradition and modernity; see Asad (1993, 2003, 2009). See also Mitchell (2000), whose work on modernity is cited extensively by Deeb (2006).

34. Deeb (2006) discusses authenticated Islam as a form of embodied piety, which is enacted through practices of veiling, prayer, not handshaking, and so on. But these "traditional" practices form part of the modernity of the Al-Dahiyya Lebanese community (99–128). Deeb states that public piety is an expression of the commitment of religious obligation (34).

35. Abu-Lughod (2013) has written extensively against the scholarship that shows Afghan women as passive recipients of tradition. See also Hirschkind and Mahmood (2002).

36. For a discussion of the emancipatory and regulatory possibilities of gender differentiation in Iranian modernity, see Najmabadi (2005).

Chapter Four

1. There was a bed in one of the rooms reserved for special occasions and special women. I saw that bed used on only one occasion and for a very special occupant: Nurzia, the female representative of the government from Nangarhar province.). She is now in hiding.

2. For an excellent discussion of how democracy and totalitarianism are intertwined in a historical context see Arendt (1958, 1966).

3. Noah Coburn has written extensively on the topic of interventionist politics. See, for example, Coburn (2016). See also Lila Abu-Lughod's (2013) pivotal work on gender and interventionist politics.

4. The role of this ministry is similar to Hisba in Saudi Arabia and Gasht-e-Ershad in Iran. These governmental bodies are given the role of policing moral behavior in the public through close surveillance mechanisms, such as checking the proper length of women's headscarves and the identification documents of couples to ensure they are legally married. For a comprehensive study of the notion of "commanding right and forbidding wrong" in Islam, see Cook (2000).

5. Yoshinobu Nagamine (2015) notes the ideological diversity of the Taliban, and gives a detailed analysis of layeha code.

6. Gulalei and other women had an impressive memory of Quranic verses, and were very well versed in Quran, sunnah, and hadith. Here is the complete surah that Gulalei cited on this day, the surah an-Nisa: "Indeed, those whom the angels take [in death] while wronging themselves—[the angels] will say, 'In what [condition] were you?' They will say, 'We were oppressed in the land.' The angels will say, 'Was not the earth of Allah spacious [enough] for you to emigrate therein?' For those, their refuge is Hell—and evil it is as a destination" (see the Quranic Arabic Corpus, http://corpus.quran.com/translation.jsp?chapter=4&verse=97).

7. Scholars have narrated the story of Hajra in different ways. Some have interpreted it to say that she ran away after disputes arose between her and Ibrahim's first wife, Sarah. The Quran does not mention Hajra by name, but alludes to Ibrahim having settled his family in a barren desert. Her story is very popular among Afghans and is often narrated in social gatherings.

8. As noted in the text, Majid's article appeared in *Shariat*, December 18, 1995. Copies of this article and the others cited in this book are on file with the author. These newspapers can be accessed via the website of the Afghanistan Center at Kabul University (https://acku.edu.af/2018/09/18/acku-rare-newspaper-collection/). These newspapers use both Pashto and Dari in their columns. I thank Nazif Mohib and Abdul Waheed Wafa for their assistance in locating these publications. I thank Roya and Professors Saeed and Anwar for discussing these primary sources with me and raising thoughtful questions.

9. (R) and (S) are Islamic honorifics used for the Prophet and his companions.

10. Cole's (2008) chapter on the Taliban is worth reading to understand how he compares the Taliban's governance to Western notions of the public sphere, specifically those of Habermas and Hegel.

11. For Foucault's notion of governmentality and how it connects with torture, see particularly his discussion of the panopticon in *Discipline and Punish* (1975) and also his

lectures (2003, 2007, 2008), which were delivered in the late 1970s.

12. As noted earlier, the Taliban fatawa are compiled in the *Taliban Official Gazette*, which the author found at the Library of Congress. A copy is on file with her. *Taliban Official Gazette: Instruments, Recommendations, Messages, Orders, and Decrees of the Ministry of the Promotion of Virtue and Prevention of Vice*, September 4, 2001.

13. Although public spectacles of corporal punishment in Afghanistan are not new and have been documented during the reign of the Iron Amir, King 'Abdur Rahman (r. 1880–1901), the Taliban revolutionized public spectacles of corporal punishment. For a detailed litany of Taliban punishments, see Cole (2008).

14. Note that the Taliban distinguish themselves from those who are in the guise of Taliban and use the name for nefarious ends, as noted by Nagamine (2015). This is the reason for developing and adhering to elaborate codes of conduct, such as layeha and pashtunwali. Paradoxically, however, the stonings are owned by the Taliban and approved by other like-minded individuals (which include both men and women).

15. To read an account of how feminist solidarities may manifest across national borders through common anticapitalist struggles, see Mohanty (2003).

16. See also Mahmood's discussion of gender performativity, where she contrasts Butler's example of the drag queen with the Egyptian pious *hijabi* woman. Mahmood notes that for Butler, the excellence of the drag queen's performativity and imitation of the dominant heteronormative gender system demonstrates its vulnerability and claims to originality. By contrast, the excellence of the veiled woman consolidates the Islamic system (Mahmood 2005, 164).

17. See, for example, Lila Abu-Lughod's discussion (2013, 9) of how the blue burqa is shown in a formless and homogenous fashion in Western media, eradicating the Afghan woman in it.

18. Nagamine (2015, 13) notes the ideological diversity of the Taliban in his book, where he includes stories of origination of the Taliban that are more rooted in justice than in violence.

19. The Taliban violated international law by taking Najibullah from a United Nations safe house where he had lived since 1992. Mutilation of a dead body is against Islamic principles and Pashtun norms.

20. Many of the Taliban's rulings were directly antithetical to Islamic principles. For example, Islamic jurisprudence has robust mechanisms for wife-initiated divorce and female inheritance of property. Although women have many rights afforded in Islamic law, even educated Muslim women in Afghanistan have a tremendously difficult time accessing those rights enshrined in Islamic law.

21. The Taliban has made a peace deal with the United States in which the United States has agreed to withdraw all troops within fourteen months. "Afghan Conflict: US and Taliban Sign Deal to End 18-Year War." BBC News, February 29, 2020. https://www.bbc.com/news/world-asia-51689443. See also the details of this peace deal on the US Department of State website: https://www.state.gov/wp-content/uploads/2020/02/Agreement-For-Bringing-Peace-to-Afghanistan-02.29.20.pdf.

22. Shia–Sunni tension has existed in Afghanistan, as Islamic practice has never been homogenous. Still, Islam remains a binding entity. Barfield (2010) states that Islam serves as basis of unity, a form of glue in Afghanistan.

23. As I write this, the American government is in renewed negotiations with the Taliban in Afghanistan, while many women's rights groups are showing concern about these

arbitrations. This time some women were allowed to be part of negotiations with the Taliban. See Ferguson (2019) and Natarajan (2020).

24. Devji (2005) discusses the audacity of donning the Prophet's cloak or mantle and the blatant disregard that this shows for Islamic values on the part of the Taliban.

25. Although the Taliban are the most memorable Afghan leaders to invoke the caliphate, the title Amir was used for previous Afghan rulers such as Amanullah (r. 1926–29) and Nadir Shah (r. 1736–47).

26. Also see Mapping Militant Organizations. 2018. "Afghan Taliban." Stanford University. Last modified June 2018. https://cisac.fsi.stanford.edu/mappingmilitants/profiles/afghan-taliban.

27. In the UAE and Saudi Arabia, local citizens make up less than 50 percent of the total population. The population that enjoys citizenship is predominantly Muslim.

28. Mahmood (2005, 76–78) defines the Egyptian state as secular-liberal a label not clearly applicable then or now.

29. Non-Pashtuns made up a portion of the Soviet resistance exemplified in such leaders as Ahmad Shah Masud.

30. The four main schools (*mazhab*) of Sunni Islamic thought are Hanafi, Maliki, Hanbali, Shafi'i.

31. This Taliban self-conception ignores some historical facts. The People's Democratic Party of Afghanistan (PDPA) had Pashtun members who fought alongside the Soviets. When it comes to ideology, Pashtuns range from conservative Islamic to modernist secular camps, but the Taliban remap these complex histories of Pashtun allegiances along ethnic and Islamic lines.

32. For a discussion of how Muslims have been categorized as good and bad, see Mamdani (2004). A significant difference between Afghanistan and other colonized spaces is that Afghanistan did not endure direct colonial foreign rule. Many local rulers instituted brutal ethnic policies against the Hazarajat, who have suffered tremendously through discriminatory policies. For a discussion of how power operates in colonized spaces to reify ethnic conflict, see Mamdani (1996, 2001).

33. Inside the United States, saving Afghan women was a popular narrative to justify the war in Afghanistan; inside Afghanistan, the Soviets are linked to the de-veiling of women, as is evident in the Taliban newspaper columns that mention the woes of communism. For a detailed analysis of the Soviet Union's governing strategies toward Muslim women, see, for example, Massell (1974).

34. There is no reliable data to support that rape incidence went down because of draconian punishment, but this remains a popular perception

35. Cole (2008, 118) notes that he uses the term *Islamic counter-modernity* "because the Taliban adopted some key motifs from high modernism and depended on modern techniques for their power (the state, radio, mass spectacle, tank corps, and machine guns mounted on Toyotas)." However, as Cole notes, these modern tools were employed toward other, different ends, which led to a different public and private divide in Taliban Afghanistan.

36. Herzfeld's (2002) notion of cryptocolonialism can be usefully applied to Afghanistan.

37. Feldman (2012) notes that the elimination of the historical central role of the Islamic *ulema* (Islamic religious scholars) by the rulers has led to the derailing of democracy in most Muslim societies.

38. See Foucault (2003, 2007, 2008) for a discussion of history and episteme.

39. The closest analogue in the present is the Islamic State movement (ISIS), which includes a similarly fraught logic of female citizenship.

40. Although some of the punishments instituted by the Taliban for sexual misbehavior are not particularly new or unique to Afghanistan, the way in which the Taliban deployed print and radio media (as evident in the Taliban newspapers and Shariat radio) to create a pious audience sets the Taliban apart.

Chapter Five

1. Sadaf's story was first introduced in Chapter Two, "Portraits of Pain."

2. For a historical account of analogous feminist processes, see, for example, Najmabadi (2005), especially her chapters "Crafting an Educated Wife and Mother" and "Vatan, the Beloved; Vatan, the Mother." Najmabadi argues that the ostensibly contradictory impulses of regulation and emancipation in fact reinforced each other to produce the modern Iranian woman in the twentieth century (183).

3. See the works of Asad (1993, 2003) to understand modern genealogies of religion and secularism. Hirschkind (2006) demonstrates how modern technologies such as cassette sermons shape counterpublics in Egypt. See also Mahmood (2005).

4. For discussions of Pashto literature, see Green and Arbabzadeh (2012) and Caron (2017).

5. Khushal Khattak's poems were compiled by Yar Muhammad Maghmoom Khattak, published in 2016.

6. See Mahmood (2005), especially the chapter "Pedagogies of Persuasion," in which she argues that classical notions of Islamic piety are reinvigorated with modernity.

7. Amanullah married Soraya after the death of his first wife. Soraya's father was a prominent literary figure, and she remained Amanullah's only wife thereafter—at least this is the public perception of Amanullah and Soraya, regardless of the intimacies of their private lives.

8. Unlike 'Abdur Rahman, who directed his reforms at the mullahs, Amanullah and Soraya employed a different strategy.

9. Motherhood is a classic theme in the Arab and Ottoman worlds, which extended to the whole Muslim world.

10. This is verse 55 from surah 20 of the Quran, called surah Taha.

11. Nawid (1999, 47) has translated *vatan* as "fatherland," but based on my reading of Khadim's Pashto and Tarzi's Persian writings, and also Najamabadi's analogous history in Iran, I note that *vatan* in Afghanistan came to be defined in the twentieth century as a (female religious) homeland. Also see Schinasi (1979) for another context.

12. As quoted in Nawid (1999, 48).

13. For discussion of an analogous intellectual project in Egypt, see Booth (2001).

14. The term *honor killing* has been analyzed by various scholars of honor. Lila Abu-Lughod cautions us against reading honor killings as the "behavior of a specific ethnic or cultural community" (2013, 114). See also Ewing (2008), Appiah (2010), and Jafri (2008).

15. This may be an oblique reference to the son of Dost Mohammad Khan (r. 1839–63).

16. For a translation of some of these texts, see Metcalf (1990).

17. For information about the ethical and historical lineages of the Taliban, and discussion of their rise to power in Afghanistan, see Devji (2005), Cole (2008), Edwards (1996,

2002, 2017), Crews (2008, 2015), Rashid (2010), and Shahrani (2008).

18. As noted in Chapter Six, "Subject of Honor," anthropological critiques of feminism have enabled us to think beyond the binaries of structure and agency, oppression and resistance.

19. *Akhlaq* is the singular, *akhlaqiat* the plural.

20. For a discussion of the relationship between the Taliban and pashtunwali, and between the Taliban and layeha code, see Nagamine (2015).

21. In this and other portions, Thanawi criticizes non-Islamic customs related to widowhood, such as sati (widow burning), and sets up a dichotomy between Hindu and Muslim women. These differences gradually congealed as irreconcilable in the writings of contemporary intellectuals such as Allama Iqbal, who had a major influence on Amanullah, Tarzi, Khadim, and Afghan intellectuals.

22. For an excellent discussion of how didactic texts become linked to grids of intelligibility (particularly via the violence of colonialism), see Mani (1998).

23. Mani (1998) suggests that misunderstanding of sati and local scripture by the colonial powers exacerbated the practice of sati.

24. "Send them to the capital" is worth noting. The state wants to take responsibility of the tribal or unruly elements, where other forms of retribution could be expected. As we saw in the case of Sadaf and many other women at the khana-yi aman, they had all run away from provinces to the capital. During my fieldwork, I attended a training for female parliamentarians and asked them their thoughts on the khana-yi aman. Almost all said that they wanted to expand shelters to their own cities so that their women did not run away to the capital, outside the jurisdiction of the provinces.

25. Here I mean social contract as enacted in Afghanistan, which has different rules than its Western counterparts.

26. For a detailed discussion of sexual slavery in Islam, see Ali (2010). For discussion of the historical oppression of the Hazaras, see Ibrahimi (2017) and Nawid (1999).

27. For more detail about moon-faced boys, see McChesney and Khorammi (2012, 2:138–39, 279).

28. The text contains the complete story. "The Murder of Qazi Shihab al-Din Khan Jawanshayr and One of His Nawkars" narrates that the "qazi had performed an indecent act of sodomy on his master" (McChesney and Khorammi (2012, 3:573).

29. Najmabadi (13). Najmabadi has an excellent discussion of how modernity narrowed conceptions of masculinity. The advent of modernity limited the scripts of masculinity and disallowed certain forms of being masculine (such as being young and moon faced).

30. See Frances Pritchett, http://www.columbia.edu/itc/mealac/pritchett/oourdu/iqbal/aurat.html.

31. Ibid.

32. Frances Pritchett, a former Urdu professor at Columbia University, has translated many of Iqbal's poems and built a website worth visiting: http://www.columbia.edu/itc/mealac/pritchett/oourdu/iqbal/aurat.html.

33. Foucault has written extensively on the nexus of power, knowledge, and resistance. See especially his lectures of 1975–76 (2003) and 1977–78 (2007).

Chapter Six

1. For example, Mani (1998, 36) discusses the descriptive and heterogeneous nature of Hindu texts that the colonials misread as prescriptive and normative. The centralization impe-

tus of the British colonial rule consolidated polyvalent traditions into singular laws that did not reflect the true meaning of the scripture. See also Spivak (2010).

2. Mahmood (2005) appropriates the notion of askesis as ethical self-fashioning from Foucault and Aristotle. For Mahmood, ethical self-fashioning through embodiment of piety in acts of shyness, modesty, and veiling demonstrates a possibility of agentival action and even political change.

3. She used the term *yakh*, which translates literally as "ice" or "very cold."

4. This reading of honor is indebted to the various governing modalities of power extrapolated by the philosopher Michel Foucault. Notwithstanding the various historical and social differences in the histories of Europe and Afghanistan, honor, as it functions in Afghanistan, particularly in how it shapes gender relations through various governing modalities, can be read in terms of the power apparatuses of sovereignty, discipline, and biopower.

5. Ali (2010, 100) notes, "By defining husbands' duty as dividing time among wives, rather than as spending time with wives, polygyny became the norm and monogamy the exception."

6. Ali's book (2010) covers all four schools of Islamic jurisprudence and, through close readings of classical texts, shows the similarities between them with respect to gender and sexuality.

7. As noted earlier in the book, 'iddat or edat is the mandatory waiting period after a divorce or death of a husband, which a woman must complete, before she can marry another man. The main purpose of this waiting period is to establish that the woman is not pregnant with the first husband's child. 'Iddat times vary depending on the pregnancy or breastfeeding status of the wife. For missing-husband cases, the courts must rule that the husband is dead after a significant waiting period has been completed.

8. The literal translation from Pashto is "What can we say? Allah will take an account of their actions."

9. For an analogous discussion of social chaos (fitna) in a Muslim society, see Abu-Lughod (1986, 144). Fitna is variously translated as chaos, disturbance, disorder, or trouble. It implies disruption of moral and social order.

10. *Haya* and *hasham* both mean modesty. In Afghanistan, modesty is often referred to as *haya* or *sharm*.

11. "*Khuruj* is a competitive practice in that one's family's place in the community—their honour—must continually be recognized by regular visits from those with whom one has connections" (Meneley 1996, 41).

12. See Wide (2012) for a brief mention of this story.

13. In this book, Irigaray critiques Freud and Lacan, saying that there is no space in their conception of the symbolic for an actual female imaginary. In other words, Lacanian and Freudian models are insufficient, in Irigaray's view, to account for a true depiction of the feminine.

14. Here the word *khazunke* is used, which may literally be translated as "like a *khaza* [woman]."

15. In linguistic anthropology, the notion of felicity is influenced by Austin (1975). There are some conditions that must be met in order for words to be felicitous.

16. Das (2007) observes that a problem of ethnographic investigation is the study of an event as an individual and collective. And thus the relation between an event and the everyday is local or localizing (135). This means that an ethnographer must be attentive to the everyday practices as well as the historical context of the everyday practices.

17. For an account of how power positions populations differentially, see Foucault's (2003, 2007, 2008) later lectures, delivered in the late 1970s.

18. For Gramsci (1971), hegemony involves both consensus and coercion and reduces the frequency of violence by creating willing subjects. Pashtunwali is hegemonic in the Gramscian sense that it has created the subject of honor as fundamental to being Afghan. Not just Pashtuns but non-Pashtuns frequently invoke the notion of honor.

19. For details on how consent is manufactured, see Herman and Chomsky (1988) and Bourdieu (1992).

20. See Foucault (2007, 207–208). Foucault has noted that there is a profound difference between "structures of obedience" and "structures of ascetism." Ascetism, he says, is "clearly incompatible with pastoral structure that . . . involves permanent obedience, renunciation of the will, and only of the will, and the deployment of the individual's conduct in the world." He goes on to say that "ascetism stifles obedience through the excess of prescriptions and challenges that the individual addresses to himself." For Foucault, ascetism carries "specific excess that denies access to an external power." In other words, askesis would require a rejection of external authority and systems of obedience and conformation. In this sense, the khana-yi aman women are practicing askesis because their sexual actions defy and disobey the sexual ethics of Islam and pashtunwali.

21. Melmastia is connected with hujra. Melmastia can be translated as hospitality or taking care of guests. Hujra is a guest house that allows for homosocial bonding among men through guest-hosting practices. Both melmastia and hujra are connected with nanawatai (refuge) and panah (sanctuary). These concepts are fundamental to an understanding of the khana-yi aman as a place for sheltering runaway women.

22. Askesis and its relation to ethical self-fashioning is detailed in Foucault's lectures delivered in late 1970s. See Foucault (2003, 2007, 2008).

23. Foucault (2019) has conducted a detailed study of the ancient concept of parresia.

24. Heidegger's notion of *dasein*, from the German "to be," "being," or "life," has a directionality, spatiality, and temporality.

Conclusion

1. The quotation here is from the original version of this essay (Spivak 1988), republished in 2010 in *Can the Subaltern Speak? Reflections on the History of an Idea*, edited by Rosalind Morris, 21–79. Morris's volume includes a revision of this essay, in which Spivak took this sentence out, as it has been misconstrued as saying that the subaltern did not have a voice.

2. In 2010, Rosalind Morris invited several intellectuals, including Spivak herself and Partha Chatterjee, to reflect on this essay in the edited volume cited in the previous note. In this version of her famous essay (which has been written in a few other iterations), Spivak discusses Bhubaneswar Bhudari in detail in a response to her original essay.

3. In the chapter titled "Sisterhood, Coalition, and the Politics of Experience" (106–123) in her book *Feminism without Borders*, Mohanty (2003) details the problems underlying the popular notion of "universal sisterhood." For Mohanty this notion creates a homogenous category of women and obscures the violence of imperialism.

4. Hangama is an extremely common Afghan name for women. In fact, even the artist for the cover of this book is named Hangama. Why are Afghan baby girls given this name at birth and then expected later to conform? It is an interesting social paradox to highlight in this context.

5. For two inspirational works on suffering in the margins, see Biehl (2005) and Gandhi (2006).

References

Abu-Lughod, Lila. 1986. *Veiled Sentiments: Honor and Poetry in a Bedouin Society.* Berkeley: University of California Press.

———. 1990. "The Romance of Resistance: Tracing Transformations of Power through Bedouin Women." *American Ethnologist* 17 (1): 41–55.

———. 1993. *Writing Women's Worlds: Bedouin Stories.* Berkeley: University of California Press.

———. 2010. "The Active Social Life of 'Muslim Women's Rights': A Plea for Ethnography, Not Polemic, with Cases from Egypt and Palestine." *Journal of Middle East Women's Studies* 6 (1): 1–45.

———. 2013. *Do Muslim Women Need Saving?* Cambridge: Harvard University Press.

Afghanistan Legal Education Project. 1977. *Civil Code of the Republic of Afghanistan of 1977.* Translated by Afghanistan Legal Education Project. https://www-cdn.law.stanford.edu/wp-content/uploads/2015/10/Civil-Code-of-Afghanistan-ALEP-Translation.pdf.

Ahmadi, Wali. 2008. *Modern Persian Literature in Afghanistan: Anomalous Visions of History and Form.* New York: Routledge.

Ahmed, Leila. 1992. *Women and Gender in Islam.* New Haven, CT: Yale University Press.

———. 2011. *A Quiet Revolution: The Veil's Resurgence from the Middle East to America.* New Haven, CT: Yale University Press.

Ahsan, Sonia. 2017. "When Muslims Become Feminists: The Khana-yi aman, Islam, and Pashtunwali in Afghanistan." In *Afghanistan Islam: From Conversion to Taliban*, edited by Nile Green, 225–41. Berkeley: University of California Press.

———. 2018. "Engendering the Taliban: A History of Women's Rights in Afghanistan." In *Revolutions and Rebellions in Afghanistan: Anthropological Perspectives. Volume 2*, edited by Nazif Shahrani, 200–12. Bloomington: University of Indiana Press.

Ali, Kecia. 2010. *Marriage and Slavery in Early Islam.* Cambridge, MA: Harvard University Press.

Althusser, Louis. 1971. "Ideology and Ideological State Apparatuses." In *Lenin and Philosophy and Other Essays*. Translated by Ben Brewster, 121–176. New York: Monthly Review Press.

Appiah, Kwame Anthony. 2010. *Honor Code: How Moral Revolutions Happen.* New York: Norton.

Arendt, Hannah. 1958. *The Human Condition.* Chicago: University of Chicago Press.

———. 1966. *The Origins of Totalitarianism.* New York: Harvest Books.

Asad, Talal. 1993. *Genealogies of Religion: Discipline and Reasons of Power in Christianity and Islam.* Baltimore, MD: Johns Hopkins University Press.

———. 2003. *Formations of the Secular: Christianity, Islam, Modernity*. Stanford, CA: Stanford University Press.

———. 2004. "Where Are the Margins of the State?" In *Anthropology in the Margins of the State*, edited by Veena Das and Deborah Poole, 279–88. Santa Fe, NM: School of American Research Press.

———. 2009. "The Idea of an Anthropology of Islam." *Qui Parle* 17 (2): 1–30. doi:10.5250/quiparle.17.2.1.

Austin, J. L. 1975. *How to Do Things with Words*. 2nd ed. Cambridge, MA: Harvard University Press.

Bakhtin, Mikhail Mikhailovich. 1983. *The Dialogic Imagination: Four Essays*. Austin: University of Texas Press.

Balibar, Etienne. 1978. "From Bachelard to Althusser: The Concept of 'Epistemological Break.'" *Economy and Society* 7 (3), 207–237.

Barfield, Thomas. 2003. "Afghan Customary Law and Its Relationship to Formal Judicial Institutions." Washington, DC: United States Institute of Peace. https://www.usip.org/sites/default/files/file/barfield2.pdf.

———. 2008. "Culture and Custom in Nation-Building: Law in Afghanistan." *Maine Law Review* 60:347–373. Available at https://digitalcommons.mainelaw.maine.edu/mlr/vol60/iss2/7.

———. 2010. *Afghanistan: A Cultural and Political History*. Princeton, NJ: Princeton University Press.

Barth, Fredrik. 1959. *Political Leadership among Swat Pathans*. London: Athlone Press.

BBC News. 2012. "Lal Bibi Rape: Afghan Policemen Sentenced to 16 Years." November 7, 2012. https://www.bbc.com/news/world-asia-20239567.

———. 2015. "Afghan Woman Accused of Adultery Is Stoned to Death." November 3, 2015. https://www.bbc.com/news/world-asia-34714205.

———. 2020. "Who Are the Taliban." February 27, 2020. https://www.bbc.com/news/world-south-asia-11451718.

Beauvoir, Simone de. 2011. *The Second Sex*. New York: Vintage Books. First published 1949.

Bersani, Leo. 1995. *Homos*. Cambridge: Harvard University Press.

Bezhan, Faridullah. 2016. *Women, War and Islamic Radicalisation in Maryam Mahboob's Afghanistan*. Melbourne: Monash University Publisher.

Biehl, João. 2005. *Vita: Life in a Zone of Social Abandonment*. Berkeley: University of California Press.

Billaud, Julie. 2015. *Kabul Carnival: Gender Politics in Postwar Afghanistan*. Philadelphia: University of Pennsylvania Press.

Boesen, Inger W. 1980. "Women, Honour and Love: Some Aspects of the Pashtun Woman's Life in Eastern Afghanistan." *Folk* 21–22:229–39.

Booth, Marilyn. 2001. *May Her Likes Be Multiplied: Biography and Gender Politics in Egypt*. Berkeley: University of California Press.

Bourdieu, Pierre. 1992. *The Logic of Practice*. Stanford, CA: Stanford University Press.

Bradiotti, Rose. 2011. *Nomadic Subjects: Embodiment and Sexual Difference in Contemporary Feminist Theory*. 2nd ed. New York: Columbia University Press.

———. 2012. *Nomadic Theory: The Portable Rosi Bradiotti*. New York: Columbia University Press.

Burki, Shireen K. 2013. *The Politics of State Intervention: Gender Politics in Pakistan,*

Afghanistan and Iran. Plymouth, UK: Lexington Books.

Butler, Judith. 1988. "Performative Acts and Gender Constitution: An Essay in Phenomenology and Feminist Theory." *Theatre Journal* 40 (4): 519–31.

———. 1990. *Gender Trouble: Feminism and the Subversion of Identity.* New York: Routledge.

———. 1993. *Bodies That Matter. On the Discursive Limits of "Sex."* London: Routledge.

———. 2004. *Precarious Life: The Powers of Mourning and Violence.* New York: Verso.

———. 2009. "Performativity, Precarity and Sexual Politics." Lecture given at Universidad Complutense de Madrid, June 8, 2009. https://www.aibr.org/antropologia/04v03/criticos/040301b.pdf.

Caron, James. 2017. *A History of Pashto Literature: Or, Pashto Histories in the World.* London: Hurst.

Chiovenda, Andrea. 2019. *Crafting Masculine Selves.* Oxford: Oxford University Press.

Chotiner, Isaac. 2019. "A Women's-Rights Activist Is Concerned about Negotiations with the Taliban." *New Yorker*, April 2019. https://www.newyorker.com/news/q-and-a/a-womens-rights-activist-is-concerned-about-negotiations-with-the-taliban.

Coburn, Noah. 2011. *Bazaar Politics: Power and Pottery in an Afghan Market Town.* Stanford, CA: Stanford University Press.

———. 2016. *Losing Afghanistan: An Obituary for the Intervention.* Stanford, CA: Stanford University Press.

Coburn, Noah, and Anna Larson. 2013. *Derailing Democracy in Afghanistan: Elections in an Unstable Political Landscape.* New York: Columbia University Press.

Cole, Juan. 2008. "The Taliban, Women, and the Hegelian Private Sphere." In *The Taliban and the Crisis of Afghanistan*, edited by Robert Crews, 118–54. Cambridge, MA: Harvard University Press.

Cook, Michael. 2000. *Commanding Right and Forbidding Wrong in Islamic Thought.* Cambridge, UK: Cambridge University Press.

Crews, Robert. 2015. *Afghan Modern: The History of a Global Nation.* Cambridge, MA: Harvard University Press.

Crews, Robert, and Amin Tarzi, eds. 2008. *The Taliban and the Crisis of Afghanistan.* Cambridge, MA: Harvard University Press.

Damon, Arwa. 2011. Afghan Women Speak out on Abuse from behind Mask. CNN. http://www.cnn.com/2011/WORLD/asiapcf/01/03/afghanistan.mask/index.html.

Das, Veena. 2007. *Life and Words: Violence and Descent into the Ordinary.* Berkeley: University of California Press.

Deeb, Lara. 2006. *An Enchanted Modern: Gender and Public Piety in Shi'i Lebanon.* Princeton, NJ: Princeton University Press.

Devji, Faisal. 2005. *Landscapes of the Jihad: Militancy, Morality, Modernity.* Ithaca, NY: Cornell University Press.

Doumato, Eleanor, and Gregory Starrett, eds. 2007. *Teaching Islam: Textbooks and Religion in the Middle East.* Boulder, CO, and London: Lynne Rienner Publishers.

Dupree, Nancy. 1984. "Revolutionary Rhetoric and Afghan Women." In *Revolutions and Rebellions in Afghanistan*, edited by M. Nazif Shahrani and Robert L. Canfield, 306–39. Berkeley: University of California Press.

Edwards, David. 1996. *Heroes of the Age.* Berkeley: University of California Press.

———. 2002. *Before Taliban: Genealogies of the Afghan Jihad.* Berkeley: University of California Press.

———. 2017. *Caravan of Martyrs: Sacrifice and Suicide Bombing in Afghanistan*. Berkeley: University of California Press.

Eickelman, Dale F., and Jon W. Anderson, eds. 1999. *New Media in the Muslim World: The Emerging Public Sphere*. Bloomington: Indiana University Press.

Emadi, Hafizullah. 2002. *Repression, Resistance, and Women in Afghanistan*. Westport, CT: Praeger.

Ewing, Katherine Pratt. 2008. *Stolen Honor: Stigmatizing Muslim Men in Berlin*. Stanford, CA: Stanford University Press.

Fanon, Frantz. 1963. *Wretched of the Earth*. Translated by Richard Philcox. New York: Grove Press.

———. 1967. *Black Skin, White Masks*. Translated by Charles Lam Markmann. New York: Grove Press. First published 1952.

Feldman, Noah. 2012. *The Fall and Rise of the Islamic State*. Princeton, NJ: Princeton University Press.

Ferguson, Jane. 2019. "Peace Talks, the Taliban, and Afghan Women's Uncertain Future." *New Yorker*. https://www.newyorker.com/news/dispatch/peace-talks-the-taliban-and-afghan-womens-uncertain-future.

Follian, John, and Rita Cristofari. 2003. *Zoya's Story: An Afghan Woman's Struggle for Freedom*. New York: Harper Perennial.

Foucault, Michel. 1965. *Madness and Civilization*. New York: Random House.

———. 1972. *Archaeology of Knowledge: And the Discourse on Language*. New York: Random House.

———. 1975. *Discipline and Punish: The Birth of the Prison*, 2nd ed. Translated by Alan Sheridan. 2d ed. New York: Random House.

———. 1978. *History of Sexuality: An Introduction*. New York: Vintage.

———. 2003. *Society Must Be Defended: Lectures at the College de France, 1975–1976*. Translated by David Macey. New York: St. Martin's Press.

———. 2007. *Security, Territory, Population: Lectures at College de France, 1977–1978*. Translated by Graham Burchell. New York: Palgrave Macmillan.

———. 2008. *The Birth of Biopolitics: Lectures at College de France, 1978–1998*. Translated by Graham Burchell. New York: Palgrave Macmillan.

———. 2019. *"Discourse and Truth" and "Parresia."* Translated by Nancy Luxon. Edited by Henri Paul-Fruchard and Daniel Lorenzini. Chicago: University of Chicago Press.

Gall, Carlotta. 2005. "Taliban Kill 6 Afghan Police in Attack on Army Arms Depot." *New York Times*, September 9, 2005. https://www.nytimes.com/2005/09/09/world/asia/taliban-kill-6-afghan-police-in-attack-on-army-arms-depot.html.

Gandhi, Leela. 2006. *Affective Communities: Anticolonial Thought, Fin-de-Siècle Radicalism, and the Politics of Friendship*. Durham, NC: Duke University Press.

Geertz, Clifford. 1973. "Thick Description: Toward an Interpretative Theory of Culture." In *The Interpretation of Cultures*. New York: Basic Books.

Göle, Nilüfer. 1997. *The Forbidden Modern: Civilization and Veiling*. Ann Arbor: University of Michigan Press.

Gramsci, Antonio. 1971. *Selections from the Prison Notebooks*. Translated by Quintin Hoare. New York: International Publishers.

Green, Nile, and Nushin Arbabzadeh, eds. 2012. *Afghanistan in Ink: Literature between Diaspora and Nation*. Oxford, UK: Oxford University Press.

Grima, Benedicte. 1992. *The Performance of Emotion among Paxtun Women: The Misfor-*

tunes Which Have Befallen Me. Austin: University of Texas Press.

———. 2004. *Secrets from the Field: An Ethnographer's Notes from North Western Pakistan.* Bloomington, IN: Authorhouse.

Griswold, Eliza. 2014. *I Am a Beggar of the World: Landays from Contemporary Afghanistan.* New York: Farrar, Straus and Giroux.

Hallaq, Wael. 2009. *An Introduction to Islamic Law.* Cambridge, UK: Cambridge University Press.

Hashmi, Ghazi. 2017. "Defending the Principle of Legality in Afghanistan: Toward a Unified Interpretation of Article 130 to the Afghan Constitution." *Oregon Review of International Law* 18 (2): 185–226. https://scholarsbank.uoregon.edu/xmlui/bitstream/handle/1794/22777/Hashimi.pdf?sequence=1&isAllowed=y.

Heidegger, Martin. 1962. *Being and Time.* New York: Harper and Row.

Herman, Edward, and Noam Chomsky. 1988. *Manufacturing Consent.* New York: Pantheon Books.

Herzfeld, Michael. 1980. "Honour and Shame: Problems in the Comparative Analysis of Moral Systems." *Man* 15 (2): 339–51.

———. 1985. *The Poetics of Manhood: Contest and Identity in a Cretan Mountain Village.* Princeton, NJ: Princeton University Press.

———. 2002. "The Absent Presence: Discourses of Crypro-Colonialism." *South Atlantic Quarterly* 1 (4): 899–926.

Hirschkind, Charles. 2006. *The Ethical Soundscape: Cassette Sermons and Islamic Counterpublics.* New York: Columbia University Press.

Hirschkind, Charles, and Saba Mahmood. 2002. "Feminism, the Taliban, and Politics of Counter-Insurgency." *Anthropological Quarterly* 75 (2): 339–54. JSTOR, www.jstor.org/stable/3318265.

Hoodfar, Homa. 1997. *Between Marriage and the Market: Intimate Politics and Survival in Cairo.* Berkeley: University of California Press.

Human Rights Watch. 2012. "I Had to Run Away: The Imprisonment of Women and Girls for 'Moral Crimes' in Afghanistan." https://www.hrw.org/report/2012/03/28/i-had-run-away/imprisonment-women-and-girls-moral-crimes-afghanistan.

Ibrahimi, Niamutullah. 2017. *The Hazaras and the Afghan State: Rebellion, Exclusion and the Struggle for Recognition.* London: Hurst.

Irigaray, Luce. 1985. "The Blind Spot of an Old Dream of Symmetry." In *Speculum of the Other Woman.* Translated by Gillian Gill. Ithaca, NY: Cornell University Press.

Jackson, Ashley. 2018. *Life under the Taliban Shadow Government.* Overseas Development Institute. June 2018. https://www.odi.org/sites/odi.org.uk/files/resource-documents/12269.pdf.

Jafri, Amir. 2008. *Honour Killing: Dilemma, Ritual, Understanding.* Oxford, UK: Oxford University Press.

Kamali, Mohammad Hashim. 2002. *Freedom, Equality and Justice in Islam.* Cambridge: Islamic Texts Society.

Kashani-Sabet, Firoozeh. 2011. *Conceiving Citizens: Women and Politics of Motherhood in Iran.* Oxford, UK: Oxford University Press.

Kfir, Isaac. 2014. "Feminist Legal Theory as a Way to Explain the Lack of Progress of Women's Rights in Afghanistan: The Need for a State Strength Approach." *William & Mary Journal of Women and the Law* 21 (1): 87–136.

Khadim, Qiam al-Din. 1936. *Loey as-Sahabah.* Kabul: Pashto Tolana.

———. 1937a. *Nawai Rana: Ijtimai Afkar* [New Light: Social Thinkers]. Kabul: Pashto Tolana.

———. 1937b. *Pashtunwali*. Kabul: Pashto Tolana.

Khan, Hamid. 2008. *Islamic Law of Inheritance: A Comparative Study of Recent Reforms in Muslim Countries*. Oxford, UK: Oxford University Press.

Khan, Tahir. 2016. "Afghan President Invokes Allama Iqbal to Garner Attention of Pakistan Leaders." *Express Tribune*. https://tribune.com.pk/story/1165834/afghan-president-invokes-allama-iqbal-garner-attention-pakistani-leaders.

Khattak, Khushal Khan. 2016. *Da Khushal Baba Kulliyat*. [Poems of Khushal Khattak]. Compiled and edited by Yar Muhammad Maghmoom Khattak. Peshawar: University Book Agency.

Kogacioglu, Dicle. 2004. "The Tradition Effect: Framing Honor Crimes in Turkey." *Differences: A Journal of Feminist Studies* 15 (2): 118–51.

Kramer, Andrew. 2018. "Shelters Have Saved Countless Afghan Women. So Why Are They Afraid?" *New York Times*, March 17, 2018. https://www.nytimes.com/2018/03/17/world/asia/afghanistan-womens-shelters.html.

Kristeva, Julia. 1980. *Desire in Language: A Semiotic Approach to Literature and Art*. New York: Columbia University Press.

Levi-Strauss, Claude. 1969. *Elementary Structures of Kinship*. Boston: Beacon Press. First published in French 1949.

Lindholm, Charles. 1982. *Generosity and Jealousy: The Swat Pukhtun of Northern Pakistan*. New York: Columbia University Press.

Mahmood, Saba. 2005. *Politics of Piety: The Islamic Revival and the Feminist Subject*. Princeton, NJ: Princeton University Press.

Mamdani, Mahmood. 1996. *Citizen and Subject: Contemporary Africa and the Legacy of Colonialism*. Princeton, NJ: Princeton University Press.

———. 2001. *When Victims Become Killers: Colonialism, Nativism, and Genocide in Rwanda*. Princeton, NJ: Princeton University Press.

———. 2004. *Good Muslim, Bad Muslim: America, the Cold War, and the Roots of Terror*. New York: Pantheon Books.

Majrouh, Sayd Bahodine. 2003. *Songs of Love and War: Afghan Women's Poetry*. Translated by Marjolin De Jager. New York: Other Press.

Mani, Lata. 1998. *Contentious Traditions: The Debate on Sati in Colonial India*. Berkeley: University of California Press.

Massad, Joseph. 2015. *Islam in Liberalism*. Chicago: University of Chicago Press.

Massell, Gregory J. 1974. *The Surrogate Proletariat: Moslem Women and Revolutionary Strategies in Soviet Central Asia, 1919–1929*: Princeton, NJ: Princeton University Press.

Mauss, Marcel. 1990. *The Gift: The Form and Reason for Exchange in Archaic Societies*. Translated by W. D. Halls. New York. Norton and Routledge. First published in French 1925.

Mbembe, Achille. 2001. *On the Postcolony*. Berkeley: University of California Press.

———. 2003. "Necropolitics." Translated by Libby Meintjes. *Public Culture* 15 (1): 11–40. Retrieved September 22, 2019, from Project MUSE database.

McChesney, Robert, and Mohammad Mehdi Khorammi, eds. and trans. 2012. *The History of Afghanistan: Fayẓ Muḥammad Kātib Hazrah's Sirāj al-Tawārīkh*. 6 vols. New York: Brill Press.

Meneley, Anne. 1996. *Tournaments of Value: Sociability and Hierarchy in a Yemeni Town*.

Toronto: University of Toronto Press.

Messick, Brinkley. 1993. *The Calligraphic State: Textual Domination and History in a Muslim Society*. Berkeley: University of California Press.

———. 2018. *Shar a Scripts: A Historical Anthropology*. New York: Columbia University Press.

Metcalf, Barbara. 1990. *Perfecting Women: Maulana Ashraf Ali Thanawi's Bihishti Zewar*. Berkeley: University of California Press.

Mir-Hosseini, Ziba. 2001. *Marriage on Trial: Islamic Family Law in Iran and Morocco*. London: I. B. Tauris.

Mir-Hosseini, Ziba, and Vanja Hamzi . 2010. *Control and Sexuality: The Revival of Zina Laws in Muslim Contexts*. London: Women Living under Muslim Laws.

Mitchell, Timothy. 1991. *Colonising Egypt*. Berkeley: University of California Press.

———, ed. 2000. *Questions of Modernity*. Minneapolis: University of Minnesota Press.

Mohanty, Chandra T. 2003. *Feminism without Borders: Decolonizing Theory, Practicing Solidarity*. Durham: Duke University Press.

Morris, Rosalind, ed. 2010. *Can the Subaltern Speak? Reflections on the History of an Idea*. New York: Columbia University Press.

Nagamine, Yoshinobu. 2015. *The Legitimization Strategy of the Taliban's Code of Conduct: Through the One-Way Mirror*. New York: Palgrave Macmillan.

Najmabadi, Afsaneh. 2005. *Women with Mustaches, Men without Beards: Gender and Sexual Anxieties of Iranian Modernity*. Berkeley: University of California Press.

———. 2013. *Professing Selves: Transexuality and Same-Sex Desire in Contemporary Iran*. Durham, NC: Duke University Press.

Natarajan, Swaminathan. 2020. "Afghan Peace Talks: The Woman Who Negotiated with the Taliban." BBC News. https://www.bbc.com/news/world-asia-51572485.

Nawid, Senzil. 1999. *Religious Response to Social Change in Afghanistan, 1919–29: King Aman-Allah and the Afghan Ulama*. Costa Mesa, CA: Mazda Publishers.

Nichols, Robert, ed. 2013. *The Frontier Crimes Regulation: A History in Documents*. Oxford, UK: Oxford University Press.

Nordland, Rod. 2010. "In Bold Display, Taliban Order Stoning Deaths." *New York Times*, August 16, 2010. https://www.nytimes.com/2011/02/01/world/asia/01stoning.html.

Olszewska, Zuzzana. 2015. *The Pearl of Dari: Poetry and Personhood among Young Afghans in Iran*. Bloomington: Indiana University Press.

Osanloo, Arzoo. 2009. *Politics of Women's Rights in Iran*. Princeton, NJ: Princeton University Press.

Parla, Ayse. 2001. "The 'Honor' of the State: Virginity Examinations in Turkey." *Feminist Studies* 27 (1): 65–88. doi:10.2307/3178449.

———. 2019. *Precarious Hope: Migration and the Limits of Belonging in Turkey*. Stanford, CA: Stanford University Press.

Povinelli, Elizabeth. 2002. *Cunning of Recognition: Indigenous Alterities and the Making of Australian Multiculturalism*. Durham, NC: Duke University Press.

Radjy, Amir-Hussein. 2019. "Overlooked No More: Forough Farrokhzad, Iranian Poet Who Broke Barriers of Sex and Society." *New York Times*, January 30, 2019. https://www.nytimes.com/2019/01/30/obituaries/forough-farrokhzad-overlooked.html.

Rashid, Ahmed. 2010. *Taliban*. New Haven, CT: Yale University Press.

Reno, William. 2005. *Corruption and State Politics in Sierra Leone*. Cambridge, UK: Cambridge University Press.

Rubin, Alissa J. 2012. "Afghan Rape Case Turns Focus on Local Police." *New York Times*, June 2, 2012. https://www.nytimes.com/2012/06/02/world/asia/afghan-rape-case-is-a-challenge-for-the-government.html.

Rubin, Elizabeth. 2005. "Women's Work." *New York Times Magazine*, October 9, 2005. https://www.nytimes.com/2005/10/09/magazine/womens-work.html.

Saussure, Ferdinand. 1972. *Course in General Linguistics*. Edited by Charles Bally, Albert Sechehaye, and Albert Riedlinger. Translated by Roy Harris. Chicago: Carus.

Scarry, Elaine. 1985. *The Body in Pain: The Making and Unmaking of the World*. Oxford, UK: Oxford University Press.

Schinasi, May. 1979. *Afghanistan at the Beginning of the Twentieth Century: Nationalism and Journalism in Afghanistan. A Study of Seraj ul-akhbar (1911–1918)*. Naples: Istituto universitario orientale.

Schulze, Reinhard. 1998. *A Modern History of the Islamic World*. New York: I. B. Tauris.

Scott, Joan. 2010. *The Politics of the Veil*. Princeton, NJ: Princeton University Press.

Shahrani, M. Nazif. 2008. "Taliban and Talibanism in Historical Perspective." In *The Taliban and the Crisis of Afghanistan*, edited by Robert D. Crews and Amin Tarzi, 155–81. Cambridge, MA: Harvard University Press.

Siddiqui, Dina M. 2015. "Scandals of Seduction and the Seductions of Scandal." *Comparative Studies of South Asia, Africa and the Middle East* 35 (3): 508–24.

Sinno, Abdulkader. 2008. "Explaining the Taliban's Ability to Mobilize the Pashtuns." In *The Taliban and the Crisis of Afghanistan*, edited by Robert Crews and Amin Tarzi, 59–89. Cambridge, MA: Harvard University Press.

Skaine, Rosemary. 2002. *The Women of Afghanistan under the Taliban*. Jefferson, NC: McFarland.

Smith, Saphora, and Mushtaq Yusufzai. 2020. "The Long Road to Peace: Four Issues That Must Be Resolved If Afghans Have a Chance for Peace." NBC News, September 23, 2020. https://www.nbcnews.com/news/world/long-road-peace-four-issues-must-be-resolved-if-afghans-n1240423.

Spivak, Gayatri. 1988. "Can the Subaltern Speak?" In *Marxism and Interpretation of Cultures*, edited by Cary Nelson and Lawrence Grossberg, 271–313. Urbana: University of Illinois Press.

———. 2010. "Can the Subaltern Speak?" Rev. ed. In *Can the Subaltern Speak? Reflections on the History of an Idea*, edited by Rosalind Morris, 21–79. New York: Columbia University Press.

Starrett, Gregory. 1998. *Putting Islam to Work: Education, Politics, and Religious Transformation in Egypt*. Berkeley: University of California Press.

Stengel, Richard. 2010. "The Plight of Afghan Women: A Disturbing Picture." *Time*, July 29, 2010. http://content.time.com/time/magazine/article/0,9171,2007415,00.html.

Sundby, Alex. 2011. "Behind 'Mask,' Afghan Women Speak of Abuse." CNN, January 3, 2011. https://www.cbsnews.com/news/behind-mask-afghan-women-speak-of-abuse/.

Taneja, Anand. 2018. *Jinnealogy: Time, Islam, and Ecological Thought in the Medieval Ruins of Delhi*. Stanford, CA: Stanford University Press.

Tapper, Nancy. 1991. *Bartered Brides: Politics, Gender and Marriage in an Afghan Tribal Society*. Cambridge, UK: Cambridge University Press.

United Nations Assistance Mission in Afghanistan and Office of the High Commissioner for Human Rights. 2010. *Harmful Traditional Practices and Implementation of the Law on Elimination of Violence against Women in Afghanistan*. Kabul and Geneva:

UNAMA and OHCHR, 2010.

Vikor, Knut. 2006. *Between God and the Sultan: A History of Islamic Law.* Oxford, UK: Oxford University Press.

Weber, Max. 1946. "Politik als Beruf." [Politics as Vocation]. In *From Max Weber: Essays in Sociology*, edited and translated by H. H. Gerth and C. Wright Mills, 77–128. New York: Oxford University Press. http://www.columbia.edu/itc/journalism/stille/Politics%20Fall%202007/Readings%20--%20Weeks%201-5/Weber%20-%20Politics%20as%20a%20Vocation.htm. Originally a speech at Munich University, 1918.

Weston, Kath. 1991. *Families We Choose: Lesbians, Gays, Kinship.* New York: Columbia University Press.

Wickens, G. M., trans. 1964. *Nasirean Ethics: Naṣīr ad-Tūsī.* London: Allen and Unwin.

Wide, Thomas. 2012. "Demarcating Pashto: Cross-Border Pashto Literature and the Afghan State, 1880–1930." In *Afghanistan in Ink: Literature between Diaspora and Nation*, edited by Nile Green and Nushin Arbabzadah, 91–112. Oxford, UK: Oxford University Press.

Wimpelmann, Torunn. 2017. *The Pitfalls of Protection: Gender, Violence, and Power in Afghanistan.* Oakland: University of California Press.

Zadran, Alef-Shah. 1977. *Socioeconomic and Legal-Political Processes in a Pashtun Village, Southeastern Afghanistan.* Ann Arbor, MI: UMI Dissertation Services.

Index

abandonment: as subject of landay, 72, 79, 83; women's experience of, 22, 56, 79, 81, 97, 103, 108

Abbott, James, 193

'Abdur Rahman, Amir, 29–30, 146

Abu-Lughod, Lila, 9, 12, 70, 76, 82, 88, 98, 100, 101, 180–81, 199

adultery: imputed to runaways, 17, 25, 26–27; legal and religious proscriptions of, 25, 62, 111–13; punishments for, 112, 123, 149–50, 158–60; rape confused with, 26, 61–62; as rationale for running away, 6–7; social chaos linked to, 173

Afghan womanhood, 137–66; binary categories applied to, 163–65; chastity as defining feature of, 152–53, 155; honor and, 147–62; modernity and, 140, 142; nationalism and, 142–62; overview of, 15; paradoxical nature of, 138; pedagogical materials on, 142–64; piety and honor as foundation of, 10; role models for, 143, 147–48, 151; wifehood synonymous with, 139. *See also* pious womanhood; women

Afghan Women Network, 23

Afghan Women's Skills Development Center, 23

Ahmadi, Wali, *Modern Persian Literature in Afghanistan*, 146

Ahmed, Leila, 9

'Aisha (wife of Prophet Mohammad), 45, 111–12, 115–16, 143, 151

'Aisha, Bibi, 53–54

Akhalq-e Nasiri (Nasir al-Din al-Tusi), 157, 175

akhlaq (ethics), 120, 146, 152, 157–58

Ali, Kecia, 173, 174, 177

alimony (mahr), 64–65

Althusser, Louis, 186

Amanullah, King, 10, 30, 141–42, 146, 162

Amin, Qasim, 146

Appiah, Anthony, 12; *Honor Code*, 1

Aristotle, 8, 101, 168

Asad, Talal, 10–11, 101, 165, 200

askesis, 8, 96, 166, 168, 170, 218n20

Atatürk, Mustafa Kemal, 146

Athmar, Nurzia, 3, 34–35, 68, 212n1

Austen, Jane, 103

Austin, J. L., 91

Awlad 'Ali, 98

baad (giving a woman in compensation), 63, 66, 153

badal (exchange to compensate a debt), 66, 153, 209n16

Bakhtin, Mikhail, 78

Balkhi, Rabia, 31

ul-Banat, Siraj, 146

Barfield, Thomas, 135, 167–68

Beauvoir, Simone de, 135

Bedouin, 76, 98, 180

Bhaduri, Bhubaneswari, 199

Bibi, Lal, 66

Bihishti Zewar (Ornaments of Heaven) [Maulana Ashraf 'Ali Thanawi], 152–56, 175

Billaud, Julie, 63

The authorized representative in the EU for product safety and compliance is:
Mare Nostrum Group
B.V Doelen 72
4831 GR Breda
The Netherlands

www.ingramcontent.com/pod-product-compliance
Lightning Source LLC
Chambersburg PA
CBHW020853270326
41928CB00006B/685